ZWINGLI

THIRD MAN OF THE REFORMATION

by

JEAN RILLIET

LUTTERWORTH PRESS

LONDON

First published 1964

This book originally appeared as *Zwingle, le Troisième Homme de la Réforme*, Librairie Arthème Fayard, Paris, 1959. It has been revised by the author for the English edition.

The English translation is by Harold Knight.

*Printed in Great Britain
by The Camelot Press Ltd.,
London and Southampton*

Contents

5

426131

PART THREE

THE PROTESTANT REVOLUTION

PART FOUR

THE THEOLOGICAL THOUGHT OF ZWINGLI

PART FIVE

DIVERGENCE OF THE WAYS

CONTENTS

Author's Foreword

IF ZWINGLI IS THE least known of the reformers, this is doubtless because of his Swiss origins. Not only is the scene on which his activity took place more restricted than the Germany of Luther, or the France of Calvin, but also the language which he used—the crude dialect of his Alpine valley—often remains incomprehensible to the foreign reader. He was born, he preached, he struggled and he died on a territory which hardly exceeded in size the limits of a province. His studies at Berne, Vienna and Basle, the military campaigns in Italy, and the colloquy of Marburg, alone free him at times from his narrow horizon. He possessed neither that passionate violence which made of the Saxon monk the inaugurator of a new era, nor the dialectical power which enabled the reformer of Geneva to publish at the age of twenty-seven his *Institutes of the Christian Religion*. The writings of the reformer of Zürich are difficult to compare with those of his two brilliant protagonists. Yet, the position which he occupies at their side is by no means a contemptible one. The lucidity of his mind and the radicalism of his views suffice to save him from oblivion. His ideas live on; a numerous spiritual progeny invokes his authority; he is the concern of the specialist in dogma. But beyond this motley crowd of admirers and critics he remains a name.

Luther died at the age of sixty-two in the bed which had been placed at his disposal by Count Albert of Mansfeld, whom through the process of a difficult arbitration he had succeeded in reconciling with his brothers. Calvin died in his room at the age of fifty-five, worn out by excessive work, and after taking solemn leave of his friends and fellow-workers. Leo X, Clement VII, ostentatious pontiffs, and

Adrian VI, a pope of austere life, were carried off by sickness. The Swiss reformer, helmeted and with sword at his side, fell on a battlefield in his forty-eighth year. Does his tragic end reveal the judgment of God? Are the length of life, and the form in which death comes, valid criteria of truth?

To the 20th century, which dreams of a committed faith, the massacred witness to truth cannot be an indifferent figure. Zwingli comes before us in all his picturesque humanity and consequently in his errors. He lived out his convictions in all the relativity of hasty decisions, characteristic of an age of upheaval and violence. Sincere and passionate, at once prudent and audacious, he made the unremitted search for God the ruling motive of his life. He was no stained-glass-window saint. His moral personality recalls that of a fighting prophet such as Elijah on Mount Carmel.

In some three hundred pages it is difficult to develop, alongside his biography, the whole thought of the writer who dramatically changed the religious destiny of his people. I have, however, been anxious to give summaries of his principal writings. Not without hesitation, I have dealt at some length with the too famous eucharistic controversy. The important place it holds in the history of protestantism constrained me to do so. The reader who is bored by these strenuous chapters will be content to bestow on them a cursory perusal.

Zürich, May 1958.

Author's Note to the English Edition

THIS TRANSLATION has afforded an opportunity of correcting some small errors. I here offer my sincere thanks to Professor L. von Muralt, who has so kindly allowed me to profit by his great erudition.

Geneva, 1963.

Introduction[1]

THE SWISS BACKGROUND

AT THE heart of Europe, under the shelter of the Alps, a community of free men established itself during the Middle Ages. Its origins are lost in what it is conventional to call the night of time. Completely colonized by the Romans on the eve of the invasions, Helvetia (Switzerland) saw the barbarians overrun it in two main waves during the course of the 5th century A.D. The Burgundians occupied the west of the country, the Alemanni the east and the centre; the limit of their territories corresponded roughly to the present division between the two linguistic zones. French and Germans join each other along a line which cuts the country from the north to the south, passing approximately through Bienne, Fribourg, and Sierre.

The domination of the Alemanni, like that of the Burgundians, was ephemeral. The Franks subjugated them at the beginning of the 6th century. Helvetia, which was subjected in turn to the yoke of the Merovingians and that of the Carolingians, passed with one of the sons of Louis the Good under the sway of the Holy Roman Empire. In the 11th and 12th centuries, this domination, which was more theoretical than real, weakened more and more on the plateau binding the Alps to the Juras, and advantage was taken of this fact by some of the local ruling families.

In the 13th century two new families increased their power, that of the Counts of Savoy to the west, and that of the Habsburgs in the centre. Rudolph of Habsburg, from being a feudal lord of the second class, rose from success

[1] The original Introduction has been shortened for the English edition. —Ed.

to success until he occupied the throne of Germany (1273).

In accordance with an eternal law, those who are perturbed by the growing power of a state, or of a family, league themselves together. The alliance of the first Swiss cantons—Uri, Schwyz and Unterwalden—formed in 1291, a few weeks after the death of Rudolph, was born of the desire to maintain a threatened independence. The signatories were mountain peasants who from time immemorial had enjoyed the traditional freedom and rights of the Alemanni. Few lords and serfs were to be found in their valleys. Basically a small landowner, the primitive Swiss administered his Alpine slopes himself under the distant and kindly eye of the emperor.

The successors of Rudolph refused to accept that in the south of their state a centre of liberty should be established. Seizing the pretext of a quarrel between the Abbot of Einsiedeln and the men of Schwyz, Duke Leopold in 1315 flung against the latter a powerful army which was crushed near the Lake of Aegeri in the pass of Morgarten. The rocks which fell from the top of the fir-covered slopes on to the knights cased in steel inscribed for the first time the name of the Swiss in the annals of European history.

By alliances and battles, the 14th century confirmed the decisions of 1291 and 1315. A series of communities, both peasant and urban, became attached to the original nucleus of the Confederation. The very fact of this progressive extension makes the history of Switzerland difficult for the foreign observer to grasp. Each of the tiny associated countries kept its personality intact, and civil wars were frequent. At most one can distinguish a first properly Alpine stage from 1291 to 1389; a century of struggle for independence made illustrious by the half-legendary figures of William Tell overcoming the Austrian officer Gessler, and of Arnold of Winkelried exposing his breast at Semprach, in contempt of his life, to the lances of the Austrian knights, by which heroic deed he assured the victorious break-through of the Swiss infantry.

With the 15th century, the Confederation, now sure of

itself, pursued a more or less deliberate expansionist policy. To men accustomed to fighting, life on the farms becomes monotonous. By dint of fighting against Austria and quarrelling with one another, the Swiss transformed themselves into professional soldiers. Were they not required—a system at that time unique in Europe—to be fitted for military service from the age of sixteen to sixty and to arm themselves on their own initiative? Shooting exercises were held in high honour. When in 1444, called to the rescue by Austria, which paradoxically enough was allied to Zürich, the future Louis XI of France, at the head of 40,000 Armagnacs, encircled and destroyed a contingent of 1,500 Swiss Confederates, the resistance of the tiny company was so valiant that their conqueror was stupefied with admiration. Where could he find better auxiliaries? Many rulers made the same observation as the French prince. Mercenary service dated from that time. The over-populated country exported its men, who returned to their villages with their pockets full of gold, delighted to have such chances of picking up wealth quickly. The determination to live better despite a poor soil, which was one day to make of Switzerland an industrial nation, led to ever-increasing engagements in the service and pay of foreign princes.

The renown of the Swiss brought them more and more attractive offers. The emperor, the kings of France and Hungary, the pope, the dukes of Lorraine, Milan and even of Austria, waited about to seize opportunities of securing contingents. The magistrates who were solicited received pensions as a reward for their good services. Primitive simplicity yielded to a growing luxury. Festival succeeded festival. To live ever more fatly, ever more money was needed. Corruption and intrigue multiplied; everybody demanded a share of the cake. Village amusements turned into orgies: "Games, dances, shooting tournaments, skittles, card-playing, oaths, riots, violence, and murders", notes the historian Ernest Gagliardi, "became more frequent than ever." Outside the frontiers, the Swiss mercenaries' reputation for cruelty became solidly established. "Give human hearts to the Swiss", implored the humanist Jacob Wimpfeling in 1507, "and take from them their hearts of stone. For there is more humanity among the Turks and the Hussites than among them. Make them more gentle so that they will not kill the enemy prisoner, but take his money rather than his life." A few magistrates of integrity tried to react and to retain on home ground a youth which was being ruined in foreign countries: their efforts had little success.

In this developing state, what was the position of the Church? As in the whole of Europe, medieval piety multiplied monasteries and foundations. Several bishops reigned over their cities as sovereign princes within the framework of the Holy Roman Empire. Their authority was, however, limited by rights conceded to the middle-class citizens. The latter, in Basle as in Lausanne and Geneva, were growing in importance. It was the same at St. Gall, where the Abbot, lord of a vast territory, found his temporal power disputed at the very gates of his cloister.

Episcopal or abbatial authority, contested from a political point of view, remained intact on the religious plane. In the course of centuries the country became covered with magnificent sanctuaries. The cathedrals of Basle, Lausanne, Chur, Geneva, the minsters of Berne, Zürich, Neuchâtel, the rich abbeys of St. Gall, Engelberg, and Einsiedeln, welcomed huge devout crowds. Yet, after the wave of piety caused by the reforms of Cluny and Cîteaux and then by the extension of the mendicant orders, laxity showed itself in monasteries that were too wealthy as in bishoprics that were too powerful. Canonries offered the nobility and the upper middle classes opportunities to place advantageously their too numerous sons. Example was set in high places.

The laity, while not touching doctrinal matters, did not scruple to criticize sharply the conduct of the clergy. In the towns, the Councils acquired the habit of intervening in ecclesiastical affairs. The manners of the citizens, however, were far from being beyond reproach. We have seen the ravages wrought by the acquisition of foreign gold. The luxury of the magistrates was insulting to the indigence of the craftsmen. At Zürich, the latter complained both of the pride of the all-powerful Burgomaster, Hans Waldemann, who was beheaded in 1489, and of the idleness of the monks.

Indulgences and pilgrimages became ever more frequent. The cult of relics was favoured by the masses. Berne possessed drops of the Virgin's milk, fragments of Aaron's rod and bits of the loam from which Adam was drawn. Mingled with the increasing superstition, sparks of pure religion gleam here and there in a few elect souls. Nicolas de Flue (1417-87), a simple peasant of primitive Switzerland, who was connected with the "friends of God" in the Rhine valley, and was the father of ten children, retired at the age of fifty to a hermitage near his family farm. He remained in close relation with his village of which he had been magistrate, and his reputation for holiness caused him to be asked to intervene at the Diet of Stans in 1481, where he successfully acted as arbiter between the divided Confederates.

When Nicolas died in March, 1487, venerated by all who knew him, Ulrich Zwingli was a merry unthinking infant of three at Wildhaus.

The country in which the future reformer was born and was to act differed considerably from the civilized regions which the tourist of today appreciates not only for their admirable landscapes but also for their towns and hotels, kept with meticulous cleanliness. A few cities had a rudimentary industry. Nevertheless silk weaving, which flourished in the 14th century at Zürich, was on the decline at the beginning of the 16th. The only discernible links which unite the Confederates of the 15th century to those of the 20th are the love of liberty, ruggedness of character, tenacity of purpose, and the liking for adventure, all of which are a direct inheritance from the Alemanni. To these traits we must add a traditional basis of Christianity, more or less keenly felt.

In his portrait of the German Swiss,[1] André Siegfried depicts them as "somewhat heavy, ponderous beings, of slower reactions" than is common among the Latin Swiss. The eminent writer also sees the people of this region as "a romantic people, methodic and even systematic doubtless, but rebellious to Cartesian habits of analysis, and always somewhat ill at ease in classical formulae of universal bearing". The German Swiss, he notes further, "is so much the more a Swiss as he is close to his native soil. Then his Germanic qualities are moderated: if he shows himself to be industrious, conscientious, thorough, respectful of discipline, and even secretly an admirer of force, on the other hand he is found to have a sense of restraint, to be immune from any touch of megalomania, in fact to be as reasonable as he is practical. If he has a clumsiness which rather smacks of the soil, he compensates for it by a great deal of shrewdness."

This remarkable analysis neglects some traits of the original. The German Swiss, more robust than his Latin brother, is, as Siegfried points out, a greater worker. He wishes to arrive, to succeed. From his mountain background, he retains even in towns and workshops the obstinacy of the peasant who brings a corner of his pasturage into cultivation or cuts his own wood. Slower and heavier than his compatriot of Lausanne or Geneva, he can however manifest an astonishing clearness of mind, though without brilliancy, without display, similar in fact to that of the Anglo-Saxon races. The work of the Zürich citizen Emil Brunner affords us at the present time, on the plane of theology, a striking proof of this gift. Solidity of reasoning is here more valued than the brilliant flights of the Frenchman or the German.

Again, his respect for discipline, his very strong sense of community life, are counterbalanced by the need to defend his opinion, the determination not to abdicate. There is nothing less sheepish than Swiss voting. Government proposals are often rejected by a recalcitrant electorate. In a

[1] *La Suisse, Démocratie Témoin*. La Baconnière, Neuchâtel, 3rd edn., 1956.

deliberative assembly, the German Swiss sometimes produces a sense of discomfort by the roughness of his interventions. He will not allow himself to be imposed upon. The old instinct which brought Tell into an attitude of defiance against Gessler's hat is perpetuated. In the sphere of politics, it has created rights of initiative and referendum, the successor of those which the citizen of primitive Switzerland enjoyed in the *Landsgemeinde* (assembly of the citizens).

The love of adventure is prolonged today on the commercial and industrial plane. German Switzerland abounds in prosperous factories. Chemical works at Basle, engineering works at Zürich, Winterthur, Baden and Zug reflect the dynamic vitality of the old Swiss halbedriers. Under an appearance of ponderosity, presidents of administrative councils go boldly ahead.

Every people has its good and bad subjects. Ruggedness of character can degenerate into coarseness, and persistence into a determination to succeed by whatever means. In the framework of the 16th century, Zwingli strikingly exhibits several of the characteristic qualities and defects of his people; a curious mixture of audacity and prudence, a common sense which glaringly contrasts with Luther's violence and lack of restraint, and an obstinacy which brings him to the tragic end of Cappel. In studying his life and his thought we must never forget that he was born on the slopes of the mountains around St. Gall, at a height where the meadows become pasture land, where the houses are chalets. A child of the 15th century, he belongs to the generation which the Renaissance delivered from the bondage of the Middle Ages to permit them to construct the first outlines of a modern church and a modern city. With him the grace of the Gospel is contained in an earthen vessel, the various constituents of which it has perhaps not been profitless to recall.

Part One

The Formative Years

CHAPTER ONE

Childhood and Education

THE FUTURE REFORMER of Zürich was born on January 1, 1484, at Wildhaus in the steep valley of the Toggenburg. He belonged to a family of well-to-do farmers. It seems that his grandfather already was *ammann*, i.e. mayor of the village. In any case, his father certainly filled this post and brought up a numerous family. Documents which have been preserved transmit the Christian names of five brothers who lived on the family estates. In the register of church tithes for 1534 the name of the Zwinglis recurs fifty-five times: they appear there—these nephews or cousins—as a robust tribe. Besides the five farmers, the immediate family of Ulrich included three sisters; a brother, Jacob, who was born in 1490, became a monk, attended lectures at the University of Vienna, and died in 1517; and also a brilliant young brother, Andrew, who was born in 1500. The latter, who was Ulrich's companion in the Zürich presbytery, was carried off by the plague in 1520.

Wildhaus at that time was a series of houses scattered over the Alpine slopes rather than a village whose streets huddled around the church steeple. The altitude—roughly 3,300 feet—made cultivation of the land difficult. Such land as was in fact usable, and which had been patiently won from the clearing of forests between the 12th and 14th centuries, left to the inhabitants hardly any other resource than that of rearing stock. The road which serves the high valley and links it with the region of Buchs dates from the beginning of the 15th century; it facilitated the sale of butter and cheese in the localities of the Rhineland plain and as far as Feldkirch. The relative prosperity of the Zwingli family was doubtless the consequence of this.

By an odd set of circumstances the parish was ecclesiastically dependent on the bishopric of Chur, while politically the valley belonged to the abbacy of St. Gall, which had acquired it in 1468 from the heirs of the counts of Toggenburg. Historians attach a certain importance to the bond with Chur, which was the capital of the Grisons; it is thought to prove the penetration of Rhaetian-Roman elements into the area and to suggest that the inhabitants of Wildhaus were only superficially Alemanni. Must we impute to these far-off origins the very Latin clarity of mind which Zwingli evinced? In such matters, schematization is dangerous. In the last analysis, both Alemanni and Franks were Aryans. It is personal aptitude rather which plays a role of capital importance.

The influence of the family circle is much more in evidence. From his father Uly and his mother Margaret (cousin of the Abbot of Fischingen) the boy received a good dose of common sense, simplicity and piety. In the house attributed to them by tradition and which the tourist respectfully visits— the Lisighaus—there was little enough room to accommodate eleven children and several servants. Education could not be a finicking business on modern psychological lines, but the mixing together of characters in a big family—shouts, arguments, games in common, smacks and rewards— achieve more, in an atmosphere of faith and hard work, than the smartest pedagogical recipes. In later life Ulrich recalled the stories told by his grandmother to the little scamps already half-asleep. She would describe Peter and Jesus on their travels sleeping in the same bed. "And Peter," she would tell them, "slept on the outer side of the bed, while our Lord rested against the wall. The woman with whom they lodged used to call them every morning, but Peter alone did she pull by the hair to awaken him." The anecdote brings to mind the mattresses on which Ulrich and his brothers slept two by two; it suggests the rustic and healthy character of such a childhood. "When father appeared with the big stick, all the children would piously exclaim: 'I won't do it again' ", wrote the reformer one day when thinking of his young days.

In the Zwingli household, love was mingled with severity. Ulrich was later to compare the goodness of God with that of a father offering his son a bunch of grapes picked from the vine-arbour. In the village which had no imported luxuries— he notes that they did not know the taste of ginger, wine of Malvoisie, spice or oranges—the grape must have been for them the most delectable delicacy.

At Wildhaus, apart from Grandmother's tales and the good advice of parents, it was impossible for an intelligent boy to learn the slightest thing. When the boy was five years old, his parents decided to entrust him to the care of his uncle and godfather, Barthelemy, who was Vicar of Wesen on the Lake of Wallenstadt. Paths which were passable from April, once the snow had melted, put Toggenburg at a few hours' walking distance from the valley. The separation was painful, but the father wanted his son to make his way in life as well as was possible. A revealing remark of his has been preserved: "I would rather have a philosopher than a play-actor!" he exclaimed when Zwingli, who was admirably gifted for music, confided to him, in a letter written from Vienna, his plans for the future, and mentioned among his other interests his favourite musical instruments. Like Luther and Calvin, Zwingli was not the child of a nonentity, but rather of a true educator who was fully aware of his responsibilities, and capable, if need be, of roughly handling his offspring.

Of Barthelemy Zwingli, who for five years watched over the moral and intellectual development of his nephew, we know but little. He concerned himself anxiously with his godson. First a priest in the village of Schännis, he was offered in 1487 the living of Wesen and officiated as dean in the area. Bullinger, Zwingli's successor, describes him as "a pious man, held in honour and esteem". Little Ulrich doubtless owed to him, along with the rudiments of Latin, the happy decision to continue his studies. In 1494 his uncle sent him to Basle, where he became the pupil of Gregory Bünzli. It was also doubtless owing to the prestige of the aged Barthelemy that Zwingli was later to find himself, while still quite young, offered the envied post of Vicar of Glarus.

With the 15th century the Middle Ages come to an end. Intellectually and commercially, towns are rapidly developing. Many ties are being created which break down former barriers. Men, merchandise and ideas are getting into circulation.

The boy who, at ten, left the quiet shores of the Lake of Wallenstadt to go to Basle, had no idea as yet that he was living in a world in ferment. He admired, at the end of another lake, the city of Zürich with its many steeples, not foreseeing that he would one day become the much-heeded preacher of the Great Minster. He took his schoolboy's lodgings at Basle without discerning the figure of Erasmus, who was to make the city a centre of letters, and to become a few years later the object of his fervent admiration. Such is the mystery of destinies which intersect and mingle. The man is born in the child without the latter realizing it, and the years which will both exalt him and make him cruelly suffer unroll before him.

Bünzli, "a good man, cultured and very mild", won the gratitude of his pupil. He ran very ably a school for Latin studies, where Zwingli spent two years; after which his master sent him back home, with the advice that, in view of his gifts, he should continue his studies. Their friendship was not to end until 1527 with the death of the older man, who in 1507 succeeded Barthelemy Zwingli as Vicar of Wesen. In 1496, Ulrich entered a school at Berne which was managed by the humanist scholar, Henry Wölflin, known as Lupulus (Little Wolf). Thanks to this new master, a Christian in the old style, a faithful servant of the Church, a zealous pilgrim, author of a life of Nicolas de Flue and translator of Samson the preacher of indulgences at the time of his round in Switzerland, the boy now made the acquaintance of

24

classical antiquity. The classics, in which he came to delight, penetrated his fresh mind. A strange episode might well have lastingly modified the course of his career: the Dominicans of Berne, enchanted by his voice and musical gifts, tried to attach him to their monastery, and even, so it would seem, went so far as to admit him as a novice. But neither his father nor his uncle agreed to the plan. On their urgent advice, Ulrich set himself afresh to his studies, and, directed by Lupulus, proceeded from Berne to Vienna.

We have very little exact information about these years of preparation, which, in their humble fashion, correspond to the years now spent at a grammar school. If they shaped the intelligence of the adolescent, they did not effectually detach him from his rural origins. His whole life long, Zwingli described himself as a peasant. A bit of straw, the manure heap, the smell of the fields, the creak of carts, the cries of the farmyard, accompanied him to the very end. It remains true that pure urban civilization is a comparatively recent creation. With its seven thousand inhabitants, Zürich was still in close contact with the fields and the woods. In consequence, Zwingli, as later Péguy, never yielded to the dizzy raptures of intellectualism: nature is the framework of his meditations up to the hour when death lays him low on the meadow of Cappel.

The years spent at Vienna are also little known. The student who arrived in the capital of Austria in the autumn of 1498 found Swiss comrades there. The names of several of them have been spotted alongside his own on the old register where he appears as *Uldaricus Zwingly de Glaris*. Mention is made further of the payment of the usual boarding fees. The adolescent was lodged, like most foreigners, in one of the houses set apart for scholars. Spent under the supervision of humanists, such as Giovanni Ricuzzi Vellini, known as Damers, and the famous Conrad Celtes, the poet crowned by the Emperor Maximilian, these eight terms procured for him a solid culture. Apart from its intrinsic value, Vienna has left hardly any traces in the work of Zwingli, but he made some excellent friends there. To one of them,

Joachim Vadian, he remained closely united; their correspondence is a precious mine of information about the later activity of the reformer.

Historians have been puzzled by a stroke of the pen which has erased the first inscription of the name of Uldaricus and by the *exclusus* which an obviously later pen has inserted into the register. Must we see in this the trace of an expulsion incurred as a result of unruly conduct, or is it a question of a later act of vengeance against the student who became a heresiarch? Whatever be the truth of the matter, if he was banished for one reason or another in 1499, Zwingli returned and pursued a regular course of study in Vienna up to 1502, when he went to Basle. In view of the tense relations between the Confederates and the Austrians, which marked this period, Oscar Farner thinks the likely cause was a political feud amongst the students. In the margin of a copy of Josephus, facing the story of Isaac athirst, driven far from a fountain by inhospitable maidens,[1] Ulrich has inscribed: "I well remember this impious woman who, when I was on my way home, at Lindau, on my return from the University of Vienna, did not allow me to enter her house, although on account of the cold I was incapable of continuing my journey, my strength was spent and I was on the verge of despair." Is this note an allusion to a flight in mid-winter or to the terminal return home at the end of an icy March? The mysterious confidence has not unveiled its secret.

His time at Basle (1502-1506) is somewhat better known. Zwingli gained there the degrees of Bachelor of Arts in 1504 and Master of Arts in 1506. He earned some of his maintenance money by part-time teaching at the school of St. Martin. He won new friends, in particular Leo Jud, who was later to be the companion of his struggle at Zürich, Nicolas de Watteville, the future canon of the Chapter at Berne who prepared there the way for the victorious progress of the reformation, and Nicolas Wyttenbach who as chief magistrate of Bienne was to bring that future industrial centre into the orbit of new ideas. Among his masters, mention should

---

[1] A Jewish legend, not found in the Bible.

be made of another Wyttenbach, Thomas, who gave lectures on the *Sentences* of Peter Lombard and on certain parts of the New Testament, especially the Epistle to the Romans. Zwingli owed to him his first serious contact with Holy Scripture, and, if we are to believe Leo Jud, the desire to study it more deeply, leaving aside the "follies of the sophists".

Is it possible that the rest of his studies aroused in him a feeling of disgust for scholastic subtleties? Such is not the opinion of Walther Köhler: at Basle, Zwingli worked especially on Thomas Aquinas and under the influence of this illustrious doctor came to feel the need for a solidly constructed theology in which reason is given a place of honour. Luther, on the contrary, through Gabriel Biel, came under the influence of Duns Scotus, the apostle of the irrational. It is said that a difference in scholastic training explains the opposition which later divided Zwingli from Luther. This thesis is not without its attraction, but skirts too lightly over the enormous difference of character which certainly played a part in the clash at the colloquy of Marburg.

However this may be, Thomism brought the Basle student into contact with Aristotle, whom he studied very seriously. The volumes of his library which have been preserved contain among other things a copiously annotated copy of the edition of this author published at Venice in 1495. The original work of Zwingli contains many a proof of his Aristotelian training, from the conception of God presented in his *De Providentia* to the knowledge of physics and natural history which is shown here and there in various writings.

To return to Thomas Wyttenbach; this scholar, in a public dissertation, was to attack indulgences several years before Luther. Zwingli pays him the homage of having learned from him that "the death of Christ alone is the price of the forgiveness of sins". Whether Wyttenbach took up his position in 1505, as some consider, or in 1515, as others insist, it is certain that his criticism is prior to the famous theses of Wittenberg, though it did not produce the same stir as the latter. In the sphere of ideas as in that of science, there can be an extraordinary coincidence in research. At the same time, in laboratories or in different university chairs, men who do not know of each other's work reach the same conclusions. In 1509, in his *Praise of Folly*, does not Erasmus also show some anxiety on this score: "What shall I say of those whose calm confidence lies in indulgences, who count so much on their efficacy that they measure as with a water-clock the time they have to spend in purgatory, calculating the centuries, the years, the months, the days and the hours with as much accuracy as if they had drawn up mathematical tables?"

In the autumn of 1506, the studies of Ulrich were suddenly brought to an end. Johannes Stucki, Vicar of Glarus, which was the chief town in the canton of the same name, died. A priest of Zürich, Henry Göldli, a man of good family and well in favour at Rome, seemed ready to inherit the incumbency. The Curia, according to a deplorable custom, had already authorized him to occupy the benefice and to have it administered by a vicar. It was about to be added to the benefices which he already had, his canonry of Embrach and his cure of Baden. The parishioners of Glarus, somewhat dissatisfied, would have preferred to an absentee, whose pockets would have to be filled, a priest residing in the parish. Meantime, old Barthelemy Zwingli at Wesen was watching carefully over his flock. His good pastoral reputation served as a letter of recommendation to his nephew. The student was asked to go and preach in the neighbouring town of Rapperswil, and shortly afterwards the people of Glarus made up their minds in his favour.

In haste, he was ordained priest and on September 29 celebrated at Wildhaus his first mass. A week later, his flock entertained him with delight. The banquet which was offered by the parish gathered around the young priest— who was not yet twenty-three—his father, the authorities of Glarus and those of the neighbourhood. But Göldli possessed his rights; to effect his withdrawal, Zwingli promised to pay by instalments a hundred florins—which was a considerable sum. When twelve years later on his election to Zürich he gave up Glarus, his parishioners, together with his Einsiedeln friends, liberated him finally from his debt by paying on his behalf a last instalment of twenty florins. This painful financial adventure was to open Ulrich's eyes to the curious way in which the Church was administered.

CHAPTER TWO

Vicar of Glarus and Chaplain in Italy

CROUCHING AT THE bottom of a narrow valley, and overshadowed by austere mountain peaks, the little town of Glarus numbered in the middle of the 16th century one hundred and thirty-six homes and some thirteen hundred inhabitants. A few years earlier, when Zwingli found himself called to be its priest, the population and benefice cannot have differed much. To the pastoral charge of the town was added that of several villages and hamlets. The task was heavy, despite the assistance of two or three curates. The young clergyman was not idle; he learnt by constant contact with children, adults and old people to know humanity in its various aspects and in the complexity of its problems.

Of the ancient township, the fire of 1860 destroyed everything with the exception of a few archives and the 14th-century chalice which was used here by the priest who was to become the convinced opponent of the mass. When he left, the people of Glarus wanted the name of their beloved priest to be engraven on the old silver-gilt cup. The inscription may still be read: *Calix Uly Zwingli 1516*. This remarkable piece of plate belongs to the treasures of the catholic parish of Glarus.

Baptizing, marrying, burying, singing the office, visiting the sick did not exhaust the activities of the new Vicar, who retained from his studies at Vienna and Basle a taste for the ancient classics and a desire to teach them. The extraordinary intellectual quickening of the Renaissance did not excite him for one moment, only to leave him drooping and inert the next. The priest remained a humanist, and very quickly a school was added to the presbytery. Zwingli got together the most capable boys of the district, taught them Latin and helped them to discover for themselves the new-found world of antiquity. In 1510, the establishment was officially recognized. The local patricians, the Tschudis, the Heers and the Schindlers, sent him their sons, several of whom later became the friends and disciples of their former master.

If he thus spent himself for others, Ulrich did not however lose sight of his own intellectual development. To improve his preaching, he read the historian Valerius Maximus and learnt by heart his most informative episodes. Similarly, he familiarized himself with Sallust and Plutarch. There is nothing to suggest that at this initial stage his contact with the Bible went beyond the level of its fine narratives, which he carefully read so as to be able to relate them later. The Zürich library contains his copy of Josephus' *De anti-quitatibus ac de bello Judaico*, heavily underlined and covered with notes dating from the years 1507 to 1508. His attention seems to be especially gripped by political and military events. The moral aspect of history interests him more than the mystical. His conscientious activity as a good priest, together with his intellectual work, suffices him. He goes straight ahead, reading the offices of the Church and in-structing youth. Must not God be content with such a priesthood?

However, between the years 1510 and 1516—although it is not possible to trace with precision the crises which marked this change—the soul of Zwingli underwent a phase of deed travail. Painful struggles matured the sprightly priest described for us by those who knew him in his youth: "he was extremely amusing and full of jokes", wrote Myco-nius, his first biographer, with reference to the Basle period of his life. Two dramas, revolving around sensuality and war, led him to a deeper level of life.

In the autumn of 1518, when the canons of the Great Minster of Zürich were planning to invite Zwingli to become a cathedral preacher, disquieting rumours began to arise about their future colleague; he was being accused, in fact, of seducing the daughter of a chief magistrate. The indulgence of the time towards moral disorders in the priesthood was immense. Example was set on the highest level: the Renaissance popes had bastards and loaded them with gifts. In the Vatican, Innocent VIII sumptuously married his daughter to a Medici and his granddaughter to a Spanish prince; Alexander VI confessed to six natural children when he mounted the papal throne, and, after becoming pope, accorded himself a generous liberty; the youth of Julius II was far from irreproachable. As for the Swiss scene, the Bishop of Constance made money out of the children born to his priests; a fine of four florins, imposed on the occasion of each birth, brought in on an average four hundred florins a year. The life of the cloister was hardly any better; the Abbot of Engelberg publicly maintained a wife and numerous offspring. Thus the rule of celibacy was more or less openly violated. But the canons of Zürich, though ready to forgive the lapses of youth, were unwilling to admit to their society an unscrupulous libertine. It is to their anxiety on this account that we owe our knowledge of the personal life of Zwingli. The latter answered their questions by frankly confessing his struggles and his falls. The poignant document, buried for centuries among the archives of Zürich, was rediscovered about 1840 by Professor Schulthess, whose first inclination was to burn the compromising papers. Fortunately, his honesty resisted the counsels of a timid prudery.

Drawn up at a period two years after Zwingli left his first parish, the text of 1518 concerns in large measure his life at Glarus. The little town on the banks of the Linth witnessed the first slip, succeeding to student years that were morally pure. From then onwards the exacting temperament of the young priest involved him in adventures which distressed him and which he tried to conceal from those around him. His pupils suspected nothing and praised the integrity of his life. "Shame", he writes, "always restrained me within certain limits and when, during my life at Glarus, I did wrong, I did it so secretly that even my intimates

noticed practically nothing." This double life and com-
promised reputation weighed terribly on an essentially
upright man, such as Ulrich was. He endeavoured to limit
the disorders by avoiding at least adultery: "My principle
was to inflict no injury on any marriage (for, as Isaiah says,
the blanket of the conjugal bed is not wide enough to cover
two men) and not to dishonour any virgin nor any nun. . . . I
can call to witness all those among whom I have lived."
Nevertheless, his situation left him morally torn asunder.
What company were the frivolous and flighty girls of a small
town for this son of the pious Margaret Meili, for the humanist
entranced by sublime sentiments! Thus he could love only
without true love.

Hence in 1515 he took the decision to remain absolutely
aloof from the other sex, for, he wrote on December 15,
1518, "Paul said that it is good not to touch women". At
Glarus, by his own confession, he remained faithful to his
oath for six months. After his transference to Einsiedeln, he
kept his resolution for yet another year, then lapsed from
grace. But the casual girl friend who then began to spread
everywhere the news of their attachment was not at all,
as she asserted, the daughter of a magistrate, still less a
virgin seduced by him. For two years, on account of her
misconduct, she had been expelled from her home by her
worthy father, a barber by trade. The wrongdoing of Ulrich
was serious: was it inexcusable? At Einsiedeln the confessional revealed to him that hundreds, even thousands of
priests were quite incapable of maintaining chastity.

If we take into account these confessions, the aberrations
of the priest of Glarus arouse pity rather than contempt.
Since marriage was forbidden him by ecclesiastical law, he
wrestled with himself in the attempt to keep an inhuman
rule of life. Before accusing the men who made this rule, he
blames himself and condemns his own weakness. These
secret struggles disclosed to him his miserable lack of will
power. God alone, beholding his wretchedness, can help him.
A great longing for purity and forgiveness now dwells in his
soul. His piety is deepened in the struggle: "I have fallen

again and am become like the dog of which the Apostle Peter speaks, returning to his own vomit", he groans.

Troubles of conscience are often a weapon which God uses to master a soul. The inner struggle of Zwingli in his presbytery recalls that of St. Augustine in the garden of Milan, but it is resolved in a different way. Whereas the 4th-century saint sternly cast out Adeodatus' mother, who had been his nameless companion for fourteen years, Zwingli was eventually to reach the conclusion—in the light of Scripture and the Fathers—that the celibacy of the priesthood is a human invention which arbitrarily excludes the normal solution of an honest marriage. But before reaching such a revolutionary decision, the unhappy man passed through a long period of moral torment which delivered him from superficiality and cast him down shattered at the feet of Christ the Saviour.

Concurrently with the struggle against the demands of his sexuality, the political life of Switzerland worried the young priest. Everything would suggest that the early years of his ministry at Glarus were spent harmoniously. A great bond of affection united Ulrich to his parishioners. For them he sang the mass with devotion. The memory has been preserved of the procession which on June 29, 1516, the feast day of St. Peter and St. Paul, he led around the church, after an extremely wet spring, in order to implore Heaven for some sunny weather: the chronicler tells us that "suddenly fine weather came, whereas previously it had persistently held off".

From 1512 the Italian wars cast a painful shadow over the presbytery. Pope Julius II, a temporal rather than a spiritual prince, aspired to bring the whole of Italy under his domination. In 1509, thanks to the French king, Louis XII, he had recovered Ravenna from the Venetians, but then he quarrelled with France. The Swiss became necessary for his victories. In 1512, an important contingent of mercenaries from Glarus contributed to the triumph at Pavia. It is not certain that Zwingli was on this occasion among the soldiers. On the other hand, his presence is attested at Novara (1513)

34

and at Marignano (1515) by his friend and successor Bullinger.

The pope paid his troops rather meanly: for the expedition of 1512 no more than a gold florin per man. Pillage was the legitimate means by which the men made up their pay. In a long letter describing the battle of Pavia, Zwingli—although it is not possible to decide whether he was the eyewitness of the facts reported—gives an account of the eulogies bestowed on the Confederate troops by the town which they had liberated from the French: preachers described them as "a people of God who had punished the enemies of the Bride of Christ", preluding thus the praises of Julius II who awarded the Confederates the title of "liberators of the Church", giving them the right to put on their blazon if they so desired the Cross of Christ or an image of the Risen Christ. At that time Ulrich was absolutely in agreement with an expedition which seemed to be justified by its success. In June 1513 the Battle of Novara was likewise settled by a French defeat. Zwingli found that, on the recommendation of Cardinal Schinner, he had been granted a yearly pension of fifty florins. Should not those who encouraged the Swiss to fight for the pope and his allies be rewarded? On September 8, 1515, the chaplain from Glarus, preaching at Monza to the assembled Swiss contingents, exhorted them to remain united and to do their duty without flinching. His exhortation was little heeded: the Bernese, together with those contingents from the Valais, Fribourg, and Solothurn, yielding to the offers of peace made by the new French king, Francis I, withdrew. Thus the men from Schwyz, Uri, Glarus and Zug were left alone to fight an enemy superior in numbers. Soon, ten thousand dead were strewn over the ground, while fifteen hundred wounded crowded the hospitals of Milan. For the first time in their history the Swiss were cruelly beaten. A wave of indignation and sorrow broke over the whole country.

At Monza, Zwingli had spoken as an advocate of the papacy. Now, these thousands of corpses began to haunt his mind and imagination. If he bore a grudge against Francis I, whose crafty distribution of gold had divided the Swiss, how should he not also examine his own conscience, face to face with the man whom history was to dub "the booted pope"? In 1516 Erasmus published the *Institutio Principis Christiani* —a treatise on the education of a Christian prince—and in it the writer expressed his horror of war. In his copy of the *Adages* of the same author, which appeared in 1515, Zwingli has underlined texts denouncing affairs with which he was concerned: "Is war anything but the mass murder of the many?" "Why should I deliver up this flowering youth to every kind of evil?" "Leo will earn more true glory if he restores peace to the world than Julius has earned in the whole world through so many wars. . . ." Meditating on this book in new-found calm, atrocious memories passed before his eyes: bloody corpses covering the Milanese plain under the rays of the splendid September sun, canals choked by dead horses. Was it right and normal for a prince of the Church, a successor of St. Peter, to unleash such massacres?

While he was thus tormented by a twofold source of anxiety, Zwingli discovered the Fathers of the Church and the Bible, and with them the path which was to make of him the founder of a church deeply transformed. From his student days he had retained a taste for literature. His correspondence—the first known letter addressed to him dates from 1510—shows him on the look out for new publications. Humanist friends keep him informed of recently published books. Thanks to printing, the ancient world lived again, and rescued the epoch from barbarism. Glareanus, a benevolent purchaser, sent him in 1511 a volume of Aristotle, while in 1513 Vadian praised him for harnessing himself to the study of Greek: "I rejoice with all my heart", he wrote to him, "that now the Muses are treading our mountains too." From 1515, with the help of the fifty papal florins, his purchases of printed volumes increased.

Oscar Farner, by a minute graphological examination of many marginal notes, has established that in 1516, when he left Glarus, Zwingli's library included works of Aristotle, Augustine, Cicero, Cyril of Alexandria, Demosthenes,

Lefèvre d'Etaples, Gregory of Nazianzus, Gregory of Nyssa, Jerome, Origen, Pico della Mirandola, Pliny, Plutarch, Valerius Maximus, and several volumes of Erasmus. In this very Renaissance collection, a folio of Duns Scotus and the *Sentences* of Peter Lombard seem strangely out of place. Another friend of Zwingli, Beatus Rhenanus, who from 1511 was established at Basle where he worked for several printers, furnished him with works of Erasmus. This illustrious writer did not yet live on the banks of the Rhine, where, from 1513, Froben published his writings. The priest of Glarus passionately admired this prince of lettered men. For was he not restoring to the Church the lost treasures of the Fathers? Did he not publish the original text of the New Testament? Was he not courageously criticizing the abuses which afflicted the Church of Jesus Christ?

In the evolution of Zwingli one may note a phase, lasting from about 1514 to 1519, which was dominated by the influence of Erasmus. The poem entitled *Jesus' Lament to Mankind*, in which the Saviour complains that believers seek elsewhere than in Himself those good things which He alone can give them, made a profound impression on Ulrich. But the palm must be accorded to the Greek text of the New Testament which came from the press in 1516. Zwingli, convinced that divine truth is contained in Holy Scripture— a conviction which he certainly owed to the influence of Erasmus—began to copy out the letters of Paul.

There is nothing so moving as to study the traces of a piece of keen research. The old folio volumes, covered with marginal notes, evoke for us the mornings and evenings when this man, avid for truth, pursued his passionate quest. Walther Köhler, with a historian's zeal equalling—*mutatis mutandis*—the reformer's own, has investigated the inscriptions and has assembled the essentials in a work which is still in course of publication.[1] The four sections which were published between 1937 and 1941 show Zwingli getting to grips with the Epistles and the Fathers and using for the

---

[1] This admirable effort, which was interrupted by the war and by death, is to be continued.

understanding of St. Paul what Jerome, Ambrose, Origen and others can teach him. The texts which have been brought to light do not all date from the period of his work at Glarus; the study is pursued from the end of 1516 at Einsiedeln and from 1519 at Zürich. An ingenious scholar of the 19th century, Usteri, has called attention to a noticeable development in the handwriting: the shape of the *d's* differs, a fact which enables us to classify chronologically (with a greater or lesser degree of accuracy, of course) the glosses of Zwingli. The latter cannot be compared with the commentaries which Luther at the same time was expounding to the students of Wittenberg. A gulf separates the clearly formulated teaching of the drofessor from the gropings of the student. The Vicar of Glarus is trying to see things clearly and for that purpose uses such help as he may. Sometimes, but rarely, a personal observation expresses his conclusion, such as that cry written in the margin of Augustine's *City of God*: "Ah, God! if only Adam had eaten a pear!"

Usually it is indirectly, through the patristic texts copied out opposite the difficult Biblical passages, that the direction of his mind becomes apparent. As Köhler points out, the keys which he used to discover the meaning of the Epistles are not those which Augustine supplied to Luther at the same time; the guide here is rather Erasmus accompanied by the cohort of his favourite Fathers. The Bible of Zwingli is the Bible of humanism.

This conclusion explains from far back the independence of attitude which the Swiss reformer was later to display towards the reformer of Saxony (Luther). The relations of the two theologians were not those of disciple and master. The path of development followed by Ulrich was truly original. If, from 1519, he began to know and to read Luther, the bases of his conviction had already been established. He openly proclaimed at a date when he had already deviated from Erasmus that the latter had marked out the path for him; in the immense effort to achieve a renewal of life, the German monk was neither the first nor the only one.

The influence of Erasmus on Zwingli was indisputably

prior in date. We have seen the admiration which the priest of Glarus, lost amid the mountain peaks, pledged to the prince of letters. In 1514 he dedicated to him a dialogue, the text of which is lost. In the spring of 1515, the opportunity came his way of meeting the author of the *Praise of Folly*. We can imagine the sentiments which filled his heart on this first contact from the letter of fervent gratitude which, on his return to the presbytery, he penned on April 29: "It was an extraordinary proof of your kindness", he wrote, "that you were not ashamed of a man so small and so unskilled in letters." Canon Cristiani accused Zwingli on this occasion of "handling the censer with admirable persistence". But is not this to forget the glow of brilliance which at that time surrounded Erasmus, who was eighteen years older than his correspondent, and the sort of ecstasy which seized the apprentice writer when a master of the pen deigned for the first time to show an interest in him? Are not enthusiasm and gratitude in a young man the intimation of humility?

The bond formed by reading, correspondence and the conversations of Basle was maintained for ten years. From 1519, reservations began to appear. But Zwingli never denied his debt to Erasmus. When the storm burst over the *De Servo Arbitrio*, he appreciated at once the damage that would be caused by this quarrel with Luther, and deplored it. He foresaw the harshness and bitterness that would mark the conflict. "The one will not have confronting him gentle souls like Budé and Lefèvre d'Etaples, nor will the other have orphan pupils such as Latomus or fools like Eck", he confided with deep anxiety to his friend Beatus Rhenanus.

CHAPTER THREE

Chaplain at Einsiedeln: The Call to Zürich

O N HIS RETURN from Marignano, Zwingli had gone
back to Glarus with a heavy heart and an agitated
mind. The useless sacrifices of an absurd war depressed
him. The thoughts which he revolved in his head found
expression in a poem of one hundred and seventy lines, *The
Labyrinth*, in which, quite in the Renaissance spirit, he
clothed his preoccupations in the form of myth. Theseus has
taken it into his head to conquer the minotaur. Armed with
the thread of Ariadne, he enters the labyrinth, where he is
welcomed by a series of threatening symbolic animals: the
lion representing the pope; the eagle, the emperor; the
cock, France; the ox, central Switzerland, and the bear,
western Switzerland. Nothing daunted, the hero gives battle
only to discover that these frightening personages are
painted canvasses. Eventually he reaches the monster in its
lair and slays it. The moral, expressed in the conclusion,
compares with Theseus the valiant citizen who is concerned
about the good of his country. Too many men plunge into
the labyrinth of life without a guide, they take appearance
for reality, they lose themselves in the windings of the corridors, and never succeed in conquering the minotaur, that is
to say, vice and sin. Happy the man who trusts in Ariadne's
thread, which is reason in the loftiest sense of the term, the
science of God. In many hearts the love of God is lacking.
That is why

> The world is full today
> Of trickery and infidelity.
> Because Christ's image shines in us no more

> Nothing but heathendom and evil power
> Or greater ill, holds sway.
> Ah, shame!

Behind this fable it is not difficult to see the wounded
idealism of Ulrich, his disgust in face of the bargainings of the
defeated Swiss with their conquerors. Francis I held in high
esteem the little people whose many sons he had laid low on
the Milanese plain. These brave soldiers, he calculated, would
make excellent mercenaries. Prodigal with his gold, with
that mixture of cunning and magnificence which always
characterized him, the king obtained in November, 1515,
the alliance of the Confederation. Thus the horrible contract
of hire signed by the pope would be perpetuated; the price
of blood would be paid by another. Francis, who moreover
paid better than Pope Julius II, lured the Swiss away into
his own service. The men of Glarus, bewitched or bribed,
plunged right into the affair; Zwingli, incapable of silencing
his indignation, drew down upon himself implacable hostility.
His ministry at Glarus became difficult. He agreed to leave
his parish temporarily for the post of preacher at Einsiedeln.
"I have changed my situation", he wrote six months later
to his friend Vadian, "not for pleasure or to earn more money;
the partisans of the French have obliged me to do so." He
left his first church reluctantly. The separation, in his own
mind, was to be for a time only; he remained the beneficed
incumbent and had himself replaced by an assistant priest.

The Benedictine abbey of Einsiedeln, situated, as the crow
flies, a mere eighteen miles or so from Glarus, but separated
from that town by a barrier of high mountain peaks, boasts
even today of a glorious past. Built in the first half of the
10th century on the site of the cell of St. Meinrad, the pious
hermit who was assassinated in 861, it has become famous
through its statue of the Virgin made of black wood, before
which throngs of pilgrims come and pray every year. The
procession has been going on since the Middle Ages; today
the motor coaches of Germany and Austria have taken the

place of the succession of carriages and pilgrims on foot. The same devout crowd prostrates itself before the richly ornate little chapel in this enormous baroque church built at the end of the 17th and the beginning of the 18th centuries. Nothing remains of the sanctuary in which Zwingli officiated. Here, as at Glarus, fire has blotted out every trace of the past. There remains only the admirable mountain setting, the slopes covered with pasture-land and forests, in particular the dense fir plantations at the foot of which squat the vast outbuildings and annexes of the abbey. Zwingli himself described the abbey as being situated in the midst of "a gloomy forest".

The spiritual life of Einsiedeln was at this time somewhat dormant. The restriction of the novitiate to young noblemen who were in a position to pay a significant dowry had reduced it to the level of a pious family concern. The number of monks had melted away to such an extent that in 1516 there were only two, the abbot Conrad von Hohenrechberg and the administrator Diebold von Geroldseck. The former, who at the age of forty in 1480 had become master of the cloister and its lands, was now growing old and devoting more time to hunting than to singing the offices. He was more frequently resident at Saint-Gerold, situated in the Vorarlberg among forests well stocked with game, than at Einsiedeln. His right-hand man, Geroldseck, the scion of a noble but poor German family, conscientiously watched over the material interests of the cloister, an upright man but lacking in breadth of view and culture. He much admired the learning of the new chaplain. Zwingli, after his call to Zürich, describing him to his friend Leo Jud, to whom he wished to transmit his office, as "not specially learned", but "having a high regard for knowledge and fond of scholars". Geroldseck gave to Ulrich, who was very nearly his contemporary, a lasting friendship. When the hour of momentous decisions struck, in 1525, he relinquished his rich prebend and died by the side of the reformer at the Battle of Cappel in 1531.

We have very little detailed information about the two years spent at Einsiedeln. From a copious correspondence, only four letters of Zwingli survive. He pursued his lonely study of scripture and the Fathers, but this did not prevent him from conscientiously fulfilling his priestly duties, and taking an interest in the people of the small town who were entrusted to his care. For their sakes above all, he sang the offices, he baptized, he married, he buried. Also he heard the confessions of numerous pilgrims; his preaching, which became ever more centred on Holy Scripture, moved them many a time. A young priest of Basle, Gaspard Hédion, acknowledged to him in November, 1519: "For a long time I have desired to be among your friends, even though it were in the lowliest place . . . for such a fine, intelligent, serious, Spirit-filled and evangelical sermon as you preached at Whitsuntide a year and a half ago in the sanctuary of the Holy Virgin at Einsiedeln on the paralytic of Luke, chapter 5, has powerfully drawn me towards you." Such a testimony is no mean thing; at one stroke the orator won the lasting confidence of his hearers.

A few years later, tracing the course of his own development, Zwingli noted: "In the year 1516 I began to preach in such wise that I never mounted the pulpit without taking personally to heart the Gospel for the day and explaining it with reference to Scripture alone." The secret work of the exegete in his presbytery sustained and inspired this ministry. Professional routine gave way before the burning desire to propagate the newly discovered truth. He continued and completed his copying out of the Pauline letters. He even learnt the sacred text by heart.

Little by little the Book of books was illuminated, while the gulf which yawned between the customs of the Church and primitive Christian piety became ever more manifest. In the summer of 1518 the monk Samson, like the notorious Tetzel in Germany, began to skim the wealth of the Swiss by selling indulgences to the profit of Pope Leo X. Zwingli, from the pulpit, sharply attacked this trafficker in forgiveness, who, beginning modestly, was now displaying increasing pomp. In a letter addressed to his friend Beatus Rhenanus, which is unfortunately lost, he denounced the

absurdity of the enterprise. "We were extremely amused,"
Rhenanus replied, "by your salesman of indulgences and the
eloquent delineation of him which you pictured for us. . . .
What frivolous methods, unworthy of pontifical legates!
Is there no limit to what they will do to enable Italy to
despoil us of our wealth? Nothing is more painful to me than
these ceremonies with which Christian people are burdened
and these old wives' tales which have nothing to do with the
faith itself. . . ." The sentiments of the humanist thus echo
those of the priest of Einsiedeln. The latter, in virtue of that
gift of humour which Myconius recognized in him, adopts
the attitude of Figaro several centuries in advance. He
pokes fun at abuses in order not to weep over them.

In such an atmosphere, the notes which become more
frequent on the folio volumes spring from no lifeless erudition. It is a lively personality which has inscribed opposite
the text of Romans and Corinthians now the interpretation
of Origen, now that of Ambrose. His meditations remained
very reserved. There were no cries of indignation, no wild
accusations. The sincere will to understand, to penetrate
to the heart of the apostle's thought, alone directed the pen
of Zwingli. He is convinced that truth lies in Holy Scripture
and he strives to master it. Behind the copied quotation or
the brief analysis, the reader feels at times a quivering pen
and a mind in travail. When for example opposite the text of
Rom. 15: 15-16, "Exercising the ministry of the gospel in
virtue of the grace which God has given me", he writes, "Let
the rectors of the churches do nothing which Christ has not
first inspired in them", it is easy to imagine the reverberation
of such words in a heart which was anxious about the
wrongful multiplication of ceremonies and the moral decadence of the clergy.

As regards the torturing problem of the flesh, the same
reserve marks the texts which have been assembled by Köhler. Zwingli does not wear his heart on his sleeve. Meditating
on chapter 14 of Romans, he writes like a wise schoolboy
by the side of verse 14, "Nothing is unclean in itself", a
comment of Origen: "Nothing in God's creation is impure

by its nature." Similarly he elucidates verse 9 of 1 Cor. 7, "It is better to marry than to burn", by this text of Ambrose: "To burn means to be led or overcome by desire". With a few rare exceptions, no personal commentary accompanies these patristic comments.

The iconography of Zwingli is extremely poor. No reliable portrait of Ulrich in the early part of his life has been preserved. The money which he laboriously earned he preferred to take to the booksellers rather than the painters. We have merely a posthumous oil painting dating from 1531, just after his death, due to the talent of Hans Asper, who knew him well, to remind us of the features of the man who turned away from Roman Catholicism an important part of Switzerland. From Einsiedeln to Cappel, thirteen years elapsed. The face, devoid of beauty, but suggesting energy and pensiveness, with its prominent chin protuberant beneath the lower lip, and its broad pug nose, cannot have changed much. The man of forty-seven, to be sure, resembled the man of thirty-four. There is a keen observant look about the eyes, as though their possessor were deeply interested in human beings and ideas; the total impression is one of a calmness and self-confidence which is not exclusive of kindness. He clearly belongs to a country where Latin mobility is as rarely found as Teutonic passion. Many faces may be encountered between the Alps and the Juras, in the neat charming villages of the Swiss plateau, which resemble Zwingli's. His complexion has the ruddy glow of health. "The red-faced Uly" was the ironic comment of his opponents. "A friendly and florid face" notes the chronicler Kessler. The traces of the farming stock from which he sprang have not been swept away by the long evenings spent in the company of Origen and Ambrose or of Erasmus. His country origin moreover is not merely reflected in his features; his biographers are at one in emphasizing that his conduct as a reformer was marked by a prudence which distinguishes him both from Luther and from Calvin.

From Einsiedeln to Cappel, through the twelve years of the Zürich ministry, an important change took place.

Ulrich's expression in Asper's portrait is grave. The eye alone betrays that a smile is not far away. Struggles and responsibilities have matured the bantering student of Basle, the young chaplain of the Benedictine Abbey.

The preaching of Zwingli, in a place as much frequented as Einsiedeln, could not pass unnoticed. In the autumn of 1517, the magistrates of Winterthur thought of him as a possible successor to their parson who had just died. The rumour of this reached Zwingli, who, even before any official steps were taken, wrote to decline the vacant post and to suggest that one of his friends should be appointed instead. He intervened in the affair not merely because he was anxious to secure for the people of Winterthur a good leader, but also from a wish to prevent the appointment of a German priest in this important city. "I would like our posts to be given to our men", he comments at the beginning of his letter; "they are not inferior to foreigners either in wisdom or knowledge —quite the contrary." As for himself, he feels that his heart is still in Glarus; that is why he refuses to stand.

At the end of 1518, however, when Zürich wished to have him for its principal church, the Great Minster, Zwingli did not refuse. The first approaches were made by his old friend Myconius. "Great would be my joy", he wrote, "if Zürich could welcome Zwingli as one of its priests." The chaplain of Einsiedeln was known and esteemed in Zürich on the shores of the Limmat, as a result of the sermons he had preached to pilgrims. That same year, at Whitsuntide, fifteen hundred men of Zürich had gone to pray in the sanctuary of the Blessed Virgin at Einsiedeln. If the preacher's life of study escaped them, the man, whom they liked, inspired their confidence. The twenty-four priests of the chapter who took the decision had no suspicion that they were inviting into their midst a reformer.

Zwingli benefited from the friendship of the Valais Cardinal, Schinner, whom he had met during the course of the wars in Italy, and in 1518 he received, on the suggestion of the nuncio Pucci, the much-envied dignity of pontifical acolyte. He saw again at Einsiedeln the first of his patrons and told him quite decisively of his doubts and criticisms concerning a decadent papacy. The Bishop of Sion was not by any means unwilling to listen. On the contrary, he affirmed that on many points he was in full agreement with such views. The hour for hunting down heretics had not yet struck. Even though Luther had nailed his theses to the church door at Wittenberg on the last day of October 1517, the Church was not yet split into two, on the one side a power defending itself sharply and, on the other, rebels attacking; it still remained in such a state of spiritual fluidity as made permissible all hopes. In an intimate talk, a cardinal and a priest could freely discuss vexed questions and burning issues of the time.

The only point which worried the three venerable and influential priests who had been charged by their colleagues to examine possible candidates was that of the morals and manners of Ulrich. The frank avowal which he made of his struggles and lapses, however, dispelled their suspicions. The candidate whom some seemed to prefer to him, a Swabian named Mär, disclosed, moreover, that he was the father of six children and the holder of several benefices. The comparison told in favour of Zwingli who, more disinterested than his rival, surrendered, as soon as he was appointed, the benefice of Glarus to one of his former pupils, Valentine Tschudi. Matters did not drag out; at Christmas, Zwingli preached his last sermon at Einsiedeln and settled in at Zürich on December 27, 1518, the feast of St. John the Evangelist. When he entered on his office in this town where he was to preach for twelve years, did he have any presentiment that he would preside over a spiritual change and upheaval which was to have lasting effects?

CHAPTER FOUR

Beginnings at Zürich: the Great Plague

W HEN, BEFORE SINGING mass, Ulrich mounted
the pulpit of his new parish for the first time on
January 1, 1519, he was celebrating his thirty-fifth
birthday. The time was far away when, as a child, he
wandered with his brothers over the meadow-lands and
through the woods of Wildhaus. There, five of them had now
taken over the paternal domain, one of the younger brothers
was dead, while the seventh, Andrew, who was devoting
himself to study, was soon to be settled alongside his elder
brother in a presbytery at Zürich.

Before leaving Einsiedeln, Zwingli, fully aware of his
responsibilities, made a decision to present to his new
hearers the integral Gospel. He resolved to meditate page by
page on the text of the Gospel of St. Matthew. In the fine
Norman church, with its sober outlines, he would expound
regularly the words and miracles of Christ, leaving aside
the legends concerning the saints with which it was custom-
ary to load sermons at the time.

The Great Minster (Gross Münster) still rears aloft its two
towers in the centre of the old part of Zürich. Its terrace,
overlooking the blue waters of the Limmat, is situated
opposite the ancient abbey of Notre Dame (the so-called
Frau Münster) which stands meditatively on the other bank,
on a level with the river. A little further away, on an emin-
ence, rises the belfry of St. Peter with its monumental dial.
The past history of the town, which at the beginning of the
16th century numbered some seven thousand souls (if the

suburbs are included), is thus reflected still in the present-day industrial agglomeration of half a million inhabitants.

In 1519, Zürich was one of the thirteen Helvetic states. A centre of fairs, it occupied an important economic and political position in the Confederation, which bears no comparison however to that which it has attained in modern Switzerland as a result of the construction of the St. Gotthard Pass. At that time, wealth had increased, bringing with it a relaxation of morals. The middle classes derived great profit from the trade in iron, salt, and wheat. The fervent piety of previous generations secured for the Church great prestige. Besides the twenty-four canons of the Great Minster and the seven canons of the Frau Münster, fifty-seven chaplains and priests of one sort or another shared among themselves the pastoral work of the three parishes of the city. In addition, the monasteries of the Dominicans, Franciscans and Augustinians, the priories of Dominican and Béguine nuns, besides other ecclesiastical establishments, formed a group of about two hundred monks, nuns and priests. A certain tension sometimes prevailed between this numerous clergy and the city's councils. The Bishop of Constance, Hugo von Hohenlandenberg, spiritual head of the diocese from 1496 to 1530 and "a peace-loving and noble lord", evoked a deferential esteem. His very aloofness from the town made him a not very formidable overseer. Intellectually, Zürich could not stand comparison with Basle, which possessed a university and upon which the installation of Erasmus had conferred the rank of a true centre of European culture.

Political power rested in the hands of two councils. That of the Two Hundred comprised a large majority of delegates from the craftsmen's corporations, together with a few members of the Constaffel, a society made up of the heirs of the ancient nobility. As has often been the case in Switzerland, a compromise had linked the new régime with the vestiges of the ancient one. The Little Council, whose members shared in the deliberations of the Great Council, numbered fifty members. Two burgomasters stood for six months in turn at the pinnacle of this complicated structure. The Little Council had the powers of administration; all important problems were decided by the Two Hundred.

Thus Zwingli found himself involved in the civic life of an independent town, accustomed to regulate for itself its own affairs. But nothing at this stage gave any intimation of a clash with the Roman control of the Church. The people of Zürich were not accustomed to discuss dogma. In their development, the influence of the new priest was to be decisive. Inaugurating his course of sermons on St. Matthew did Zwingli contemplate setting up Scripture in opposition to the Church? Nothing would lead us to suppose so. A strong desire for simplification and return to essentials inspires him. His tendencies recall that humanistic evangelical spirit, of which in France Lefèvre d'Etaples and Bishop Briçonnet were at this time the outstanding representatives. Two very different events of the year 1519 deflected by their impact the course of his development: his encounter with Luther, and the great plague.

In 1519 Zwingli discovered Luther; not the man, but his books. The first mention, in his correspondence, of the Saxon monk goes back to a letter dated December 6, 1518, in which Beatus Rhenanus tells him that he knows him ill. The name, invested in an aureole of glory, has crossed frontiers. What did the theologian of Wittenberg want exactly? Ulrich, his interest stimulated by vague echoes in connexion with the struggle over indulgences, had for the time being to remain hungry for news. But on December 26 Luther's books reached Basle. Rhenanus expressed his delight. News relative to the reformer and his works then appeared frequently in the epistolary discussions of the two friends. It is characteristic that Zwingli's admiration, expressed in February 1519, did not separate Luther from Erasmus. "Luther and the *Compendium* of Erasmus", he wrote, "reap applause from all intellectual men, the latter in particular from myself; I never remember having derived so much profit from so small a volume." When the manuscript of a lampoon denouncing the avarice of the clergy reached him through Rhenanus, he showed it to Cardinal Schinner, who whispered into his ear: "Try to get it printed by Froben" (letter of March 9, 1519). Thus a member of the higher clergy, a humanist, and a future heresiarch were at this moment still walking in company. In this extraordinary phase, it was still legitimate to cherish every hope of a peaceful reformation.

Ulrich continued, in the Great Minster, his cycle of sermons on St. Matthew. Did the *Our Father* of Luther confirm his own criticism of the invocation of saints? If so, he offered to buy an important number of copies so as to circulate them widely and gain support for his preaching from the authority of the monk. Is it right to imagine Zwingli, as does Oscar Farner, recommending the writings of Luther without taking the trouble to study them? Being excessively busy often obliges one to read quickly, too quickly. The evenings spent at Zürich, with many friends and much discussion, ceased to afford the meditative calm which he had enjoyed at Einsiedeln. The correspondence contains complaints about his lack of leisure, such as will recur regularly from now on. But to suppose a total abstention from effort at study in a matter so basic seems to be going too far. On many points, evidently, the position of Zwingli had already been established. He read, not so much to enlighten himself as to rejoice in the company of a contemporary who was reaching the same conclusions. His native prudence was shaken, indeed painfully shocked, by the verbal violence of Luther. In a letter dating from the autumn of 1519, he depicted him to a hesitant humanist of Freiburg in Breisgau, one Zasius, as a new Elijah—a description which his correspondent found exaggerated. But the qualification is illuminating. Zwingli admired the courage of the man who denounced abuses with the frankness of the prophet challenging Ahab, the criminal ruler. He was interested not so much in the theologian as in the revolutionary. In this respect the dispute of Leipzig, with its denunciation of papal authority, assumed capital importance for the future of the reformation in Switzerland.

The extant letters show Zwingli quite clear in his own mind about his faith. He was no longer a student. Pastoral work occupied the greater part of his time. He made every endeavour to proclaim the Gospel faithfully. The correspondence with Rhenanus, which from that summer onwards was doubled by messages addressed to Myconius, now settled at Lucerne, contains the echo of many criticisms and acts of resistance. The abolition of abuses would not proceed without entailing hurt and damage. "But I keep ever in mind that word of Paul: if I wished still to please men, I should not be the servant of Christ"—thus in May he confided to his friend at Basle. In December it was with the man at Lucerne that he discussed the same subject. Myconius had given some objectors a good setting-down. "I applaud the fact that finally you gave them their answer, but I would prefer to win over obstinate men of that kind by kindness and a courteous welcome rather than to clash with them by an irritated and violent attitude." From such comments we gain the impression of a Christian anxious to be firm but conciliatory, of one who was desirous of avoiding useless clashes.

In the summer of 1519 a terrible epidemic of the plague rolled over Switzerland. One after the other, the Helvetic cities were ravaged by it. Winterthur lost five hundred of its two thousand inhabitants. Lucerne counted as many as thirty-two burials a day. When the scourge reached Zürich, Zwingli was resting at the baths of Pfaffers; in conformity with the duties of his office, he braved the danger and returned to his parish, visiting the dying and burying the dead. This dreadful malady seized him in September. Outside, it was rumoured that he was dead. The papal legate became anxious and placed his own doctor at the disposal of Ulrich, who swallowed on the orders of the physician every kind of medicine. One of his colleagues, Canon Hoffmann, suspecting him of heresy, went to see him on what he supposed to be his deathbed in the expectation of some retraction. But Zwingli's robust constitution resisted the disease. Of the seven thousand inhabitants of Zürich, two

thousand according to one chronicler, three thousand five
hundred according to another, succumbed. At Basle his
friends rejoiced when the good news reached them. For a
long time still, he complained of weakness and bad head-
aches. It mattered little: he was saved. A few months later,
the terrible disease snatched away his brother Andrew,
who returned too soon from Glarus to Zürich where the
epidemic seemed to have died away. The harsh blow over-
whelmed Ulrich when he was as yet scarcely recovered
himself.

The feelings aroused in him by the nearness of death and
the return to health are known to us by a hymn which he
wrote most probably just after his healing:

> Help, Lord God, help
> In this sore strait:
> Death, my soul knows,
> Is at the gate.

He implores God, if it be His will, to withdraw from him the
arrow which has wounded him, to remove the evil which
leaves him not an hour of repose. If God wills that he should
die:

> . . . . Far then from earth
> My spirit Thou wilt bear,
> Never to sin again,
> Never to soil with my corrupting stain
> Hearts that are true and fair.

In the extremity of his illness he invoked divine consola-
tions. When he recovered he sang of his joy and gratitude:

> More than of old
> In health's new days
> My song shall tell
> Thy truth, Thy praise.

The suffering through which he had passed was the seal for
him of a new lease of life. The heart which had been furrowed
by affliction gave itself more unreservedly to God. When

53

Andrew was taken away from him, he wrote in his agony (November 25, 1520): "I am far from nourishing resentment against God, for I have learnt to submit myself utterly to His divine will." However, at the first moment, he confessed that he "wept like a woman". He recovered his equanimity but his pen trembled between his fingers when he recalled the vanished life: "He was so highly gifted a young man, and one whose life allowed us to hope for the finest things." For several weeks, at the urgent entreaty of his anxious friends, he stayed away from the presbytery which death had visited. When he established himself there again, together with the boarders for whose instruction he was responsible, the familiar place welcomed a man who had been matured by grief.

Part Two

The Reformer

CHAPTER FIVE

Zwingli, the Biblical Preacher

WITH THE GOSPEL of St. Matthew open on the pulpit desk of the Great Minster, Zwingli's proposal to explain it in its entirety, page by page, need not in itself have worried either Constance or Rome. Those who were alert to his intention thought it but the passing fancy of a young priest. None the less, the central principle of the reformation is enshrined in the will to heed the divine word of Scripture. The statues remained fixed against the pillars, the mass unfolded itself according to the normal rite; but the focal point of interest and consequently of authority had shifted. God is in the very words of Christ, of the apostles and of the prophets. Through those words, the Church enters into communion with its Lord. It submits itself to the sacred text which invites it to new life, and to the constant renewal of life. Scripture now dominates tradition.

There was, however, a priest of Zürich who appreciated the scope and implications of the discreet revolution. This was Conrad Hoffmann, a guardian of morals, he who had visited his dying colleague to bring him back into the right way. The venerable canon sent a written complaint to the Provost of the Great Minster. The latter forwarded it to Zwingli, who defended himself by invoking the example of Augustine and Chrysostom and urging that the lists of prescribed passages dated only from Charlemagne. In comparison with this system of reading only fragments of scripture, the saints of the 5th century were invested with the authority and the halo of antiquity.

Free to preach according to his own understanding of the task, during the twelve last years of his career Zwingli adhered to the principle he had adopted. After St. Matthew, in 1520 he commented on the Acts of the Apostles; in 1521, on the First Epistle to Timothy, and on Galatians; then, to silence the criticism of those who contested the authority of Paul, he took the two Epistles of St. Peter. In 1522 he tackled Hebrews, then came back to the Gospels; in 1523 St. Luke, in 1524 St. John, while in the first term of 1525 he went back to various Pauline texts. In the second term, he had recourse for the first time to the Old Testament: he goes through, one after the other, Genesis (which he finished on March 2, 1527) Joshua, Judges, Ruth, Samuel, 1 and 2 Kings (1527), Isaiah (1528). Jeremiah and other prophets, Ezra, Nehemiah, Esther, Chronicles, fill up the last years. A few question-marks are to be noted at the end of the list.

There are no extant manuscripts of the sermons. Ulrich spoke with fluency and copiousness. Writing on December 29 to Haller, the future reformer of Berne, who had been in his congregation and asked him for the text of his sermon, he apologizes for his inability to satisfy him: "I never write out my sermons, a fact which might be annoying to one who has no idea of my many duties."

Calvin, who preached quite as often and enjoyed as little leisure, possessed the pen of a clever and ready writer. His commentaries normally contained the substance of his sermons. Moreover, in Geneva he had the advantage of a skilful secretary in the person of a French refugee, Denis Ragueneau, who copied down and established the text of more than seven hundred sermons. Others collaborated with him in this work, leaving a rich heritage, which the negligence of a librarian at the beginning of the last century has unfortunately much diminished. Zürich was far less well equipped. For a long time the preaching of Zwingli was accessible only through some important discourses, formulated as a result of special circumstances, or through the reports and notes of occasional hearers. Recently a manuscript long buried in the public library of the town has been found to contain notes taken under the arches of the Great Minster during the years 1528-29, and which were recopied and put in order long afterwards by a country pastor, Henry Buchmann. Was the latter himself among the congregation of Zwingli or has he used a manuscript of Leo Jud, the close friend of Ulrich? This detail however concerns only scholars.

However it may be, the sermons which the reformer preached on Isaiah and Jeremiah were published in 1957, thanks to the labours of the diligent Oscar Farner, who translated them into modern German. The two prophets have been studied chapter by chapter. In spite of the fact that Buchmann's notes are certainly incomplete—they were not anything like a shorthand report—it is impossible not to recognize the vital and challenging character of many of these exhortations. Despite the distance which separates us from the preacher, we feel that we are here confronted by a man with a great heart. Such sermons are conversational in tone and leave far behind the inevitable coldness of a formal theological treatise. With the exegesis are mingled counsels, apostrophes, consoling words. The soul of the pastor here unveils its tenderness and its concern for the weak.

Consider his explanation of Isa. 9, which contains the famous prophecy, "Unto us a child is born": "The 'us' is emphasized. This child will be ours. And he, who is ours, will be the one through whom all will come about. Children never wound anyone, they never kill anyone. The child is kind, gentle, and candid." Continuing his meditation on the passage, he dwells on the following words: "And the government shall rest on His shoulders." By means of this comparison, he goes on to show that government and rule are above all a very heavy burden. "Like the thoughtful father of a family who watches over his own, so as to organize his family well and promote its interests, to the end that all may be in good order, so kings and superior officers should conduct themselves. Many imagine that their life will be comfortable and rich in pleasures, permitting themselves to seek their own good and not that of their people. Christ was very different: He died for His people and carried the cross on His shoulders. All who wish truly to be kings should follow His example."

If the imitation of Christ is one of Zwingli's favourite themes, if he constantly portrays their Master to his flock as one who was meek and lowly of heart, elsewhere he invites them to discern the hand of God in the trials of life. "I will give them a heart to know that I am the Lord" (Jer. 24: 7). "The prophet clearly explains here why God punishes His people with captivity or other misfortune. It did not happen by chance. God does nothing without a reason. Hence we should not impute these troubles to the nearest cause, as when people complain: 'If only there had not been such sharp frosts this spring, the vintage would have been abundant. . . .' God has willed it so, He who is the primal and original cause. . . ." "If God resolves to inflict a universal punishment, He begins with His own house, i.e. with His own people, for they too are sinners. . . . If as Christians we had only this one vice, that of swearing, we should not be surprised that God decides to send a punishment on all His people. We call ourselves the people of God, even the people of Christ (Christian derives from Christ) and we swear scandalously . . . by all the wounds or by all the sufferings of Christ, for example. . . ."

This unadorned style, popular in the best sense of the term, betrays the preacher's desire to reach the simplest hearts. In this respect he reminds us of Luther and the Curé d'Ars much more than of the subtle and brilliant Erasmus. His Christian charity banishes useless complications, those of language as well as those of ritual. "The essential, in My religion, says God, is that you should obey Me", he explains with regard to Jeremiah 7; and on Isaiah 1:17, *Defend the fatherless, plead for the widow*, he says: "These are the works which are well pleasing to God. You must cast off the burden of sin and then at once the joy of a good conscience will fill your life. If any one bears a heavy burden and asks, 'How shall I manage to dance?' he is mad. We likewise: if we bend under the weight of sin and if we try by means of ceremonies to please God, and to gain peace of conscience, we are fools."

Anyone studying these sermons, which are three years later than the great reformation decisions, but hardly ten years distant from his first Zürich homilies, is surprised to find so little of confessional polemic in them. Ulrich aimed essentially at producing in his hearers a change of heart. Yet, here and there, he lets fall from the pulpit some point of doctrine. Thus the commentary on the verse (Isa. 43: 11) *I am the Lord, and besides me there is no saviour*, provides the occasion to note that we should not adore the saints alongside God like those people who "apart from God wish to have gods for themselves". Verse 25 of the same chapter, *I am He who blots out your transgressions*, is accompanied by the terse remark: "Here falls the power of the keys claimed by the papists." It is to be noted that in Zwingli's interpretations the New Testament constantly penetrates the Old, illuminating it with its light.

Buchmann considerably shortens the sermons of Ulrich and is content to give the main points, but a number of the sentences must have been spoken as they stand. The sobriety and lucidity, the gentleness yet firmness which characterize them are also found in Zwingli's letters and other works. Despite a mode of speech which smacks of the soil, he is far removed from the violence of Luther. He hates also grandiloquence. Leo Jud praised him for his simplicity. If he did not write much, it was not simply a question of time: improvisation seemed to him a more direct method of communication, devoid as it was of the flourishes common in the written word. His voice was rather weak and his delivery rapid. When in 1528 he preached in Strasburg Cathedral, many complained that they had not understood him.

Sometimes it would happen that Zwingli mingled with his serious exhortations ironic and saucy comments which amused the faithful and caused Canon Hoffmann to raise his eyebrows. His biographers quote several examples. One needs to have lived in his country if one is not to be too severe with him in this respect. The sense of humour of one race does not correspond to that of another. What brings a smile to the lips of a German Swiss does not necessarily amuse his compatriot of Geneva or Lausanne. When Ulrich advises the priest who is anxious to preserve extreme unction to keep his oil for his salad, adding: "We become blessed through faith, not through oil, otherwise it would be containers that would be happiest", we must not forget his native farm and the crudities of the Middle Ages only just past. His reading of the ancients and his contact with humanists have not altogether effaced the roughness of the mountain peasant.

It is said that one of his hearers was once provoked by the personal allusions heard in the course of a sermon at the Great Minster. How much truth and how much slander is contained in this criticism? It is difficult to say. The prophets are sometimes ruthless in their frankness. The vindictive Hoffmann reproached him for denouncing too openly the vices of the monks, for giving too much prominence to local events, and, in his appeals for penitence, for confounding grave with venial sins.

Before preaching, Zwingli was accustomed to utter a short prayer inspired by Ps. 119: "Almighty God, eternal and compassionate, whose Word is a lamp to our feet and a light to our path, open and enlighten our hearts, that we may understand purely and clearly Thy words; may they transform us according to this exact understanding, that we may never be displeasing to Thy divine Majesty, through Jesus Christ, our Lord. Amen."

CHAPTER SIX

Ways and Means: the Temporizer

IN 1517 LUTHER WENT straight ahead. His militant temperament, goaded by Eck in the Leipzig dispute, provoked him to those utterances which caused him to be dubbed a Hussite. In April, 1521, he threw down as a challenge to the assembled Diet at Worms his glorious refusal: "I can do no other; so help me God." As soon as Zwingli realized the risk of a decisive clash, he felt a desire to avoid it. Between Wittenberg and Zürich there was no wall of partition. News circulated rapidly. In the summer of 1520 the text of the papal bull *Exsurge Domine* became widely known. The term "Lutheran" was rapidly becoming synonymous with "heretical". The wave of indignation, suspicion, and repression which broke over Germany reached Switzerland.

In consequence of the correspondence which went on unceasingly between Zürich, St. Gall, Lucerne, and Basle, we can picture Ulrich alert to the trend of events. On May 4 he noted with displeasure the journey to Rome of Eck, Luther's adversary. A few weeks later, he told Rhenanus of the lectures given by Commander Conrad Schmid of Küssnacht, who explained the Epistle to the Romans to his monks, and pointed out the moral support afforded him, in public opinion, by this effort, which was parallel to his own: "My hearers become kinder when they have heard him", for they have lost sight of the Gospel, "which has grown so old that nobody any longer discerns its true face." His friend Myconius, in a letter of November 2, 1520, described the delicate situation in which the evangelists of

Lucerne found themselves: "Everywhere in the town people are crying out that Luther should be burnt and with him the schoolmaster [i.e. Myconius], and yet I never speak of Luther except to my intimate circle and even then very rarely."

Ecclesiastical authority as such did not yet seem to be stirred. Zwingli remained on good terms with the bishop. On October 8, 1520, Geroldseck, the administrator of Einsiedeln, and Faber, the Vicar-General of Constance, spent the day with him and Myconius. All three added their greetings to those which Ulrich sent to his correspondent, Rhenanus of Basle. This was a curious moment when nothing was as yet decided, when friendship still united those whom on the morrow hate would divide, when the pleasures of the table and conversation held off the smell of the fires of persecution.

At the moment when the men of Lucerne were fulminating against their schoolmaster, Zürich remained relatively calm. Should we admit, as Bullinger asserted years later, the publication at the end of 1520 of an order by civil authority asking priests to confine themselves to the preaching of the Gospel alone? Köhler believes there has been some confusion and that Zwingli's successor antedated a measure taken in 1523 or 1524. Oscar Farner and Emil Egli, on the contrary, urge the authenticity of this early political intervention in ecclesiastical matters. One fact seems certain: as early as 1520, Zwingli, under the fire of criticism, found among the laity the solid support which three years later enabled him to resist the thunders of episcopal authority. The Council of the Two Hundred, composed especially of craftsmen and small tradespeople, lent him support. Whether or not official authority adopted an attitude as early as 1520, the sympathy of the middle classes was his, and it was on that basis that he was to win the day. The German reformation with the princes, the Swiss reformation with the middle classes, represents a victory of the laity and the lower clergy over the hierarchy.

But, if the storm yet spared Zürich, the credit was due to

the patience which Zwingli showed. With the year of Worms, the fateful pontificate of Leo X was approaching its end. The pope, whose chief concern had been to build a sumptuous sanctuary, died at the end of 1521. He had showered wealth upon artists and adorned basilicas with marble. Did he realize that his superficiality of outlook was destined to produce a lasting schism in the Church? Before the tomb of the frivolous Medici pope one might have hoped for a successor whose mind would be open to new ideas, who would be animated by the desire to rescue the Church from corruption, and capable of discovering means of achieving a peaceful reform. Cardinal Schinner, the friend and protector of Zwingli, played an active part in the conclave. Through his influence, the papal tiara fell, after long debate, on Adrian of Utrecht, a Dutchman of austere life.

Zürich and Rome remained in military alliance as a result of the treaty of 1515. When the town refused to enter, with the rest of the Swiss, into the alliance concluded with France at the Diet of Lucerne (May 5, 1521), it granted to Leo fifteen hundred of the six thousand men whom he demanded through the intervention of the prelate of Valais and the nuncio Ennio Filonardi, on condition that the contingent would be used solely for the defence of the papal states. Zwingli opposed the decision, but it does not seem that his prestige at the Court of Rome suffered in consequence. In January, 1523, the pope addressed to him a personal message in which he assured him of his goodwill, and expressed the desire to see him more closely associated with the work of the papal see.

As soon as he was appointed, Adrian VI asked Schinner to draw up a plan of reform. The memorandum composed by the Bishop of Sion contained some interesting suggestions, but its author was not to witness their execution. The plague which ravaged Rome carried him off on September 12, 1522; a year later his master also succumbed. The tiara was restored to a Medici, Clement VII, an Italian prince who was more preoccupied with dynastic problems than with the Gospel.

So long as Schinner lived, the presence at Rome of the

prelate to whom Ulrich had talked familiarly about the abuses in the Church maintained in him the hope that the Church would be transformed by a decision of the hierarchy. In spite of obstacles and opposition, the possibility of a peaceful evolution remained. Did not the cardinal—immediately on the election of the new pope—write to the Council of Zürich of his delight, and put forward Adrian as a prelate of irreproachable conduct, deeply versed in the knowledge of Scripture? The priest of the Great Minster desired a progressive and legitimate development in harmony with the men who, like Erasmus, Lefèvre d'Etaples, and William Briçonnet, had been striving for some years to restore the Gospel to the centre of piety. He was concerned for the weak, who must not be offended, and at the end of December, 1521, enjoined his friend Berchtold Haller to spare the feelings of his bears—that is to say, the Bernese, whose spiritual guide he was. One must not cast pearls before swine, but win them over through gentleness and persuasion. Did not Paul set us an example when he "fed the Galatians on milk and not on solid foods"? Speaking to Myconius a year previously about the futility of relics—"everyone desires to become happy through the labours of others rather than his own"—he abounded in the same counsels of prudence.

CHAPTER SEVEN

Lent, 1522: the Dramatic Affair of the Sausages

THE DAMP AND inclement climate of central Switzerland demands a substantial rather than a fine diet. As everywhere in the valley of the Rhine, the foreigner is amazed to see the abundant collations of bread and pig meat consumed right in the middle of the afternoon. At the fairs, the vendor of grilled sausages does well; their savoury smell carried on the wind is sniffed on the merry-go-rounds and at the shooting stands, sharpening the appetite. That the reformation should be inaugurated by an alimentary drama will not shock anyone who has lived in this part of the world.

In his sermons at the Great Minster, Zwingli invited his congregation to distinguish between the eternal Gospel and the rules of the Church. Did he not declare one Sunday morning that Church tithe was a human and hence relative arrangement, to the great fright of several of the canons? Following the text of St. Matthew, he must have come upon that fifteenth chapter in which Christ denounces external ritual purifications as being of mere secondary importance: "It is not what goes into the mouth that defiles a man", proclaimed the Saviour. But, anxious to avoid irritating and often useless discussions, eager to lead his flock to Christ rather than to anticlericalism, Ulrich abstained from proposing immediate reforms.

When the guns of the peoples have been loaded for some time, popular wisdom has it that one fine morning they go off on their own. In ideological warfare it is the same. One evening in the Lent of 1522, a dozen men were discussing in the house of the printer Froschauer. He had had a very strenuous day. He was preparing for the Frankfurt fair a new edition of the Epistles of St. Paul, and his printing presses had been going day and night for weeks. In order to refresh his exhausted workmen, he had told his wife, in view of the high cost of fish, to get some meat from the butcher.[1] Sausages were served, not only to the weary typographers, but also to the guests of the printer, among whom there happened to be three priests: Zwingli, Leo Jud, and a country parson, Laurence Keller. Ulrich had not been fore-warned: when the reeking hot dish was held out to him, he refused, while the other guests, including the two remaining priests, guzzled. The episode had resounding repercussions. The magistrates were quickly informed and were much disturbed. The attitude of Zwingli is explained by his often-expressed desire to respect the weak; his fellow-guests were for the most part violent men, with whom prudence passed as pusillanimity. Every religious or political group includes some fanatics. The subsequent career of those who partici-pated in the famous sausage party is revealing. Several of them are found among the hotheads of other quarrels, and at their head was the iconoclastic bootmaker Hottinger, who was beheaded in 1524 in the county of Baden, where he was railing against the mass. Madmen outnumber the wise; the soundest ideas falling into the hands of the excitable become a formidable dynamite.

The scandal having become public, what was to be done? Zwingli does not hesitate: an important principle, that of Christian liberty, extolled by Luther in an immortal little work, was at stake. In order to defend both his friends and his own conduct, on March 29 he preached on the theme of fasting and had his sermon published. After passing in review the chief texts of the New Testament concerning foods, Ulrich declared with Paul that "to the pure all things are pure". Fasting is an act of personal renunciation. Christ commanded nothing on the matter: "Do you, of your own

[1] The eating of meat during Lent was forbidden by the Church. Fish was permitted.—*Tr*.

free will, wish to abstain from meat? then do not eat it! But allow your brother his liberty." The rich man who is idle does well to avoid too substantial a diet: he can, moreover, buy himself fish. But religion, it is said, becomes a pretext for disputes. For the sake of peace, Zwingli advised the Christian who is free not to make use of his undoubted right: "If the use of your freedom provokes your brother, you must not scandalize him without cause. . . . Use your liberty if no trouble ensues. . . . Instruct the weak, so that the number of the strong grows so great that no one is any longer offended."

The Council appointed a commission, consisting of the Provost of the Great Minster and the three parish priests of the city. This followed the lead of Zwingli, justified the rebels basically, but, to avoid further trouble, maintained the practice of fasting.

The Bishop of Constance, alerted by the enemies of Ulrich, resolved to intervene. A delegation of three priests arrived on April 7 at the town on the banks of the Limmat. Its instructions were to defend the value of the traditional rules, while avoiding a public clash with the preacher of the Great Minster. There was to be a discussion in his absence with the Council. These shrewd tactics nearly succeeded; already the magistrates, deeply impressed, were bowing to episcopal authority. Finally, it was decided to call to a second session the three parish priests of the town. When the representatives of the hierarchy grew dissatisfied and spoke of withdrawing, murmurs of disapproval passed through the ranks of the convocation. They had to remain, whether they liked it or not.

Zwingli had spent a restless night up to the moment when he decided to commit everything into the hands of God: "I was beginning to grow calm", he relates, "and with sighs to cast the burden of my anxiety on Him who hears the groans of the captives: do not Thou abandon the truth, and defend Thy gospel, whereof Thou hast willed me to be a preacher." The confident prayer was heard. Ulrich replied with compelling force and dignity to accusations which it was obvious were directed against him, although the delegation, in conformity with its mandate, carefully avoided mentioning his name. In conclusion, the Council on April 9 begged the Bishop of Constance to see that the matter was taken up by "pope, cardinals, bishops, and councils, so that there should be no conduct contrary to the precepts of Christ". Fasting was provisionally upheld. The transgressors were to refer themselves to their confessors and accept a penance. All were implored to entertain henceforth peaceful sentiments and avoid disputing. This, however, did not prevent Ulrich from publishing on April 16 his sermon of March 29. We have seen that this too contained an invitation to foster calmness and mutual respect.

CHAPTER EIGHT

Final Attempts at Conciliation: the Rupture

ONE INCIDENT SET in motion another. At the moment when he was defending Froschauer and his guests, while counselling prudence, Ulrich was contemplating taking a step of capital importance. Like the canon law concerning fasting, the requirement of ecclesiastical celibacy seemed to him ever more arbitrary. By what right should a priest be forbidden to engage in holy matrimony, instituted of God? Did not the Levites have wives and children? Does not the New Testament imply that, with the exception of St. Paul, all the apostles were married? In the spring of 1522, Zwingli married secretly Anna Reinhart, the widow of a patrician of Zürich, Hans Meyer von Knonau.

This action was unacceptable by ecclesiastical law, but authorized in civil law. Many of his friends took the same step. A situation which was by circumstance complicated —for Anna lived with her children in a house belonging to her late husband's family—together with the desire not to defy public opinion, explains the air of mystery which surrounded the decision for two years. However, the situation worried the priest of the Great Minster. Might it not be possible to obtain from the bishop, Hugo von Hohenlandenberg, such measures of reform as would free the diocese from unjust laws? In spite of the hardening of tone reflected in an episcopal charge, printed on May 2, condemning quarrels and revolts; in spite of the delivery at Zürich by a delegation on the 24th of the same month of two threatening letters, addressed the one to the Council and the other to the Chapter of the city, Ulrich drafted a petition, signed along with himself by ten of his friends, imploring that priests should have the freedom to marry. In the *De votis monasticis* (about monastic vows) Luther shortly before had attacked the same problem.

Zwingli addressed himself to his spiritual head with trustful respect. He recalled the humanistic tendencies of Hugo and begged him not to join forces with the enemies of a Gospel which had for too long been neglected. He considered that the present state of division in the Church would only cease with a unanimous return to its source—that is, to Christ Himself. "You should not merely tolerate this bold undertaking, but vigorously support it. It is Christ's affair, not ours." On the particular point of celibacy, the petitioners emphasized that Hugo should intervene without delay. Chastity is reserved to some: only those can keep it to whom God has granted it as a gift: "As we have sadly discovered through experiment—before the doctor one must boldly uncover the wound—this gift has been refused us." The vow of chastity is a fruit of pride, a vain effort to escape the human condition. Sexual life should be regulated by matrimony: to each man his wife: such is the teaching of Genesis. "If a virgin marries, she does not commit a sin", says St. Paul.

Along with the petition, a parallel text intended for the laity came from the press. To the reminder of Biblical teaching, Zwingli now added some facts drawn from ecclesiastical history. Priests and bishops in the early age of the Church had wife and children; thus, for example, Saint Hilary of Poitiers, the Pope Hosius, himself the son of a sub-deacon. Other pontiffs, like Boniface, Agapetus, Felix III, Gelasius, were sons of priests or bishops. Do not the priests of the Greek church marry, he asked, and are they not, none the less, as good Christians as ourselves?

The humble petition, dated July 2, met with the rebuff of a contemptuous silence. Ulrich waited for weeks, hoping for a message from Bishop Hugo. He had humiliated himself

and had opened his heart to his superior. The path of conciliation was being blocked. On August 22 he published a
cry of indignation, the *Architeles* (his first and last word).
In essence he wrote that it is not enough to command, it is
necessary to convince by the help of Holy Scripture; "the
more you intervene as a master, Bishop Hugo, the more
you will render yourself odious to all." Ulrich defended himself passionately against the complaint that he was a heresiarch. "Unremittingly I shall endeavour to restore the
unity of the primitive church. . . . I will never be a party
man. What is my crime? For four years I have done nothing
but preach the New Testament. I have not despised tradition.
The nearer ancient customs are to the Gospel, the more
should we honour them." One after the other, Zwingli
takes up the points made in the charge of May 24, which,
although it did not mention him, was certainly alluding to
him. The Gospel, he protested, does not need the approbation of the Church, nor even its unity, to remain valid. In
the time of Arius, the Holy Book survived in the midst of
schism, both parties invoking its authority. Who disputes the
fact that there is one Church alone? The long protest ends
with a prayer addressed to Christ the sole Head of Christians:
"Thou knowest how far I was, from the start, from wishing
to bring about strife and trouble, and yet, in spite of all my
efforts and my resistance, Thou hast led me to fulfil this
task."

With his conscience torn asunder, Ulrich repeats in his
own words the "I can do no other" of Luther at Worms. He
has done the impossible to effect a peaceable reform of church
institutions. If he has sinned, it was rather by excessive
slowness than excessive haste. The dice have rolled in spite
of him on the table of the century; the Church will now be
split for generations to come. After the *Architeles* was
printed, his desire for compromise was again expressed in
the touching letter of September 17 which the reformer
addressed to his brothers. Criticism and slander had penetrated even as far as Wildhaus. Evil tongues accused Ulrich
of despising Mary, Mother of God. He sent to the five

companions of his childhood the text of the sermon on which this ill-natured gossip was based. They would see from it that his sole concern had been to declare "what great grace and salvation the Son of God, born of the pure servant Mary, has brought to mankind". This little treatise on the Virgin Mary, the only one, notes Gottfried Locher, which the reformers drew up, expounds the evangelical doctrine concerning Mary, both virgin and mother by a divine miracle. Ulrich never depicted her as a poor half-mad woman, as was affirmed.

Malicious detractors continued to pursue him with their spite. In this very year, they were alleging that he had many children, and that princes were showering wealth upon him. In face of these imputations affecting his private life, he remained silent. But he could not admit the accusation of blasphemy. For him, Mary conceived the Son of God without spot of sin, as is proved by the story of the Annunciation and the visit to Elizabeth. He confined himself to suggesting that the Ave Maria should not be used as a prayer; it is nothing more than the angel's praise and salutation. In regard to Mary, the instrument of salvation, Ulrich professed a deep respect, but vigorously opposed those who believed that the multiplication of Ave Marias would procure the remission of sins. To prove his true veneration for the Mother, let the Christian rather sing the praise of those benefits which flow from the passion of the Son. The greatness of Mary is to have brought forth the Son of God who saves us.

From August to December 1522 the atmosphere became more and more electric. Partisans and adversaries of Zwingli wrangled bitterly. If congratulations and encouragements reached him from Toggenburg, his native place, from Thurgau, from St. Gall, from Basle, from Berne and even from Constance where the new ideas were winning adherents; if in Zürich itself the support of the civil authorities seemed increasingly assured, everywhere else in Switzerland conservative minds were accusing him of heresy, and breathing out threats. His friends began to fear for his life. The bishop, enclosed in an attitude of disdainful reserve with regard to him, exercised severe discipline wherever possible. Priests from Knonau and Höngg were summoned to appear before his tribunal. The priest of Fislibach, outside the domain of Zürich, in the province of Baden, was arrested and thrown into a cell of the castle of Gottlieben near Constance where he was to remain from November, 1522, to June, 1523. Had it not been for the protection of the Council, Zwingli would certainly have suffered a like misfortune.

While committing his cause to God, while encouraging his friend John Zwick, a preacher at Constance, by reminding him of the promise, "He who endures to the end shall be saved", Ulrich keenly desired to see the matter he had in hand publicly debated and adjudicated upon. Since Hugo von Hohenlandenberg refused to answer, the priest turned for help to the temporal power. At his request, the Council fixed for January 29, 1523, a meeting to which were summoned the clergy of Zürich. As well as the Bishop of Constance, delegates from other Swiss cantons were invited. In Switzerland as in Germany, the laity took control of Church matters, but whereas Luther entrusted his cause to the princes, in Zürich, with its democratic traditions, it was the citizens themselves who sat in debate, pending the calling of a general council.

After the despatch of the invitations, Zwingli formulated sixty-seven theses which constitute the charter of the Zürich reformation. Written in a style which every one could understand, they embrace the whole scope of piety as practised at the time. The pastor of the Great Minster knew how to talk to the people. There was no abstract theology in this cascade of affirmations which, even today, are in conformity with the faith of the Swiss Reformed Church.

The first fifteen extol the Gospel as the source of truth, and celebrate Christ as the only Saviour. "Christ is the only way towards blessedness for all those who were, are and shall be. . . . Christ is the captain promised and sent by God to the human race." He is the Head of the Church:

75

"All those who live in Him, the head, are members, and children of God." To act independently of Him is madness: that is why the declarations of ecclesiastics with regard to their splendour, their wealth, their state, titles and laws are absurd, for they do not conform with the spirit of Christ. Finally, the Gospel is sufficient for a knowledge of the truth, and to lead men to a new life: it is enough therefore to preach it. The customs of the Church are then sifted in the light of these basic principles. Zwingli proceeds to a severe pruning process. He rejects the pope (for Jesus is the supreme, the only and eternal priest), the idea of the mass as a sacrifice (it is a memorial which refers us to the sufficient sacrifice of Christ), the invocation of saints, the wealth of the clergy, and the ordinances relative to fasting, pilgrimages, monastic orders, the tonsure and the frock. The clergy should be able to marry: the vow of chastity is an abuse to be condemned. Excommunication is the right of the local church. The wealth of the cloisters must be used to supply the needs of the poor. Civil authority is based on a divine ordinance and must be honoured for this reason. It is part of its duties to promulgate laws which are in conformity with the divine will. If the magistrate acts contrary to the commands of God, he may be deposed.

Three theses concern prayer, which must be quiet and unobtrusive—and this implies the abolition of litanies— and seven others concern the forgiveness of sins which is granted by Christ alone: "That is why one must regard confession made to the priest or to one's fellow man not in the light of absolution for sin, but as a seeking of advice." As well as the imposition of penance, the reformer rejects purgatory. His article on this point, however, is accompanied by an interesting reservation: "If a man in his trouble prays to God for the dead, I do not reject the idea." But such a practice must not be bound up with certain moments nor with financial transactions.

The doctrine of predestination which, in 1525, Luther with his *De Servo Arbitrio* was to bring to the centre of interest, is absent from Zwingli's document, where attention is

concentrated on the compassionate Christ, whose full sufficiency for salvation Zwingli emphasizes. If he attacks the power
of the Church, he re-establishes the value both of marriage
and of lay institutions. In Reformed Switzerland, the magistrate will be given a place of honour. The State school will
be accepted without discussion. The clergy no longer have
the monopoly of religious knowledge. The laity will be
placed henceforth on a footing of equality with the ordained
ministry. The certitude of divine creation and redemption
illuminates the whole field of human activity. Everywhere
man can with benefit pray to God. The work of the craftsman
and the peasant is as valuable as that of the priest, provided
it is done to serve the common good. The Reformed pastor
receives the honourable charge of proclaiming the Word of
God. In recognition of this spiritual service, other believers
will honour him—that is, will provide him with material
support.

The crowd thronged into the assembly room of the town
hall when, on the morning of January 29, 1523, the Burgomaster, Mark Roüst, opened the historic session. The members of the Little and of the Great Councils, the priests of
the city and of the countryside, had hastened to the spot,
anxious to see and hear everything. In the vast room, the
presence of Helvetic notabilities might have been observed
—namely, the Capuchin Hofmeister from Schaffhausen, the
Dominican Sebastian Meyer, from Berne, and the Burgomaster of St. Gall, Vadian. But attention was directed especially to the episcopal delegation, which was led by the Vicar-
General, Faber, flanked by three dignitaries of exalted rank.
After a brief welcome from the President and some kind
words from the Chevalier d'Anwil, one of the four representatives of the bishop, leave was given to Zwingli to speak. He
declared that he was ready to defend his theses. Faber,
wearing the red cap of a doctor in theology, and holding two
Bibles, one in Hebrew and the other in Greek, expressed
himself in conciliatory terms, calling Zwingli as ever "my
good friend" and "my dear brother". He reminded his

audience that only a general council of the Church was competent to discuss the questions raised, and, in default of it, universities such as Paris, Cologne, and Louvain. "And why not Erfurt or Wittenberg?" interrupted Zwingli, raising a laugh in the assembly. "Luther would be too near," answered the Vicar-General. Had not the Diet of Nuremberg decided to convene a national synod? "Very well," exclaimed Zwingli, "but why delay? Are we not—those of us who are gathered here—sufficiently numerous and sufficiently learned? Is it right that souls held under the tyranny of unjustifiable customs should have to wait for a council which might never be convened? O men of Zürich, you may take the matter into your own hands. It is a great honour that God has bestowed on you."

A long silence followed this passage of arms. The passionate appeal of Ulrich had had its effect. But in vain did he try to renew the debate. Faber complained that he had received too late the sixty-seven theses, handed to him at Winterthur, on the way to Zürich, a few hours before the discussion began. He outlined a defence of the invocation of saints and the celibacy of the clergy. "For twelve hundred years now priests have not been allowed to marry. . . ." "But they have been allowed to take prostitutes!" shouted someone present. The theme of Scripture and tradition was also touched on. Some friends of the reformer intervened. At noon, the Burgomaster proposed an interruption of the sitting, an interval which the councillors used in order to discuss among themselves and to draft the text of a declaration favourable to Zwingli. Not only was the latter encouraged to persevere in his chosen way, but all the priests of Zürich territory were enjoined to confine themselves, like their leader, to the preaching of the Holy Gospel.

Eagerly welcomed by the priest of the Great Minster and his friends, the decision of the Council none the less encountered opposition from Faber, who offered to prove the invalidity of the theses. "Well, do so, Reverend Sir. We will listen to you with pleasure," exclaimed Zwingli. The debate was resumed, only to get bogged down at the end of the afternoon in a clash of contradictory assertions. "There must be a judge to decide these controversial issues," opined the Doctor of Constance. "The Spirit of God on the basis of Scripture is the only judge," retorted Zwingli. Nothing remained for the representatives of the hierarchy but to go back to Constance with their minds inflamed and with the painful feeling that they had lost the contest. As for their opponent, whom this victory faced with a Church in need of reconstruction, he formulated between February and June his *Commentary on the Sixty-seven Theses* which was printed about the middle of July. Ulrich dedicated it to Glarus, his first parish. The famous Zwinglian symbolism appears for the first time in this important book in connexion with the 18th thesis, which defines the Lord's Supper as a memorial. As the thought of the author was more amply expressed in the *De vera et falsa religione,* two years later, we shall explain it when we come to discuss the latter work.

Part Three

The Protestant Revolution

CHAPTER NINE

Abandonment of Ancient Practices

A REVOLUTION IS LIKE an avalanche. The first sections of snow which slide away bring others in their train. Soon an immense sheet of snow is in movement, threatening to sweep away everything in its path. The time for calm meditation in a library had now gone by. What was necessary now was to tear up and remake, at once, in the sphere of concrete realities.

From June, 1523, Zwingli was carrying on a daily struggle to maintain the equilibrium of a Church which was involved in a process of transformation, torn as it was between the conservatism of those who wished to change nothing and the spirit of the innovators to whom the slightest survival from the past became suspect.

At Zürich, those personages who, in 1522, had been involved in the scandal with regard to fasting were now clamouring for changes in the cult. They were brilliantly led by two recruits of good family, Conrad Grebel, son of the councillor Jacob Grebel and brother-in-law of Vadian, and Felix Manz, son of the Provost of the Great Minster. In the country, peasants were demanding the abolition of tithes paid to the monasteries. On June 22, six parishes adjoining the city sent a delegation for this purpose to the Council. Why should money be poured out, they asked, for the purpose of maintaining futile customs? The canons ought to devote themselves to useful activity: baptisms, ringing of bells, and burials. They ought to go, with the exception of about six who would be devoted to the service of the people, declared the delegates.

Ulrich, who had just finished his *Commentary on the Sixty-seven Theses*, took up his pen again to revise for the press his sermon of June 24, *Divine and Human Justice*, which dealt with social problems. At the same time, with his friend Leo Jud, he began to consider the question of liturgical reform. On Monday August 10, 1523, on the occasion of a baptism celebrated at midday in the Great Minster, the Latin of the office was replaced by German. In the evening, in another sanctuary, the ceremony of the morning was repeated: for the second time the sacrament was celebrated in its renewed garment. The pastors had come to an understanding and were resolved to put into practice the exhortation of 1 Cor. 14, to make church worship understood by all. The rest of the rite underwent few modifications: the sign of the cross and the insufflation were retained.

At the end of this same month of August a new monograph by Ulrich, the *Essay on the Canon of the Mass*, left the press. Written in Latin, it subjects to the scrutiny of a scientific criticism the liturgy of the sacrament. The *Commentary on the Sixty-seven Theses* contains on the other hand a doctrinal study of the rite ordained by Christ and is the prelude to later discussions. Zwingli attacked the medieval notion of a repetition of the sacrifice. The Supper added nothing to the sacrifice of Christ on the cross. It depicted it anew to the minds of the faithful; it was a memorial. The work completed on Calvary suffices. Bread and wine proclaim the redeeming death. They are the concrete signs of a marvellous spiritual reality: they do not repeat the sacrifice, but render it present for faith. Zwingli's symbol theory is intimated here and there; he emphasizes, on the basis of John 6: 60-65, that in the Communion it is not a question of physical eating, for "the flesh is of no avail". It is faith in the sacrifice of Christ which feeds the soul and quickens it: "I am not concerned about the speculations of theologians with regard to the transformation of the bread and wine." There is not yet apparent any divergence from Luther on this point. Yet, in this first analysis of the sacrament, Zwingli affirms his independence of the Saxon reformer. It is not Luther who has instructed him, but the Gospel itself. At Einsiedeln and Wittenberg, the same Master has led to the same conclusions. Between the two reformers there is only a difference of terminology: for the rite which Luther calls a *sacrament*, Zwingli prefers the term *memorial*.

The *Essay on the Canon of the Mass* draws from these theological premisses the inferences affecting divine worship. Once the sacrificial interpretation has been abandoned, the rite itself can be simplified. It must be centred around the death of Christ, and those expressions which present it as an ever-repeated sacrifice must be changed. The readings, taken solely from sacred Scripture, will be in German and the Gradual reduced. Ulrich did not, however, reject eucharistic vestments; and further, out of regard for the weak, he accepted the sign of the cross and retained the traditional singing.

Zwingli wished the reformation to take place in an orderly fashion in accordance with decisions inspired by the magistrates. The *Essay on the Canon of the Mass* is put forward as a basis of discussion rather than as a programme to be carried into effect at once. For some months, the mass continued to be sung as before, but conviction was now lacking. Some of the clergy were beginning to murmur against it.

The storm broke, not in connexion with worship, but in regard to pictures and statues of which the churches, both in town and country, were crammed full. Leo Jud bears a heavy share of responsibility in this matter. On September 1 he thundered against images from the pulpit of St. Peter's Church. Shortly afterwards torn-up pictures were found on the floor of the chancel. On September 11 the same kind of disaster occurred in the Church of Our Lady. Then the city was lashed to a pitch of bubbling excitement by the removal of the great carved crucifix which stood above the gate of Oberdorf. The Council was angered. The bootmaker, Hottinger, who was responsible for this act of vandalism, was imprisoned together with his accomplices.

Such tension could not last much longer. A second public

debate, to which were convened the Bishops of Basle, Chur and Constance, opened on October 26 in the presence of eight hundred persons. The prelates were conspicuous by their absence. The first day was devoted to the discussion of images, the second to that of the mass. The partisans of rapid decisions clashed fiercely with the moderates. A deep impression was made by the wisdom of Conrad Schmid of Küssnacht, who spoke at some length in the last session. For him, idolatry lodged itself essentially in the heart of man. Instead, there should be implanted there first of all a true knowledge of Christ. Pilgrimages brought the mountain-dweller to the plains and the townsman to the mountain, the German to France and the Frenchman to Germany. Every Christian should learn to discover the Source of all good wherever he lived, and should cease to say to wood and stone: "Help me." Hence serious instruction should precede the justified removal of images and statues.

Zwingli desired that the decision as to the right moment for action should be left to the wisdom of the Councils. His point of view prevailed. A conference called at the town hall on January 19, 1524, brought together once more the body of ecclesiastics. Decisions were taken at the close of the following spring. On May 14, 1524, the pilgrimage which took about fifteen hundred people of Zürich every Whit Monday to prostrate themselves before the Virgin of Einsiedeln, ceased. A decree of the Council on June 15 ordered the removal of all images "so that the people might turn away from idols and draw near to the living God". With an orderliness and thoroughness altogether in the spirit of the country within two weeks the churches were cleared; altars, saints, madonnas vanished under the expert supervision of people whose job it was: blacksmiths, locksmiths, carpenters, stonemasons. Extreme austerity succeeded the profusion of ornaments. The bareness of protestant worship banished the ceremonies and display of catholicism.

CHAPTER TEN

End of Chapter and Cloisters

THE CHALLENGING OF one authority puts others in danger; hence the collusion frequently observable among those who have vested interests to defend. One column shaken and the whole edifice totters to the ground. If bishop and pope are no longer in control, if the mass is useless, what is the point not only of church tithes, but also of civil taxes and interest payable on borrowed money?

The step taken by the peasants of Zürich on June 22, 1523, revealed the peril. Advanced as he was in his ideas, Zwingli had not by any means the character of a revolutionary. He knew too well the ambition which cloaks itself beneath lofty proposals: "Come out of your place that I may jump into it." On the other hand, he noted crying injustices. Usurers squeezed their debtors. Tidy fortunes were built up at the expense of the unfortunate. On June 24, 1523, he mounted the pulpit and offered to the congregation of the Great Minster some reflections on the theme *Divine and Human Justice*—reflections which do credit to his sagacity. Printed at the request of his hearers, the sermon was dedicated by Ulrich to his friend, Nicolas de Watteville, son of an outstanding citizen of Berne and Provost of Lausanne Cathedral. Through him as spokesman, the reformer wished to reach the Bernese, to whom at this time Zürich was being pictured as a hotbed of anarchy.

Divine justice claims the whole man for God and for the service of his neighbour. It seems inaccessible, but none the less it must be preached. It compels each one to appreciate his imperfection, to disclose himself as a sinner. But repentance does not lead to despair, for Christ came and lived for the sins of many.

In comparison with the transcendent divine demand which wills us to be like God, human justice is concerned only with the coarser vices, with outward transgressions. A man who is righteous in the eyes of his neighbours may still be a scoundrel in the eyes of the Most High. In spite of their rudimentary character, the regulations of human law must not be despised. When a father takes his son to the schoolmaster, he says: "Teach him this and that and chastise him without sparing," for he knows his child and realizes that blows will often be necessary to compel the youngster to pay attention and work. Civil authority, like the schoolmaster, uses the rod so as to obviate the anarchy wrought by human passions, and to maintain in this world a minimum of order and peace. It would be a good thing, moreover, if it gained inspiration from the Word of God, so as to refine its conception of justice. If we must render to Caesar the things that are Caesar's, too many princes are children avid of filthy lucre and worldly glory, whence arise many troubles and wars. We must obey them except in regard to religious faith, which is outside their authority. If some potentates ruin their people, God will raise up an avenger who will strike down the tyrant.

Zwingli then develops the teaching of Rom. 13: 1-7, and in particular the verse concerning taxes and debts, "Pay all of them their dues", which justifies State revenue.

He who buys must pay the seller. Tithes sanctioned by authority are likewise payable as a matter of conscientious obligation. With regard to interest, Zwingli makes some careful distinctions. Loans ought to be made gratuitously. Private ownership wrongly grabs the earth and its fruits which are due to God. Nevertheless, God permits it, on condition that the proprietor realizes his debtorship and administers his wealth accordingly. It is not enough that the rich man should have regard to human justice: he must also remember his responsibility before God. In contrast with absolute requirements, interest appears as an evil which should be controlled. The rent of land will be proportionate to the area of the land rented and payable in kind. A valuation will establish objectively the worth of capital loaned. The interest rate should not exceed one in twenty, that is, 5 per cent. As for usury and other abuses, Zwingli condemns them severely. Let the magistrates look out for squalls.

This short treatise appeals to the conscience of every man and warns the rich as well as the poor. Several protested that it was a compromise. Ulrich knows the realities of life too well to attempt to build a Utopia. He has no wish, on the pretext of attaining perfection, to undermine the social order. If he appreciates the limits of human justice, he believes the latter indispensable, as is the rod to the schoolmaster. He desires a limit to the absolutism of princes without stating exactly what its nature or the mode of its introduction might be. By subordinating the right of the king to divine judgment, however, Zwingli helped to discover the basis on which constitutional monarchy might one day be built.

One point in particular he was anxious about—namely, that of ecclesiastical tithes. The twenty-four canons of the Great Minster, together with their chaplains, demanded money wrongly. It was not the purpose of taxes to perpetuate sinecures or the recitation of vain prayers. After belief in the power of masses had been swept away, the revenues of the cathedral chapter could be diverted to the building of the theological school which the new clergy needed, and of hospitals which the poor urgently required.

The desired reform took place speedily. The majority of the canons became convinced and followed the lead of Ulrich. At the end of September his plan was submitted to the Council and approved. The revenues received would henceforth be used to pay the stipend of the pastor and his assistant, and all perquisites abolished. Baptisms, confessions, the administration of extreme unction, the ringing of bells, were to be performed freely. No successors would be appointed to deceased canons and chaplains. The school dependent on the Great Minster was enlarged; its schoolmaster received a better salary; to the country parishes was appointed a spiritual pastor residing in the village; the poor were welcomed and maintained by the hospitals, and the desired theological school came into being. Future priests would be able to study in Zürich. By 1525 already this formidable programme was being put into execution. Zwingli passed to the rank of professor, together with Leo Jud, Gaspard Grossmann, and Johannes Ceporinus.

On November 25 the suppression of convents was begun by a move of the Mother Superior of the Dominicans, Küngolt von Langenberg, who was supported by two nuns, Anna and Barbara von Meggen. Two years previously, Leo Jud had been authorized by an order of the Council to take the place of their chaplain and thus to bring their circle into the orbit of the new ideas. His preaching had struck home; the three women sold their convent to a nobleman from Lucerne, Nicolas von Meggen, a cousin of Anna and Barbara. Five days later, Catherine von Zimmern, who had ruled the convent of Notre Dame since she was nineteen, made a gift of her abbey and of the immense forests she possessed around Zürich, reserving to herself solely the right of residence during her own lifetime. She enjoyed it, however, for but a short time, since she married the knight Aeberlin von Riesebach, who lived at Schaffhausen. The three monasteries for men seem to have offered a certain degree of resistance: they were secularized on December 1 by a decree which ordered that the young monks should be made apprentices so as to be in a position to earn their own livelihood. The older ones were bidden to form a group in the Capuchin house, where they were to end their days, or, if they preferred, they were allowed to retire to their own families.

The wealth thus freed was devoted to what today would be called, according to the area of the country, a charity bureau or social security department. Walther Köhler has examined the early registers of this institution, thanks to which the poor were effectively helped. Those who were in charge of it made every effort to discover the truly needy and to restrain professional mendicancy. The sick and pregnant women received food, wine, wood, and various remedies for their ills. Children were clothed and apprentices encouraged by the offer of financial aid. The expenditure rose from 2,737 pounds[1] in 1525 to 8,734 in 1528, which was a considerable sum for a town of 7,000 inhabitants. The inscription which heads the old compilation of rules concerning mendicancy proclaims the evangelical inspiration at the source of this effort: "Be merciful", says the Lord, "as your Father in heaven is merciful."

[1] *Livres*, the unit of the old French money system.—*Tr.*

CHAPTER ELEVEN

From Mass to Lord's Supper

O N MAUNDY THURSDAY, April 13, 1525, and on the
following Good Friday and Easter Day, under the
amazed arches of the Great Minster, divine service
took place according to an absolutely new rite. The German
language completely excluded the Latin of the liturgy.
Choral music was absent. Only the voices of Zwingli and his
two assistant priests could be heard at the entrance of the
choir, reciting antiphonally texts taken from psalms or
the creed. At certain moments the crowd which thronged the
Cathedral church supported them by its responses: "God be
praised, Amen", or again, kneeling, would recite with them
the *Our Father*. The Lord's Supper supplanted the mass.

The decision to effect this change had been taken only
after long hesitation. Finally, on April 12 the Council of the
Two Hundred, on the proposal of the two burgomasters,
admitted that in all churches the mass should be abolished
and that in its place the holy table of apostolic times should
be set up. For the last time, the Roman rite was celebrated
on the Wednesday of this week.

Zwingli spent a restless night, disturbed by a terrible
nightmare the horrors of which he was able to describe the
next day. He was debating with one of his opponents, the
under-secretary Joachim vom Grüt, who on the previous
day had vigorously intervened during the sitting of the
Council to defend the Real Presence. In his dream, Ulrich
found himself face to face with an old man; his tongue was
paralysed and he was incapable of making any answer to
some very weak arguments until a mysterious being suddenly

appearing said to him: "Why are you dismayed? To reply to him, make use of the text of Exodus 12—it is Easter—that is, the passing over of the Eternal Lord God." Thereupon he woke up and jumped out of bed, dashed to his Bible, and extracted from it the essential ideas of a sermon which finally convinced the majority of those who still hesitated.

The elements of the holy meal were placed on an ordinary table. Zwingli officiated facing the congregation, instead of taking as in the Roman rite the eastward position. Assistant ministers then distributed the bread to the congregation who remained in their seats, each taking a piece and placing it in his mouth. The cup, carried round in the same way, then passed from one communicant to another. Zwingli insisted that the wine should be poured into wooden chalices, so as openly to reject any suggestion of pomp.

These sensational innovations met with little opposition. The facility with which the Church freed itself from an age-long tradition is amazing. For several years, those who upheld the ancient faith were authorized to go to church on Sundays in Aargau or Schwyz territory, at Dietikon, Baden or Einsiedeln. There they found again sacerdotal vestments, incense, the Kyrie Eleison, the Gloria, the confession, all of which had disappeared from the churches of Zürich.

When relations between the Confederate states grew strained, shortly after the adoption of the reformation in Berne in 1528, toleration came to an end. For a long time, catholics had been persecuting protestants. In 1524, as a result of troubles which broke out in the frontier village of Stammheim, the pastor Wirth and his son, who had been unjustly accused of causing a fire at the monastery of Ittingen near Frauenfeld, were condemned to capital punishment by the Diet of Baden. With the consent of Zürich, they had been taken to the town for questioning. Their trial, however, was decided in advance. Introduced as witnesses, they passed at once to the status of the accused. When, on September 28, they were led to the place of execution, their courage deeply impressed all who witnessed the scene. "I beg you, father," cried the younger, "do not turn aside from what you have learnt." "Certainly," replied the older man, "with the help of God, I shall persevere in it to the end." Then, turning towards the people, he exhorted them to live at peace with God, and to help him by addressing to God in his favour an *Our Father*; if he had done wrong to anyone, he begged to be forgiven as he himself forgave all. Shortly afterwards, their heads rolled to the ground. A catholic witness of the scene wrote in his journal: "Thus they died, with a fine Christian chivalry. . . . A stone would have been moved, and many men wept."

Against this background of blood, the three years of relative confessional peace which Zürich enjoyed from 1525 to 1528 deserve a mention.

Among the decisions taken by the Council at the instigation of Zwingli, there is one which remains infinitely regrettable. The celebration of the Lord's Supper was limited to four times a year: Easter, Whitsuntide, one Sunday in autumn, and Christmas. Why confine to this extent the Christian's contemplation of the cross, the commemoration of that sacrifice which is essential to salvation? The usage of Zürich was taken over by Berne in 1528, and thence passed to Geneva, where Calvin had to accept it with reluctance.

Part Four

The Theological Thought of Zwingli

CHAPTER TWELVE

A Book for France: the "De vera et falsa religione"

ON JULY 12 a colourful traveller, the monk Lambert d'Avignon, entered Zürich by the gate of Rennweg mounted on an ass. He did not know a word of German, but preached four times in Latin, very well, in the Church of Our Lady. His last sermon concerned the topic of the invocation of saints. Afterwards he offered to discuss this subject with Zwingli, only to declare after a few hours that he had been completely convinced by the arguments of the reformer: "He swore", relates the chronicler Bernard Wyss, "that he would never again, in all his difficulties, call upon any one but God, and that he would give up the use of the rosary."

This first contact with a French visitor was followed by several others. Through his friend Glareanus, who had lived in Paris a few years before returning to settle in Basle in 1522, Zwingli knew by repute the humanists who were gravitating around Lefèvre d'Etaples and Bishop Briçonnet. He had read the works of the former in his presbytery at Glarus. The growing tension which induced the Bishop of Meaux in April, 1522, to send away several of his collaborators caused William Farel, the future fellow-worker with Calvin, to flee France in order to settle at Basle where the presence of Erasmus assured him of a liberal atmosphere. Humanism and the reformation went hand in hand. The city of the Rhine had in May, 1523, adopted a conciliatory position in the far-reaching religious dispute which had been going on since the Diet of Worms, and the magistrates recommended preachers to adhere to the Gospel while respecting ancient traditions. The same city seemed to the innovators "a truly royal port of salvation, since the King of kings wishes to make flourish there, to be read and proclaimed there, His Gospel and its eternal laws". Thus John Canaye, who had remained in Paris, expresses himself in a letter which he sent from that city on July 13, 1524, to Farel, who, he supposes, breathes on the banks of the Rhine a lighter air.

A refugee banished for his convictions has difficulty in holding his tongue in check. The climate of opinion in Basle authorized considerable difference of views, but the excitable southerner, joined by a little group of hotheads, openly attacked after a few months those who did not follow him in his condemnation of priestly vestments, fasting, and monastic institutions. He announced that he would hold a public discussion. One of his theses was aimed at Erasmus, whose anxiety to spare ecclesiastical authority was becoming exasperating: "He who hopes to be saved by his own strength and power, and not by faith, exalting himself and making himself a god by his trust in free will, such a one is blinded by impiety." The university reacted sharply and, in agreement with the Vicar-General, forbade professors and students to take part in the dispute. The Council retorted by ordering them to attend, under threat of sanctions. Hence on March 3, 1524, Farel had the advantage of a numerous, if reserved, audience. A few weeks later he began a series of lectures on the thought of St. Paul, broke off after he had delivered a few of them, and left Basle accompanied by a refugee from Lyons, a banker by profession, named Antoine du Blet. The two friends, who had taken it into their heads to go to Saxony to see Luther, changed their itinerary for an unknown reason and contented themselves with going to Zürich, which was nearer, where they met Zwingli.

The conversation turned on France and its religious situation. Ulrich did not know the language of the one-time Gauls. Latin was used as a medium. Farel showed that he was appreciative of the publications of the Zürich reformer. "You ought," he said in substance, "to write a work that will propagate in my country, which at the present moment is in the full swing of development, those ideas which we have in common." He painted an optimistic picture of King Francis I and his favourable disposition towards the new faith.

Zwingli did not forget this conversation. A few months later, when writing the book which, by common consent, contains his thought in a mature form, the *Commentarius de vera et falsa religione*, he provided it with a preface in the form of a letter addressed to the king of France. Anyone reading this text today is amazed at the unreserved confidence of the Zürich reformer. The impetuous Farel took his desires for realities. The honest Ulrich was incapable of discerning through enthusiastic reports the double face of the man of whom the keen-sighted Louis XII, when trying to reorganize the finances of the kingdom, said to one of his intimates: "Alas! we are working in vain; this big lad will spoil everything." Francis was essentially a humanist and a friend of progress out of concern for modernity. He wished his court to eclipse the courts of Italy. He liked the new style of speech, he liked castles with bright rooms, but there persisted in him a background of cruelty and medieval superstition which from 1534 onwards would lead him to shed the blood of the reformers.

Farel's influence is betrayed in Zwingli's effort to rouse Francis against the Sorbonne, a centre of ignorance and a haunt of self-interested clerics. After denouncing the retrograde theologians of Paris, the reformer commends to the benevolence of the monarch other scholars who are ornaments of his kingdom, more expert in the things of Heaven than in those of earth, and who have an admirable knowledge of the ancient tongues. This account is evidently an allusion to Lefèvre, whose *Psalterium quincuplex* Ulrich possessed and used. His copy, beautifully printed in 1513, with its wide margins in which is inserted here and there the fine hand of the reformer, is to be found at Zürich on the shelves of the public library.

"Scripseramus maxime in usum Galliarum" (we have written

especially with a view to France); hence it was but right to dedicate the book to its king. By this declaration which closes the preface, Zwingli proclaimed his desire to offer his work to the compatriots of Farel. To what extent was his wish realized? The friends to whom he talked in 1524 did their utmost to make known the writing, which was the fruit of their solicitations. No French translation seems to have popularized it; Calvin read it and a part of Zwingli's message is reflected in the *Institutes of the Christian Religion*. The enormous success of the latter book was to overshadow the *De vera et falsa religione* in France itself. Zwingli had been sleeping his last sleep for five years when the masterpiece of the French reformer left the printing press of Basle.

CHAPTER THIRTEEN

Doctrine of God and of Man: Origin and Nature of Religion: the Christ

THE OPENING OF the treatise recalls Cicero's definition: *religio* derives from *relegere*, it is that which binds God and man together. "By religion I understand the whole piety of the Christian, his faith and his life, the divine commandments and institutions, the sacraments." True religion is based on the Word of God, false religion is indistinguishable from superstition.

Since religion unites the Creator to the creature, we must come to know the two partners: God may be discovered by reason, which concludes with the idea that there is a first cause. But if the philosophers hail in this the source of life, they do not lead us to do its will.

The essence of God eludes our meditation. In His infinity He remains inaccessible to our limited minds. Whence the cry of Isaiah: "Truly, Thou art a God that hidest Thyself." The pride of philosophers and theologians should not deceive us. Their chatter is "carnal temerity"—*carnis audacia*. Outside the Spirit of God and His guidance, the presumption to define the One on whom all depends repeats the futile enterprise of Prometheus.

Moses obtained from the Lord the reply: "I am what I am" (Exod. 3); God is what He is by His very nature. Every other existence derives from His. Moreover He is identifiable with the good. God alone is good, proclaims the Christ (Luke 18). If the creation is good, it is as St. Paul says because "all things are of Him, and through Him and in Him". The pagans themselves have recognized Him and the apostle takes from one of their poets this judgment: "In Him we live and move and have our being" (Acts 17).

Zwingli admits—following St. Paul—that there is a *natural* knowledge of God. This seems to him to flow not so much from the activity of the human mind as from fragmentary revelations, "one or two pearls" under a mass of dung, he notes picturesquely.

If all springs from Him who said "Let there be light", must we attribute to Him also the creation of noxious creatures, such as the wasp and the flea? Our tiny intelligence will never be able to explain everything. A craftsman has his secrets: so has God. Let it suffice us to know that He loves us and watches over us. The Old Testament bears witness to this by miracles and angelic appearances. To inspire a total trustfulness, the New Testament relates the resurrection of Lazarus and the healing of the man born blind, and describes at length especially the gift of Christ.

Face to face with the God of love, whose being is surrounded by mystery, Zwingli then puts man, His opposite, a creature impenetrable by his own mind, resembling the cuttle-fish, that inky fish which secretes a black cloud to escape its pursuers: "The heart is deceitful above all things and desperately corrupt; who can understand it?" (Jer. 17).

We do not like to look into ourselves and confess our wretchedness. However, since Adam, who aspired to exalt himself above his true condition, the human soul has ceased to live. It is controlled by egoism. Man is evil from his youth (Gen. 8: 21)—a fact which is confirmed by other texts drawn from Ecclesiastes, St. John, and Romans. At this point, the *De vera et falsa religione* echoes the severity of Luther and foreshadows that of Calvin. With them he attacks the pride of theologians who exalt the freedom of the will. Are they not contradicted by Cicero himself, who depicts man as attracted towards the good by a desire of glory?

After the Fall, Adam's eyes are opened. He discovers his own nakedness. This lack of clothes symbolizes our wretchedness. We encounter difficulties, we come up against an inexpressible poverty which God alone can fill. And behold, a mysterious voice is heard speaking to the crippled being: "Adam, where are you?" This appeal is a sign of concern and pity. With this question, true religion is born, outside of which there exists only a vain search for the absolute. A bond is created, constituted of trust and hope. Faith brings before the rebel the Father's countenance. Reconciliation presupposes, it is true, one condition: the confession of sin. Definitions flow, one after the other, from the pen of the writer: "Piety, religion, consist in this: God reveals man to himself in such a way that, like Adam, he recognizes his act of betrayal and his misery." In consequence, "he utterly despairs of himself", but discovers the "vast abyss of divine mercy". Thus piety is a relationship in which man entrusts himself to God as to a Father, and has an unshakeable faith in Him as the only Good. One sign of its presence is the desire to live according to the will of God. The believing soul clings to the Lord. heeds His word, in a divinely exclusive way. It desires only God and His commands, without adding to them or subtracting from them. No authority balances His, whether it be that of pope or councils.

Christ is the centre of faith, He who came not to seek the righteous but sinners. Zwingli extols Him as God's gift to us, which reconciles justice and love. The scholastics saw that He appeased the divine wrath, for His innocence alone can atone for our sins: His sacrifice avails more than alms-giving which is dictated by the egoistic desire to escape the torments of hell. Several pages exalt the love of the Son, proclaimed by ancient prophecy as the One who would crush the head of the serpent. He is the second Adam, whose obedience compensates for the rebellion of the first. The sweetness of the forbidden fruit led to death: the bitterness of the cross engenders life. A piece of wood—that of Calvary —repairs the damage caused by another piece of wood, that of the interdicted tree of paradise. Jesus, the paschal lamb, unsullied by sin, son of an immaculate Virgin, rests in the manger, a sign that He will feed the life of souls.

Aglow with a tender fervour, the reflections devoted to Christ are free from the coldness which is so common in theological treatises. Here a believer communicates his faith and expresses his love. From Bethlehem to Calvary, the priest of the Great Minster follows the progress of the Author of our salvation. To those who, without studying him, condemn the *moralism* of Zwingli, we must recommend the reading of these texts. They will find reflected here the true face of the reformer, mystical and thoughtful, and with it the foundation of the Zürich eucharist, which was a celebration of the victorious cross.

CHAPTER FOURTEEN

Gospel and Penitence: Law and Sin

STILL MORE REMARKABLE than the thoughts about God and Jesus Christ, summarized in the preceding chapter, those on the Gospel, on penitence and the transformation of a heart which grace has touched, are as good as the best pages of Luther and Calvin. Zwingli is in fact even better than these two theologians in virtue of his sheer lucidity. He proposes to be a popular exponent, a popularizer of doctrine, one might almost say, if the intimate, personal character of a study which turns into a confession did not forbid the use of such terms: "I approach with you now some high and difficult thoughts", he writes to his reader, "but in a simple language: I adjust my mode of speech so that it may penetrate your understanding."

We know that the extant volumes from his library disclose his long preparatory meditations in the solitude of Glarus and Einsiedeln. Throughout the *De vera et falsa religione* Zwingli spares his reader, with a few exceptions, patristic references and quotations. None the less the extreme clarity of his style springs from the patient study undertaken concurrently with his pastoral activity and inner struggles. Zwingli utilizes both what he has read and what he has experienced.

That Christ has suffered for us, that He expiates our sins on the cross, is the heart of the Gospel, the good news. This has a twofold implication. Forgiveness of sins and penitence are closely linked and must be preached in the name of Jesus. He who enters into contact with the Son of God is sorry about his past life. Closed eyes are opened. Under the breath of God's Spirit, man knows himself and his face is covered with shame. "Repent!" proclaims John the Baptist. Baptism, affirms Peter, is a restoration of conscience, an act of lucid self-examination.

Hence penitence is something different from external acts, such as pilgrimages, recitations of *aves*, or purchases of indulgences. It is connected with the inner despair of the man who condemns himself. In this impasse, which is produced by the Spirit, the troubled soul encounters Christ the Saviour and takes refuge in His mercy. Zwingli seems here to have been inspired by St. Augustine: *"cor nostrum inquietum donec requiescat in te"* (our heart is restless until it finds rest in Thee). Jesus dispels the anguish of the penitent. He is the source of salvation, the Son who dispenses life eternal (John 3), the light of the world (John 8), the door of the sheep (John 10), the redemptive bread and wine (John 6), the way, the truth, and the life (John 14).

On the completion of this analysis woven from Johannine texts, Ulrich deals with the objection which catholicism flung in the face of the reformers, as soon as the first treatises of Luther had been published. If Christ freely blots out man's sins, if in the heart of the believer the fear of hell is effaced, will not the latter draw the conclusion: "Let us sin that grace may abound"? The unfair criticism is as old as St. Paul. Zwingli makes a frontal attack on it. It is, he explains, relative to theoretical considerations. In the living reality of souls, such an aberration is impossible. Does the man who has been sick desire to renew his fever because he knows the address of a good practitioner? Will the victim of an accident, after the proper setting and healing of his broken leg, say to himself: "You are lucky to have discovered such a doctor; break your leg often, for your doctor can do all things"? *"Beatus es quod talem invenisti medicum, crebro crus franges nam medicus iste omnia potest."* Amid his learned reflections, the theologian forgets the pain that has been felt.

An elementary train of reasoning, which it is difficult to dispute! Zwingli is not satisfied with it, however. In the chapter entitled *De poenitentia*—concerning penitence—he goes deeply into the problem of the relation in the Christian life between the spirit and the flesh. If the despairing man, he notes, looks towards the fountain of pity, if he rejoices in forgiveness, his joy does not make him forget the basic wretchedness of his condition. As long as he lives in this mortal body, he continues to be penitent. Desires ceaselessly spring up which must be deplored: "This travail, this struggle, this vigilance, what are they if not penitence?" When Christ, John, and the apostles say: "Repent!" they are calling man to a new life, wholly different from the previous one.

The Gospel always combines with the note of forgiveness the summons to make a break with the past, to change, to self-renunciation. He who puts his hand to the plough must not look back (Luke 9). In the parable of the wedding feast, the guest who has not put on the festal garment is banished (Matt. 22). Zwingli considers that this symbolizes a faith that is unaccompanied by penitence. And he draws from the armoury of the New Testament some of his most famous warnings: you must be a *new creature* (Gal. 6), it is not sufficient to repeat "Lord, Lord" (Matt. 7). The Christian life is nothing other than a "firm hope in God and an innocent life following the example of Christ" (*firma spes in Deum per Christum Jesum et innocens vita ad exemplum Christi expressa*).

However, we continue to sin. Is it possible to satisfy the mind that is eager for clarity in face of the paradoxes of the Christian life?

The mind of the theologian who wishes to explain everything is moving within scholastic categories. The drama of the Christian life—which Luther in an unforgettable formula sums up as *simul peccator et justus*—is connected with experience and only he who participates in it can understand it. "*Res enim est ac experimentum pietas,*" cries Zwingli; piety belongs to the sphere of reality and experience. It has nothing to do either with speech or knowledge: "*non sermo vel scientia*". The Christian, like Abraham, is plunged in contradiction. Had not God promised to the patriarch an innumerable posterity? Hence what could be the meaning of the command to sacrifice Isaac? Abraham, however, believed and obeyed. Likewise the Christian believes in forgiveness without inferring from it laxity of morals, and he welcomes the requirement of a pure life without concluding from it the supreme value of works.

The law is intimately connected with the gospel. Divine mercy, far from annulling the law, sustains it. Written in the heart (Rom. 2: 15) or in the ten commandments, it remains valid for the Christian who fulfils it with joy and no longer because of the curses of the Old Testament. "Thou shalt love thy neighbour as thyself": such a command is eternal.

In view of the ever valid nature of the law, Zwingli analyses further and at great length the nature of sin. Hereditary sin, the evil tendency (*morbus*) which comes from Adam, must be distinguished from particular transgressions of the law which are its consequence. Sin as a disease, or the tendency to evil, impels man to avoid struggle and difficulties and to seek pleasures and voluptuous living (*jucunda et voluptuosa*). Man is unaware of his egoism, or rather finds it natural up to the moment when there shines in his heart the divine command to love.

From then on, torn between instinct and the ideal, he leads a difficult life. The wicked man, whose conscience is troubled, has recourse to external guarantees: he offers money to some pious foundation, he fasts in honour of the Virgin Mary, he raises heavenwards a troubled and half-hearted prayer, but meantime, under a façade of religion, he continues his disorderly life. The true Christian takes the law seriously. It seizes his very being, kindles in him the fire of which Christ speaks (Luke 12), the flame of charity. Now that it is freed from the ancient curse by the certitude of forgiveness, the will harnesses itself joyfully to the service of God. Yet it constantly comes into conflict with the impulses of a rebellious heart. Sin, as an ingrained malady, still inclines it towards evil. Zwingli takes up, in the form of a paraphrase, the famous texts of the Epistle to the Romans: the law reveals sin, it is not a poison, but its illumination overwhelms us. It does not slay; it reveals death. In the believer, once he has passed through the painful initial phase of discovery, and has received forgiveness, the inner conflict goes on. What I expound, says Zwingli in essence, is my own experience: the spiritual man approves the divine law, but the old man pulls me in the opposite direction. I am divided; I hesitate, and am neither a crow nor a dove. "Neither an angel nor a beast", Pascal will exclaim a hundred and twenty years later.

This tension would reduce the believer to despair if the memory of Christ did not come to his aid. The certainty of His love revives the fainting soul: "The God who has given up His son for you cannot disclaim anything and He knows your weakness." The weight of fear is lightened and the soul breathes better. But already a new clash is intimated, and it will be succeeded by others: "The life of the Christian is like the ship which is tossed hither and thither by a horrible storm; at times the sailors succeed in controlling it a little, thanks to the rudder; at other times they are obliged to yield to the violence of the winds."

The painful cry of St. Paul: "The evil I do not want is what I do," finds an echo in the heart of this priest of Zürich, who does not seek to disguise this inner life: he surrenders it as it is, quivering and tormented, to our moved attention. These are poignant confessions for anyone who remembers the drama of Einsiedeln, the barber's daughter and the self-mastery purchased at such painful cost. "We suffer", said Pascal," in proportion as the vice which is natural to us resists supernatural grace." And again: "The most cruel warfare which God can wage on men in this life is to leave them untouched by the conflict which He came on earth to unleash."

When Ulrich questions himself to try to distinguish in the Christian life the pledges of ultimate victory, he situates them in the death of Christ crucified, who has destroyed the empire of sin, and, secondly, in the permanent reign of the Spirit, which is its corollary. The latter cannot now be defeated by the assault of temptations. "To live according to the flesh"—to quote another Pauline expression—is to make total surrender to the flesh. The Christian resists. "The citadel must be firmly held lest we should deliver ourselves over completely to the dominion of the flesh." If inherited sinfulness persists, the heart is nevertheless renewed; it knows God, it is illuminated by divine grace. Instead of trusting his own wisdom and strength, the Christian relies on God alone; his life becomes a perpetual act of penitence (*paenitentia perpetua*).

A comparison comes to the help of the writer, who forgets neither the orchards of his childhood nor his vicarage gardens. The nurseryman uproots in the woods a wild stock, transplants it to good soil and grafts it. The new branches produce some excellent pears, but from the old trunk ceaselessly spring useless branches, covered with prickles, which must be cut away lest in growing they should draw to themselves all the sap, with the result that the good branches weaken and die. So is the disciple of Christ with his new heart engrafted by grace, and his old Adam. The image expresses more effectively than all the subtle analyses of the scholastics the moving complexity of the Christian life.

Zwingli's train of thought does not move within scholastic categories, but the problem which he approaches, that of justification by faith, will for a long time overshadow the disputes between reformers and catholics. It plays an enormous part in the work of Luther, fills the 14th chapter of the *Institutes*, and occupies a conspicuous place in the decisions of the Council of Trent. The *De vera et falsa religione* emphasizes both the reality of salvation (the Spirit penetrates the life of the Christian) and its frailty (we must wage an unceasing struggle). By the close tie which he establishes between penitence and forgiveness, he escapes the temptation to set these two aspects of the spiritual life in opposition to each other. There is no mercy without repentance, but likewise there is no penitence without hope for him who truly heeds Jesus Christ. The soul breathes and struggles, at once strengthened and stimulated by one and the same message. The appeal which liberates man strikes home to the deepest places of the heart, determining a fundamental choice. The love of one's neighbour replaces the external secondary works which tranquillized superficial consciences while bringing no peace to the anguish of those who were more deeply disquieted. The bracing vision of the incessant struggle against self opened wide the doors to a real and manly saintliness—and, if I may dare to use the paradox, far removed from gilt pasteboard halos, from Sulpician or pietistic finicalness.

CHAPTER FIFTEEN

The Power of the Keys—the Church: the Idea of the Sacrament: Baptism and the Lord's Supper

THE MEDIEVAL CHURCH assumed an immense share in the communication of salvation. Zwingli brutally reversed the trend by flinging forth the revolutionary formula that the power of the keys is identifiable with the Gospel itself. The ritual words: "May the Lord Jesus Christ absolve you, and I absolve you by His authority whose exercise is entrusted to me", he remarked, conferred upon the priest an excessive mediatorial role. The keys, in the thought of Christ, were intended to unlock the door of souls. He does not give them to Peter alone: the words of Matt. 16 concern the whole group of disciples and behind them the pastors of all ages. The latter will bind or unbind human spirits in proportion as they convey the good news of Christ.

Tu es Petrus: Thou art Peter: "Do you not in fact confess firmly, clearly and steadfastly that which is the saving truth for all mankind?" It is not you personally who are Peter, you are Peter in virtue of the message that you bear. God alone is the rock on which the Church is built. "The gates of hell shall not prevail against it"—this means that they will never be able to resist the power of Christ.

Thus the keys are a metaphor exalting the power of the Word. That power liberates and consoles men: "To unbind means nothing other than to raise up the spirit which despairs of salvation by leading it to a sure and certain hope."

When the apostles spread abroad in the world the message of peace, they were fulfilling the mission with which Christ had entrusted Peter as their representative. "As the Father has sent me, even so I send you" (John 20). "He who believes and is baptized will be saved; he who does not believe will be cast out." These two sayings of Christ refer to the keys.

Catholics and protestants are further apart "than heaven is from earth. The popes make of the keys an authority conferred on man by God. Christ defines the keys as the faith by which man believes in the message of the Gospel." This brings grace and new life.

When the preaching of the Gospel arouses unbelief, Christ commands His disciples to depart shaking off the dust of their feet. To *bind* means to leave in error. The instrument of salvation becomes one of rejection.

Such a conception deprives the clergy of the power of disposing of souls and brings them back to the status of instruments in God's service. Zwingli desired to cleanse the keys "of the rust of tradition". For too long, they had turned in the locks of the Church through the power of money and for the profit of souls still burdened with sin: they had tranquillized such souls without delivering them.

The dismantling of the traditional edifice of the Church is continued by a direct attack on the hierarchy. Men have mistakenly confined the Church to a small group wielding authority; a mistake similar to that of those who identify the state with the king. "Pure and spotless" because of the Saviour, the Ecclesia is distinct from the bishops. The totality of souls illuminated by the light of the Gospel constitutes the infallible people of God. The latter is not tied to Alexander, Julius, Leo and Adrian. The various communities—formerly Antioch and Corinth, "today the Greeks and ourselves", form the *catholic church and the communion of saints* of the creed. This includes solely those who are attached to Christ, excepting hypocrites who are the tares mingled here below with the wheat of sincere believers.

Does the "church of the pontiffs" share in the *communio sanctorum*? Zwingli answers negatively, contrasting the flock of God with the flock of Belial. The thought that a Christian element may persist at the heart of the condemned organization does not occur to him. He, the heretic, whom his former chiefs would condemn to the stake, becomes exclusivist in his turn: *"Ecclesia pontificum est ecclesia inimici hominis, hoc est diaboli"*—the church of the pontiffs is the church of the devil, the enemy of man. Violence provokes violence, intolerance reaps intolerance, as the wind the whirlwind. The slow passage of four centuries will be needed before Roman Catholicism and the people's church arising from the reformation will come to regard each other without hatred, and will discover, despite tremendous divergences, that they have in common their invocation of the name of Christ, the supernatural sign of unity.

For the ordinary person, Zwinglianism can be reduced to its idea of the sacraments, with the result that the Zürich reform is confused with the Marburg debate. The preceding pages show the injustice of this limitation. Nevertheless, Zwingli's interpretation of the communion bread and wine occupies an important position in the *De vera et falsa religione*.

The word *sacrament* is not much to Zwingli's liking. Many, he observes, understand by this word "something great and sacred which by its inherent power liberates the conscience from sin", thus confounding the symbolic action with the Gospel itself. Others reduce it to the rank of a sign (*signum*). Zwingli would approve of the latter, if they did not at once postulate a necessary coincidence between the external action and the reality of inner cleansing. A third group consider the sacrament to be a sign confirming a spiritual transformation which has already taken place. "I do not willingly part company with great men who are like shining lights in this storm and write so felicitously," he notes, alluding thus discreetly to his difference with Luther. When a writer thinks differently from oneself it is wrong to despise him. One must try to understand his thought, in the expectation that he will reciprocate this.

Coming back to the word *sacrament*, Zwingli lays it down

as a principle that no physical element—whether it be water, fire, oil, milk, or salt—has any power to affect the soul. God alone can change the dispositions of the heart by faith. The latter operates in the depths of man's being and is not to be confounded either with knowledge or dreamy contemplation or with an illusion. It arises when man begins to despair of himself and to cling to the one true God. The sacrament is therefore an *initiatio* or an *oppignatio*—that is to say, a pledge. It commits the man who receives it. It is like depositing a surety. By its means, "man presents himself to the Church as a disciple or a soldier of Christ". The sign does not confirm faith, "for if faith is completed only when it is confirmed by a sign, then it is not faith". True faith is based solidly on God, and cannot be shaken.

The conception of Zwingli effects a radical break with that of the catholic church. Bread and wine no longer feed the soul; the water of baptism ceases to regenerate. All three symbolize the self-committal of the Christian to the service of Christ who alone nourishes and cleanses souls. As compared with Luther, the divergence again is enormous, since Luther's thought remains centred on the idea of the sacrament as a power of communication.

Baptism, of which the author of the *De vera et falsa religione* states that "it effects nothing", becomes an act of self-committal to penitence: no essential difference separates the baptism of John from that of Christ. Jesus did not rebaptize Peter or John.

As for the Lord's Supper, concerning which Ulrich expressed himself with prudence in the apology of his sixty-seven theses, for fear of shocking the weak, he now speaks without reserve: his conception, he remarks, must be looked for in his second book, not in his first. The holy meal is a joyous act of thanksgiving, the eucharist of the New Covenant. Every Christian should take part in it so as to declare his membership of the Church of Christ, while hypocrites, whose wicked life reveals their impiety, will be turned away from it. Basing his thought on John 6, Zwingli recalls the fact that the essential work of salvation is to believe. The bread is Christ Himself, who has come down to earth, Christ seen as God. The word *bread* might be rendered by that of *Gospel* and *eat* by *believe*. The transference of these terms to the Communion service has for centuries caused the most frightful confusion: "Many eat and drink sacramentally the Body and Blood of Christ who however are not in God. Neither is God in them, except to the extent to which He is also in an elephant or in a flea." Jesus was in conflict with the Jews who understood His words in a materialistic way: the 6th chapter of St. John is a "mystical discourse". Only he who believes in the redemptive sprinkling of the blood on the cross, gains liberation. "It is the Spirit that gives life," says the Saviour, "the flesh avails nothing." There is nothing so absurd as the conviction of eating "spiritually His carnal body". The very words clash with each other and are mutually exclusive.

The reformer foresees that these frank reflections will raise a storm. What matters it to him? The clamour of his adversaries does not impress him. They raise the cry of heresy: let them discuss rather on the basis of Scripture. He, Zwingli, offers to do so. Estimable men—and this evidently is an allusion to Luther and his friends—stress the "This is my body." Does Christ by these words truly identify the bread and His physical being? The real problem lies in the verb "is" which corresponds to "signifies" (*significat*) here as in many other texts. The question of the cup— "This is my blood"—may be solved in the same way. The wine too recalls the offered sacrifice. At this point, Zwingli breaks a lance for the suppression of masses for the dead. Let the revenues of the foundations be left to the priests who serve them for their lifetime, but after their decease they should not be replaced.

This summary gives but a feeble idea of the seriousness of the study which Zwingli wrote for his French readers. Gospel and Epistles are ceaselessly quoted. The theologian here sheds his reserve and draws upon the arsenal of his patristic knowledge. Tertullian, Augustine, Origen, Hilary, Jerome are invoked in his support. The struggle promises to be long and difficult. Luther, paradoxically allied to catholicism, will contest Zwingli's conclusions. The transubstantiation of Rome, like the consubstantiation of Wittenberg, implies a quasi-physical communion.

Zwingli seems to have been dominated by the desire to make a complete break with the mass. Long assailed by doubts, he chanted a liturgy in which his heart had ceased to share. Like Luther, who had recently attacked indulgences, he fought against the danger of providing the soul with an external security. The soul, he considered, was merely lulled into slumber by the sacraments. What was the use of a serious repentance, if, after death, money had the power to multiply redemptive ceremonies?

The distinction between the physical and the spiritual, which the reformer stressed, is of capital importance. Who, if he gives a little thought to the matter, will not agree with his point of view? The manuals intended for use in seminaries teach today that saving grace cannot be mediated by the eucharistic bread apart from the inner dispositions of the communicant. "The conditions of worthy reception" enumerated by the Council of Trent envisage the case of the dying who are burdened by mortal sin. Before receiving the eucharist they must undergo the sacrament of penance, or, at the very least, show a perfect contrition. None the less, Catholicism and Zwinglianism remain poles apart. The permanence of the Real Presence, affirmed by the same Council of Trent, closely binds the living Christ to the Host which is jealously reserved and adored.

Calvin who, in the 17th chapter of the fourth book of the *Institutes*, disputes the catholic and Lutheran formulae of a divine presence enclosed in the eucharistic species, insists on the communicant's participation in the Risen Body which is in heaven. "There are some", he notes, "who briefly assert that to eat the flesh of Christ and to drink His blood mean simply to believe in Him. But it seems that He Himself wished to convey a loftier thought in that noteworthy discourse in which He enjoins the eating of His body: the meaning is that we are made alive by the true participation in Himself which He bestows on us and which He has signified by the words eating and drinking, lest any should think that it was a question of mere knowledge. . . . By calling Himself bread and wine, He wished not only to denote that our salvation is bound up with trust in His death and resurrection, but also that, in virtue of our real communion with Him, His life is transferred to us and is made ours: just as bread, when it is taken as food, strengthens the body" (*Institutes*, 4, 17-5).

For the French theologian, Jesus verily communicates Himself to the faithful, but it is not a question of the eating of His fleshly body. The "This is my body" was uttered by the Lord while He was still incarnate. The sacrament does not refer to the earthly Christ, but to the heavenly glorified Christ. The latter "is always present with His own", sustains them, confirms them and fortifies them. Calvinism is differentiated from Zwinglianism by the assertion of this real mystical communion between the Risen Lord and His disciples. In the last analysis is it a matter of a mere verbal difference? Behind the words which clash, do believers—as is so often the case in theology—envisage one and the same spiritual reality? It is impossible for us here to go deeply into this problem. If Calvin insists on a substantial communication of living power, while Zwingli stops at faith in the sacrifice wrought by the Son of God, the picture of a mystical Calvin confronting an intellectualist Zwingli contradicts the portraits of the two reformers which are suggested by their biographies. To the impartial observer the Zürich reformer appears as much inspired by Jesus Christ as his Genevan contradictor, and certainly more Christian than the voluptuous pope Alexander VI or the ostentatious Leo X. As for Luther and his theory of "impanation" (or consubstantiation), we shall consider them in the chapter devoted to the colloquy of Marburg, where the discussion of this whole problem will be resumed.

CHAPTER SIXTEEN

Confession, Marriage, Monastic Vows, Invocation of Saints, Images, Merit, Prayer, and Purgatory

"HOLY SCRIPTURE", declares Zwingli, "contains only the *confession* of the man who knows himself and commits himself to the mercy of God, in accordance with this cry of the Psalmist: 'I said, I will confess my transgressions to the Lord; then Thou didst forgive the guilt of my sin.'" God alone can heal the sick heart. The sinner, however, in his confusion, may open his mind to a servant of the Word. The latter will point out to him the way that leads to the true physician; like the Good Samaritan, he will pour wine into the wound, that is, the bitterness of penitence, and oil, which is the joy of meeting Christ. "Auricular confession is thus nothing more than a consultation, in which we receive from the minister to whom God has committed this trust the counsel which will help us to discover the way of peace for our heart."

Confirmation completes, at the age of discretion, the baptism which has been received in infancy. It belongs to the category of customs, as does the visitation of the sick (extreme unction) recommended by James, ch. 5. The visitor will pray with the sick man for his recovery, after anointing him with oil. Ordination must be considered a human invention. *"Functio est, non dignitas, episcopatus":* the episcopate is a function, not a dignity. Whoever preaches the Word shares in the episcopal office; whoever does not fulfil the ministry of the Word does not deserve the title of bishop.

With regard to marriage, Zwingli notes that it cannot be classed among the sacraments, for it does not represent, like the Lord's Supper, a mystery of the faith. None the less, it is a holy institution, sanctioned by the divine will. Hence no law should forbid the pastor to be the husband of one wife. The plea which had in vain been addressed just previously to the Bishop of Constance reappears here in an abridged form after the marriage of Ulrich. He combines it with a severe condemnation of monastic vows. It is sheer folly to promise what God does not require. Chastity,[1] a special gift, is reserved to the few. Other men will do well to extinguish the fires of the flesh by undertaking marriage, rather than endure in their minds the trouble and impurity of unquenched desires. In this respect, each one is the best judge of his capacity for resistance: "Revolving the matter in your own mind in solitude, you yourself can best decide whether you ought to marry or not." And since no one can in advance be expected to answer for his constancy: "All vows of chastity are impious." Even husband and wife ought not to separate from each other for a time except by mutual consent, teaches St. Paul. Let it suffice us to fulfil the commandments of God without wishing to go beyond them. To love one's neighbour as oneself is already difficult enough.

Similarly, the vow of poverty is liable to criticism. All Christians ought to be poor in spirit. It is enough, if God so commands, to distribute one's goods to the poor: why accompany this decision by a promise? If God entrusts someone, a king or prince, with the task of faithfully administering the wealth of a country, why should such a believer decide of his own initiative to live in indigence? Moreover, the poverty of monastic orders is far from being true poverty. Nowhere is to be found so much wealth combined with so much leisure as in the life of the cloister. He who remains in the world has a much less easy time of it. "Are you supposed to be rich and comfortable in the life of the city? You must, however, worry about very many things, going up and down staircases, for instance, the rain, the hail and all the other caprices of the weather."

As for obedience, the Christian owes this to all men:

[1] See above, p. 72.

"Whatever you wish that men would do to you, do so to them" is what the Gospel commands. And again: "If any one forces you to go with him one mile, go with him two." The Church is a body, and life in community demands mutual understanding. Christians should submit themselves in turn to each other. Ulrich sharply reproaches the monks with egoistically establishing themselves in a world apart. They refuse the payment of taxes and, in case of war, refuse to take their part in the defence of their country. "Even Solomon in all his glory did not enjoy the delights of this world in such ease and tranquillity."

The invocation of saints is condemned on the basis of the principle that *God alone is good* (Luke 18). The believer whose faith lifts itself to the merciful Father in heaven can do without special protectors. What need have we for a celestial advocate, when we possess the Christ, the sole Mediator? "Come to Me, all who labour," He says (Matt. 11). The pagans, not knowing their Creator, attributed their healing to gods such as Apollo and Aesculapius, or if they went on a sea voyage committed themselves to the care of Castor and Pollux. The Bible sweeps away the promptings of superstition: "I lift up my eyes to the hills: from whence does my help come?" asks the Psalmist. His answer is clear: "My help comes from the Lord, who made heaven and earth." The patristic texts cited by a theologian of Paris, John Clichtove, failed to impress Ulrich. *"Scio Hieronymos, Augustinum, alios, sed simul scio Christum et apostolos"* (I know Jerome, Augustine, and the others, but I also know Christ and the apostles).

Closely connected with the veneration of saints, that of images is discussed in the final pages of the book. Statues and pictures should be removed only if acts of worship are rendered to them. That is why Zwingli proposes to leave untouched stained-glass windows which no one thinks of venerating. Those who defended images maintained that they instruct man and influence him in the direction of piety. But if they had this power, Zwingli asserted, Jesus would have spoken of it. Has He not said on the contrary: "You always have the poor with you"? Hence it is to the poor and unfortunate that we must give the gold, silver, precious stones and pearls which are used to decorate the statues and portraits of saints. The Old Testament forbids idols. Any representation of God is sacrilegious.

But are not the calvaries showing Christ hanging on a cross of wood on a different footing? If you wish to expose His divinity to the eyes of men, objects the reformer, you are trying to express what cannot be expressed. If it is His human nature which is being depicted, the image ought not to be adored. The reader will recall the incident of the big calvary surmounting the gate of Oberdorf which was hurled down by the iconoclasts. If Zwingli did not approve the violence with which it was done, he nevertheless desired the abolition of crucifixes in general. In this respect, as in some others, he went further than Luther. Oscar Farner emphasizes his radicalism in such matters. With the extreme logicality which is characteristic of him, the Zürich reformer pushes his principles to their uttermost conclusions, regardless of tradition. He reacts violently, because he knows so well the aberrations of false religion: "Have we not all revered as holy the touching of images? Why have we kissed them? Why have we bowed the knee before them and given so much money for the privilege of gazing at them?" Einsiedeln glories in its black Madonna. Zwingli had been accustomed to welcome there pilgrims from all parts. He knows what he is talking about. Such a grave ill requires surgical remedies.

For Ulrich the problem of images is envisaged from a purely religious point of view. He has no objection to art in itself, whence the reservation which closes this paragraph: "We do not speak from prejudice, for no one is fonder than we are of pictures, statues and images."

The merits of the saints have been transferred to dissolute persons through the payment of money. Zwingli, who opposed Samson, the seller of indulgences, does not recur at once to this aspect of the problem. He goes first to the heart of the matter, namely the origin of good in the Christian. In the last analysis, all goes back to the will of God, who by His providence guides the life of the world and of human individuals. The mind of man controls the visible movement of his body: his feet, his hand put to the plough, obey him. *"Hoc est deus in mundo quod ratio in homine."* God fulfils in the world the function which reason fulfils in the life of the human being. Events depend on Him. We are afraid to take this conviction to its extreme conclusion lest we should make of God the author of evil. But we do not notice that in man things which are frightening—illnesses and sufferings —are salutary. He is tormented by fever; he becomes sober and recovers. Gout draws the harmful humours to the extremities of the body while making healthy the rest of it. We fear to attribute to God acts which would shock us in a human being. But is God subject to the same rules as ourselves? The moral life of an animal is not the same as that of a man; why should there not be a similar difference between the ethics of God and those of His creatures?

The problem of evil and that of predestination are only lightly touched on here. Zwingli confines himself to expressing the view that the omnipotence of God eliminates human free will and therefore human merit. Predestination and foreknowledge cannot be distinguished from each other. God knows and ordains everything. A true Christian attributes to God the faith which illuminates him. But, it will be said, why does not the Almighty enlighten every man? Here, the theologian refuses to reply, and seeks refuge behind the Pauline image of the potter: "Ask Him who created them! Ask Him to render you accounts! We were not His counsellors. . . ."

A few years later, Zwingli took up this problem again in the *De Providentia*. For the moment, he concentrates above all on denying merit. Armed with many texts, he shows that the good works of Christians flow from the action of Christ in them. He is the Vine; we are the branches. Our fruits are His fruits. God is love: "If you have recognized the sovereign good, it is not possible for you not to love."

Participation in ceremonies is not the surest indication of a true faith. Obedience to the divine will is still better. Let us be filled with zeal to gain truth and innocence, and ready to expose our lives for our brothers: thus we shall live for the glory of God.

With regard to prayer, Zwingli protests against the selling of prayers. Prayer is an uplifting of the soul to God. The exploitation of intercession is a scandal. "You must not appear before God with your hands empty," say the priests. This they make a pretext for holding the faithful to ransom. There is nothing so abnormal as the division of labour suggested by the monks: "While you work, I will pray." The Christian must in turn join his hands together in prayer and labour. "Love suffers with others, struggles and gives help."

Purgatory offers a good target for the irony of the ex-canon. Speculation has postulated for the lukewarm an intermediary sphere between hell and heaven, unknown to the scriptures. The clergy seized on the idea and have exploited it for financial gain. Masses are recited, psalms sung. Money can put out the flames! Self-interested preachers are hardly better than quacks; they make use of man's fear to acquire for themselves plenty of custom: prison, serpents, flames, torrents, fire, sulphur, all serves their purpose. The Gospel texts cited by the advocates of purgatory, when submitted to the test of judicious criticism, cannot be said to bear such an interpretation.

CHAPTER SEVENTEEN

Temporal Authority

THE LAST PARAGRAPHS of the *De vera et falsa religione* reflect the internal dissensions of the reformation. Confronted by German illuminism and the Swiss anabaptism of Manz and Grebel, Zwingli defends the necessity of the State. Several demand its abolition, convinced that all constraint contradicts the spirit of Christianity. A true believer, they assert, ought not to occupy any civil office. The reformer replies that he knows many honourable, pious, and faithful magistrates who fulfil their trust for the greater glory of God and the good of their fellow citizens.

Is it right to separate the Church absolutely from the State? In theory, the former institution includes only the disciples of Christ, while the latter is content with a conscientious administration of the laws, quite apart from the question of religion. In regard to the sphere of the State, each member must—as the Gospel directs—forget his own interests, work for the good of the community, accept his share of responsibility and risk, and avoid partisanship. The Church lays stress on a charity which is concerned about others. It requires us to weep with those who weep and to rejoice with those who rejoice. The programmes of the two cities, temporal and spiritual, overlap: *"utraque requirit quod altera"*, each seeks the same thing as the other. The difference lies in the means used to attain the common end. The State uses compulsion; the citizen is placed under the yoke of the laws; he often does his duty hypocritically and reluctantly. The rule of the Church is spiritual. Everything within its sphere is voluntary. The Christian does not require from his brother the sharing of goods. In case of necessity, he freely puts his own wealth at the disposal of others. Christ has loved us; following His patterns, we try to love our neighbour as ourselves. If Christian love is added to the sense of civic duty, the pursuit of egoistic interests will disappear. Hence the State cannot find better citizens than its Christian members. *"Nulla civitas beatior erit quam in qua vera religio simul degit"*: no city will be happier than that in which true religion flourishes and abounds.

This observation which concerns private citizens is still more true when it is a question of the prince or magistrate. The Christian government will be the best. Heads of State who have not the fear of God before their eyes rapidly degenerate into tyrants. Should a wicked prince be converted, he becomes a father to his people.

What are we to think of the thesis that the Church of Jesus Christ should be perfect to the point where political authority is made useless? Zwingli brings out the utopian aspect of this proposition. He would like to see the advent of such a reign of innocence. Alas, it does not exist. Those who most ardently demand the abolition of the State are violent men, incapable of holding themselves in check, and refusing to accept any criticism. It is madness to remove the barrier of constraint before the conditions for such removal are fulfilled. When sin has disappeared in acts and words, only then will it be time to abolish the magistracy. Not before. Scripture contains several texts enjoining obedience to authority, I Pet. 2 and Rom. 13 in particular. Furthermore, it praises pious chiefs like Abraham, Moses, Joshua, David, Solomon, Josiah, and Hezekiah. The New Testament quotes examples of Christian magistrates like Erastus, the city treasurer (Rom. 16), and the proconsul Sergius Paulus. The history of the Church honours the Emperor Theodosius, and other princes famous for their piety.

The absolute insistence on independence is an aberration. Every society requires organization, otherwise it crumbles. The heads of State, for their part, must be vigilant to serve God. If Paul writes, "All authority comes from God", the text does not excuse the exercise of arbitrary power by princes. Providence punishes wicked peoples by sending them bad kings, but these last only for a time. The task of government is not easy; let the magistrate not play at being master, but aim at ruling his subjects with fatherly care.

In these pages devoted to the theme of authority, Zwingli hardly touches on the problem of Church government. Does not the Church, which is an association of free consciences, need either bishops or synods? The reformer criticizes the use which the popes have made of their power. For centuries, papal bulls and excommunications have brought trouble to the Church. The papal tribunal is the only one in the world which condemns without hearing the accused, whereas Christ (Matt. 18) asks that the guilty brother should first of all be taken to task in friendly fashion, man to man, "between you and him alone". "If he listens to you, you have gained your brother." The stubborn sinner must then be denounced to the Church, not to the pope. The latter excommunicates the innocent. "*Vide, quam atrox imperium.*" Atrocious rule, even more inhuman and harsh than that of the Persians, a veritable tyranny! Excommunication is the business of the local church, which knows the accused, not that of a remote authority.

When should the necessary reform of doctrine and rites be put into effect? Zwingli advises prudence. First let Christ and His grace be solidly rooted in the hearts of men; the rest will follow. It is pointless to scandalize timorous or hesitant spirits by insisting from the first on the negative aspects of the new faith. Is it a question of fasting? Although the individual Christian alone is the judge before God of his habits in the matter of food, a slow evolution is better than a sharp break with the past, if such a break arouses in the heart of many a hatred of the Gospel. The marriage of a priest may remain secret for a time, if the publication of it should have as its consequence the death penalty or expulsion. As for consecrations, unctions, and other such rites, which are destined to disappear, the wisest course is to have patience.

The caution characteristic of Ulrich thus reappears in the final pages of his book. Did Farel and his friends understand the importance of the foreword addressed to them? If the excitable southerner sometimes moderated his impetuosity, others were unable to bridle either their tongue or their pen. The famous placards of 1524, posters insulting to the mass and which at Amboise were introduced into the royal chamber itself, provoking the murderous wrath of Francis I, furnish sad proof of this. Charity, combined with circumspection, advised progressive changes rather than revolutions; but the temporizers were regarded as cowards by foolhardy spirits. Zwingli believed in the legitimacy of carefully planned steps. Ignatius Loyola, in the opposite camp, went much further by the same means.

Part Five

Divergence of the Ways

CHAPTER EIGHTEEN

Rupture with Erasmus

THE CRUEL COST of religious convictions lies in the
separations which they cause. On a certain spiritual
level, concord seems to have been attained. Souls
communicate with each other in the same fervent way;
eager for truth, they progress harmoniously in quest of their
goal. Suddenly, contradictory affirmations are sparked off;
paths diverge; the sometime friends are enemies.

As early as 1515, Erasmus had opened the eyes of Ulrich
to a new vision of the faith. Ulrich was enormously indebted
to the *Praise of Folly*, to the *Summary of True Theology*, to
the *Enchiridion*, to the *Manual of the Christian Soldier*,
to the *Annotations of the New Testament*, and above all to
Erasmus's Greek text of the New Testament, which Zwingli
copied out as soon as it appeared. In the author of these
volumes, which were carefully read and annotated by him,
Zwingli admired both the scholar and the believer, and he
never disowned his debt. In 1527, when the die had already
been cast three years previously, he rendered homage to his
former master in a writing in which he refutes the claim of
Luther to be the first discoverer of the Gospel. "Already,"
he writes, turning towards a past which is receding, "there
were a good number of people who had reached the essential
faith, if not better—which you would never admit—at
least as well as you. Yes, truly, there were men who, twelve
years ago now—and at that time I was on a footing of friendship with them—proved very useful to me and led me to a
joyful zeal."

The clash between Luther and Erasmus cannot altogether

surprise us. They never really understood each other. The rough, austere monk moved in an utterly different world from that of the subtle intellectual. Their first contact was grating. Spalatin, the secretary of Duke Frederick "the Wise", writing at the end of 1516 to the prince of the lettered world, conveyed the esteem in which the Elector held him, but added to his compliments a note of theological reservation. A certain Augustinian monk, who was a great admirer of the writer, wished to draw his attention to the inadequate exegesis of the idea of *justitia* which marred his Commentary on Romans. He suggested that the reading of St. Augustine would provide him with useful further understanding.

Did Erasmus remember the name of the obscure professor who thus permitted himself to give him advice? Nothing is less certain. In 1518, he read the *95 Theses*, and sent them to his friend More with some comments on the impudence of those who trafficked in indulgences. In 1519, it was Luther who took the initiative in making contact with the humanist. For the furtherance of the new ideas, it would be useful, he suggested, if the world realized that they were in agreement. But the façade of eulogy ill conceals the mistrust which already had been openly expressed in a letter which he addressed about the same time to his friend John Lange: "I read our Erasmus, and day by day my esteem for him diminishes. . . . . I fear that he does not sufficiently preach Christ and His grace. In these matters he is much more ignorant than Lefèvre d'Etaples. The human element in him triumphs over the divine. . . . He who concedes something to the freedom of the will judges otherwise than he who knows only grace." In 1518, Erasmus addressed to the same Lange a eulogy of the *95 Theses*: "I see that the monarchical rule of the pope in Rome, as at present exercised, is the plague of Christianity." But he expressed his fear of debates in the public squares and thought that the princes should settle the matter.

This mixture of esteem and criticism foreshadows the storm which broke over the *De Libero Arbitrio*. As early as

1519, Erasmus tried to dissociate his cause from that of the heretic. The fear of troubles ahead played the chief part in his reaction: "I see that the affair is becoming a revolution," he confided in June, 1520, to Melanchthon. It may also be that the vain desire to remain the first thinker of his time was a motive with the susceptible Batavian. In any event, he had always detested war. Intellectual jousts had their attraction for him on condition that they remained purely academic. His prayer at the thought of the rent in Christendom is well known: "Bring order out of this chaos, Lord Jesus, send Your Spirit to move over these evilly turbulent waves of dogma."

In 1521 his situation became uncomfortable. A monk denounced before the king four precursors of Antichrist among whom were Erasmus and Lefèvre. In 1522 began the quarrel with Noël Béda, Syndic of the Sorbonne, which reached its climax with the publication in 1526 of Béda's *Adnotationes*. In this work the humanists, sharply attacked, are made responsible for the successes of Luther. It became absolutely necessary to make apparent that a wide gulf yawned between the friends of scholarship and the reformers. In 1524, the *Diatribe de Libero Arbitrio* endeavoured to do this. "As long as Erasmus refuses to write against Luther," said the theologians of Louvain, "we consider him to be Lutheran." The lampoon directed against the man of Wittenberg was intended to whiten the calumniated scholar. It provoked in particular the stinging reply of the *De Servo Arbitrio*, which, a year later, pilloried the writer and his subtleties: "the evasive and veering manner in which you constantly sail between Scylla and Charybdis, more cunning than Ulysses, never affirming anything which you do not retract."

Zwingli had been one of the first to see the storm looming. His lucid mind measured the abyss which separated the two thinkers. If he appreciated the writings of Luther, the works of Erasmus formed the basis from which he had set out for his encounter with Christ. In 1885, Jean-Martin Usteri, in a study which is still of value, enumerated the theological ideas of Erasmus which influenced Zwingli: the call to go back to the sources of Christianity, which restored to the Bible its authority; the full sufficiency of Christ for salvation; that infants who die without baptism are "saved"; the conception of faith as a *fiducia* (trust); the criticism of the superstitions with which the Church was encumbered, and of papal absolutism. Even as regards the doctrine of the sacraments, there exists more than one point of contact between the two doctors. In the matter of church life and worship, Erasmus protested against the transformation of Christianity into a series of external ceremonies. Perfection does not consist in a special way of dressing or eating. The *Praise of Folly* stresses the futility of pilgrimages: one may enter into communion with God at home; the *Enchiridion* deals with the folly of precepts concerning fasting. The repudiation of scholastic subtleties is also traceable to the influence of Erasmus. The editor of the Fathers, while promoting the study of them, did not scruple at times to call attention to their contradictions: his disciple owed to him the great liberty of his attitude when confronted by the doctors of the past and present. The life of the believer, the *Enchiridion* also teaches, consists in struggle. The Christian, enlightened by his Saviour, learns to know himself. He tries to imitate Jesus. The best relics of the saints are the examples they have left us.

The ardent moral inspiration which exalts the writings of Zwingli was fed by his reading of Erasmus. The pupil also owes to his master his reliance on family and social virtues. For Erasmus the fulfilment of simple daily duty towards wife and children is quite as worth while as the works of monks and their vows. Marriage deserves the fullest respect. Finally, the severe comments of the *Enchiridion* on war helped the military chaplain of Marignano to appreciate the scandal of conflicts provoked by pontiffs who were eager to enlarge their states. In his copy of the *Adages*, Zwingli heavily underlines the famous *"dulce bellum inexpertis"* (war is sweet to those who have no experience of it).

If re-read in the light of this catalogue, the work of Zwingli loses some of its originality. But the man who has been able to assimilate the thought of others without losing his independence of mind is not thereby diminished in stature. Who does not live on mental and spiritual borrowings from one source or another? Originality consists sometimes in a new disposition of ideas, sometimes in the presentation of them in a new light; it is very rarely a creation *ex nihilo*.

Ulrich adds to this Erasmian heritage a keen sense of sin which was the result of his inner spiritual wrestlings. The reading of Luther confirmed him in the cruel lucidity of his insight as a penitent. The mercy of Christ alone is able to efface the stain of our sins. Our merits weigh nothing in the balance with our failures. We are saved *fide sola*, by sheer faith.

In his meticulous study of 1949, *Die Anfänge der Theologie Huldreichs Zwinglis*, Professor Arthur Rich has shown that from 1520 onwards there was added to the Erasmian element in the reformer's thought the conviction of being an instrument in the hands of God. God, he felt, determined and controlled the play of human affairs. He also moulded the heart of the Christian. This certitude, won in the everyday struggle to guide Christian souls, and strengthened by the reading of the *Acts of the Leipzig Dispute*, did not, however, annul Zwingli's gratitude towards the author of the *Enchiridion*. He never wrote anything at all resembling the *De Servo Arbitrio*. If, from 1524, he abandoned the prudence which Erasmus advised, and attempted a reformation of Church customs and worship, the reason was that he was not working in a library, but in a parish. Men are more tumultuous and more exacting than books. They insist on the embodiment of ideas.

The correspondence of the years 1521 to 1526 yields some information about the break between the two men. Their relations gradually became chilled. Ulrich ceased to write to Glareanus, who was fighting at Basle on behalf of the conservative-minded group and who in 1529 followed Erasmus to Freiburg in Breisgau. On the other hand, he became closely linked with the ex-monk Oecolampadius, with whom the prince of the new learning was at daggers drawn. In the city of the Rhine a complex political game was being played. The innovators, among whom Farel had been for a time resplendent, were encountering opposition from the bishop, Christopher von Utenheim, and from the university. Erasmus, frightened by the example of Zürich, allied himself with them in order to restrain the movement of impetuous minds. The last missive he sent to Zwingli dates from the end of August, 1523.

A painful incident provoked the indignation of his Zürich correspondent. Escaping from Germany, the hot-headed knight Ulrich von Hutten, ill and ruined, knocked in vain at the door of Erasmus, with whom he had been recently linked by the tie of their common devotion to scholarship. The writer distrusted this personage, who was discredited and, into the bargain, penniless. The unfortunate man fled to Mulhouse, there to give vent to his anger at this churlish inhospitality in a little vindictive pamphlet. When in June, 1523, he settled at Zürich, where Zwingli and Conrad Schmid of Küssnacht generously attended to his needs, Erasmus deemed it advisable to write to the city council to warn them against him. Coming shortly after the death of the paladin, about whose weaknesses Ulrich entertained no illusions, the denunciation brought to a head the growing opposition of the two friends.

In 1524 the author of the *Enchiridion* read the *De vera et falsa religione* and expressed his judgment of the work. As often happens, a report of his comment, repeated from mouth to mouth, reached the ear of the chief person concerned, who on May 28, 1525, wrote about it to Vadian: "When Erasmus of Rotterdam received my Commentary, he exclaimed according to the account of one of his intimates: 'O good Ulrich, what have you ever written that I have not already previously written?' I tell you about this that you may see to what false assertions the love of self can lead men. If only Erasmus had treated my theme with his own style! The whole world would already be of our opinion, and such hatred would not now make my life difficult. I would have preferred to remain in obscurity. But the Lord has not willed it: may His will be done! If only my book bore the name of Erasmus on its title page! My modesty would not suffer, for I don't care about my renown. I say it before God: if my books were read everywhere, I should be happy to see my name once again forgotten by all mankind. Glareanus does not fulminate against me only, but he uses every resource in his hostility to Oecolampadius."

If Glareanus was publicly running down Zwingli, the prince of the lettered seemed more anxious to defend his originality than to vituperate his former admirer. However, a few months later, the booksellers were putting out for sale an anonymous writing attacking the Zwinglian conception of the eucharist. Is it true that the author of this was Erasmus? enquired the disturbed Ulrich of Oecolampadius. The style of the lampoon is violent and the method of discussion unworthy of the great writer, who agreed, moreover, to be a member of the commission of four appointed by the Council of Basle to examine it: "Either the language of Erasmus is no longer the same or else the man conceals in his heart sentiments contrary to his words." If Zwingli judged with the same severity Erasmus' weak reply to the *De Servo Arbitrio*, he never allowed himself to indulge in a facile attack on the ageing humanist. The bitterness of the present dissension did not efface his gratitude. The text of 1527 quoted at the beginning of this chapter does credit to the objectivity of Ulrich. The latter continued to regard the thinker to whom he owed his first contact with the Gospel as the intellectual author of the reformation. In the correspondence subsequent to 1526, Erasmus is frequently mentioned by Bucer, Capito, and Oecolampadius, who refer to the malicious tricks which the great man plays on the reformers. Zwingli's only answer is silence, with one single exception. A letter of February, 1530, betrays his irritation against the writer who was plotting behind the scenes to frustrate the innovators. Hence Capito, in September 1527, praises the "marked kindness" of Ulrich, who, "although superior to Erasmus and Luther", is patiently awaiting the moment when truth by its own action will create a new bond of unity. Do we not find the kind-hearted Zwingli, in 1528, going so far as to explain to Ambrose Blarer why his former master now pursues him with his hatred? "If what people say is true", he notes, "my crime is that formerly in a letter I defended Luther against Erasmus with all my strength, and the old man is vexed because of this."

It would be pleasant to discover in Erasmus traces of a similar generosity. He had decided to support catholicism more because he was dubious about the innovators than from any genuine conviction." It is easier", he wrote in 1526, "to put up with the faults to which one is accustomed. Hence I support this church until I find one that is better." He keenly desired to emphasize the distance which separated him from the revolutionaries. Was it not being murmured everywhere that Erasmus laid the eggs and Luther and Zwingli hatched them out? He deemed it wise to tone down his criticisms of the old church. In 1531, the Zürich reformer fell on the battlefield of Cappel. Oecolampadius followed him to the tomb shortly afterwards: "It is good", wrote Erasmus, "that these two leaders have succumbed. Had Mars been propitious to them, we ourselves should have been undone." The glacial funeral oration shows that, if in Zwingli's heart the memory of Erasmus held a place, the old master nevertheless repudiated the too enterprising disciple whose crime it was that he attracted a few rays of glory to his own head, and that, by precipitating Erasmianism into the living realities of church life, he let loose the storm which shook the foundations of Christendom.

CHAPTER NINETEEN

The Anabaptist Drama

THE FANATICS WHO, after applauding the preaching of Zwingli, had begun to berate him for lukewarmness, were not satisfied with the abolition of images and the promise of reform in church worship. They considered that still more decisive steps were necessary before the purity of the true Church of Jesus Christ was attained. At the head of the group stood Grebel and Manz, whose connexions with Ulrich's friends we have already noted. "They have sprung from us", remarked Zwingli with melancholy. Most of the partisans were simple-minded people who took the Bible literally and wished to embody its teachings in everyday realities without making the necessary spiritual effort at translation and understanding. A touching but dangerous literalism inspired them, and ten years later this was to be manifested in the communism of Münster in Westphalia. In that town, which fanaticism was leading to ruin, a tragi-comic episode illustrates the prevalent confusion of mind. On the morning of Easter Day, 1534, the chief magistrate, Jan Bockhold, went round the streets of the city proclaiming: "All that is abased shall be exalted." At his command, the excited crowd pulled down the spires of churches and monasteries.

At Zürich things did not get to this pass. The removal of images, as the reader will remember, was accomplished with perfect order. The reformation took place by degrees and was carefully prepared by teaching given from the pulpit. But this very prudence appeared to Grebel to have been dictated by a devilish shrewdness rather than by the impetuous motions of the Holy Spirit. Felix Manz, who had studied Hebrew with Zwingli, gathered into his mother's house a little community who scrutinized Biblical texts. The circle was frequented by several country pastors, who demanded the abolition of tithes. The group proposed to reach a state of perfection worthy of the early church; the members communicated to each other their visions and prophecies. The spiritual temperature gradually rose, recalling that of certain contemporary sects such as the pentecostists.

Manz and Grebel were in correspondence with Carlstadt, Luther's future opponent, whose bold initiatives precipitated the return from the Wartburg. Thus here a popular, fervently mystical and anti-social religion was being opposed to that of the reformers, whose tendency it was to come to terms with princes and magistrates. Every period of change sees the emergence of such generous, unbalanced spirits, who are unaware of the complexity of reality, and aim at reconstructing the earthly city in a few weeks on the plan of the heavenly Jerusalem.

Opposition to the baptism of infants entered rather late into their programme and then doubtless under the influence of Thomas Münzer. They held that only adults, fully aware, should be baptized. Joining practice to theory, at Zollikon they demolished the baptismal fonts of the parish church. The Council, faithful to its method of examination and reflection, appointed a commission composed of the three pastors of the town and representatives of the anabaptists. The sittings, held on a series of consecutive Tuesdays, were painful. Grebel wrote a defence of his ideas to which he hoped that Zwingli would reply at length. The latter feared an interminable and useless palaver. In a letter addressed on January 19 to his friend Vadian he recounted the course of events. "Greet all the brethren", he wrote to his correspondent; "also tell them they must not make a great to-do by rejecting infant baptism." The previous day he had, for his part, spoken against the anabaptists and had expressed his convictions with regard to baptism in quite an original manner.

In fact, on January 12, the Council had invited a public discussion for the following week. This took place on January 17, and its consequence was that the next day an order was issued to the effect that all children who had not yet been baptized were to be baptized. All who dissented were to leave the territory of the city with their wives, goods and chattels. It is clear that the gentlemen of Zürich were in no mood for joking and were treating the anabaptists more harshly than, after deciding on the reformation, they had treated the adherents of the ancient faith. It is true that the repudiation of infant baptism formed only a part of the sectarian programme. The confessed desire for a perfect community, without tithes, without private property, and without priests played its part in determining the governmental decision.

Ulrich's judgment on his opponents is to be discovered in a curious pamphlet entitled *Who Are the Trouble-makers?* published in December 1524. In it, Zwingli surveys all the forms assumed by opposition to the Gospel. On the one hand, bishops and abbots deplore the abrogation of their privileges, foreshadowing those *émigrés* of another revolution of whom it was possible to say that they neither learnt anything nor forgot anything. Their speech is full of threats, observes Ulrich; they talk of wars and cry out every day: "Soon things will be different." But to this hostility of the reactionaries lusting for revenge is to be added that of the enemies within the camp. Zwingli divides them into four classes. In the first place come those who have embraced the reformation only out of hatred for the pope and not from a true love of Jesus Christ. Then come the lovers of pleasure, for whom the preaching of grace and the abrogation of the canonical rules of life become a pretext for gay worldliness and sensuality, like those women who, having heard denounced from the pulpit the wearing of voluminous and sombre coats in Lent, now go to church "done up [in tight-fitting gowns] and ornamented like peacocks". In the third category appear the shrewdly calculating who profit from the general upheaval by refusing to pay tithes and interest on loans, taking as their excuse that debts are contrary to the teaching of the Bible. The fourth category includes the idealistic anabaptists of the stock of Manz and Grebel.

Without naming them, the pamphlet depicts them with merciless irony. They are more "puffed up by their knowledge of the Gospel than aflame with the spirit of charity. . . . They ceaselessly criticize other men, discern what they lack to be good Christians, but do not look at themselves. Besides this, they are full of contradictions. Sometimes they will not have magistrates, at other times they want them while insisting that no Christian should exercise public office. It so happens that they accept the idea of a church, but assert that authority should not protect the preaching of the Gospel by the use of force. One moment they exclaim that erring priests should be put to death; a little later, that they should be allowed to preach freely. Infant baptism, to hear them talk, is the worst of sins. In addition, their talk is replete with slander, jealousy, anger, and hatred. They cease to greet those who displease them, and, if an estimable man continues to greet the opponents of the Gospel, him too they exclude from their acquaintance. They fail to understand that this contentious spirit is not spiritual but carnal. They forget that strife over words can serve no useful purpose, as St. Paul reminds us (2 Tim. 2) and everywhere they argue, in the streets and in the shops. They believe themselves to be moved by the Holy Spirit, and do not perceive that they are being controlled by a Saturnian spirit of melancholy. They have no joy. In their opinion, grace is too much preached about, and they do not rest until they have plunged their hearers into a despair like their own. Anxiety and anguish overshadow their lives. The preacher of the Gospel knows all about struggle and trial, but this suffocating gloom has a different origin. We must discern the spirits: these anxious ones are obedient to Satan who has brought them again under the yoke of works."

This witty portrait of the sectarian type remains astonishingly true. The anabaptist of the 16th century has many successors who all alike display the same officious and melancholy zeal, crazily discussing truths which they ill understand and judging the piety of others by external signs. The Gospel knows them by the name of Pharisees. With their overwhelming seriousness of mentality, they confuse the appearance of faith with its reality. In their minds the whole question of baptism is distorted by their desire to discriminate in this world between the genuinely convinced and the lukewarm. When, on any particular point, the teaching of the New Testament is not clear, Zwingli considered that we should have resort to the Old Testament, and proceed by the method of analogy. In his view, the baptism of infants was related to circumcision among the Hebrews; hence it should be maintained.

The brochure, *Who Are the Trouble-makers?*, written at a time when Zwingli was preparing to ask for the abolition of the mass, shows clear signs of nervousness. The opposition of former friends was more cruelly wounding than that of declared enemies. The anabaptists were casting ridicule on the reformer's efforts to restore order in the Church on the basis of Biblical teaching. "See," people were saying, "the theologians of the new school are not in agreement." At Zürich, however, Ulrich's prestige was secure: he had gained the lasting confidence of the councils. But, outside, what was not being suggested?

The decision of January 18 did not have the looked-for success. The anabaptists clung to their ideas. A few days later, by way of protest, they proceeded to the baptism of adults, and decided to celebrate separately the Holy Communion. The Council ordered the main culprits to be shut up in the Dominican monastery. The three pastors of the town had a talk with them, and on their advice the magistrates released the fourteen prisoners, demanding the payment of a fine and the deposit of a surety of one thousand florins.

To explain these decisions, two further facts should be noted. Zürich, a city of liberty, saw the influx of many refugees, among whom was a particularly fanatical priest from the Grisons named George Blaurock. The town dreaded being transformed into a religious dumping-ground. Furthermore, the news from Germany indicated a wave of increasing social agitation. In November, 1524, a revolt had broken out in Swabia among the peasant subjects of the Count of Lüpfen. At the beginning of 1525 the peasants' revolt was fermenting in the whole of South Germany. The excitement of men's minds was constantly increasing. At any moment the anabaptist movement might turn into a revolution.

The feverish agitation of the sectaries appears in the following narrative written on February 7, 1525 by one who had been present at a rebaptismal scene: "The room was full. There was much talking and reading. Then Hans Bruggmann, of Zumikon, got up, began to weep and to cry out that he was a great sinner. He begged all those present to be so good as to pray for him. Blaurock asked him if he wished to receive the grace of God. After he had given an affirmative reply, Manz rose in his turn and asked: 'Who then will prevent me from baptizing him?' When Blaurock had replied that there was nothing against it, he took a bucket of water and baptized him in the name of God the Father, God the Son, and God the Holy Ghost."

The spiritual climate disclosed by this description explains the futility of appeals to reason. Whereas nothing essential theologically separated Zwingli from Manz or Grebel on the central point of Christ's all-sufficiency for salvation, whereas all three were in agreement to repudiate, along with the mass, the invocation of saints, images and the devotional customs of the Middle Ages, the question of the age at which baptism should be performed became an occasion of schism. During the whole of the 19th century and the first half of the 20th, movements similar to that of anabaptism have periodically agitated protestantism. The tolerance to which the modern world is accustomed has favoured the creation of dissident churches. The latter, once the first enthusiasm has passed, usually decline with fair rapidity to the rank of conventicles divorced from the great mass of believers and with no power to influence them.

Fettered as it was to a medieval conception, the Council of Zürich considered it essential to maintain the religious unity of the people which had just broken with catholicism. During the year 1525, attempts to solve the painful conflict followed one after the other. All were bidden bring their babies to baptism. A second trial went on from March 16 to 25, concurrently with a second public debate on the 20th of the same month. A third on November 6 saw such a vast crowd congregate that it became necessary to leave the town hall and to hold the session in the Great Minster. Zwingli had an answer to every objection and manifestly carried the day. When the dispute had ended, he urged the Council to treat the recalcitrants with leniency. "Conrad Grebel has been arrested at Grüningen with George (Blaurock), that madman, and incarcerated", he writes to Vadian on October 11, 1525. "The unhappy man always wanted a drama with a sad ending. He has it now."

The leniency which in the end the Council felt inclined to show proved useless. On March 7, 1526, a second judgment was pronounced against Grebel, Manz, and Blaurock, who were once more cast into prison for disobedience to authority. In the new Tower they were put on a diet of bread and water. At the same time, the magistrates announced their decision not to tolerate a repetition of the offence. On January 5, 1527, these threats were carried out. Manz, who in the meantime had been freed, together with his companions, was flung, bound hand and foot, into the Lake of Zürich. "By water he had sinned, by water he must perish" ran the judgment. Blaurock, who was expelled as a foreigner after a public whipping, passed into Austria, where he was to be burnt as a heretic by the catholics. Balthasar Hubmeyer perished in the same way at Vienna in March, 1528. As for Conrad Grebel, he was carried off by the plague at Maienfeld, where he happened to be in 1526. This dramatic end was doubtless not the one to which, according to Zwingli's statement, he aspired. But tragedy was also to overtake his father, the old councillor Jacob Grebel, who on October 30 of the same year was condemned to capital punishment. The next chapter will give us an opportunity of returning to this painful episode.

On March 7, 1526, at the time of the first arrests, Zwingli, recounting events to Vadian, expressed his disapprobation. "I deplore the incorrigible rashness of these people, but I cannot say that I am satisfied [with this decision]. It is not my wish that the beginnings of the Christian awakening should be hallowed by such examples." The following months belied this hope. Added to the drowning of Manz, the blood of two scaffolds sullies the glory of the reformer. The third case deserves hardly more than a mention. It concerned a rather obscure citizen, Hans Bülmann, whose fault it had been to insult the spiritual head of Zürich, calling him "a rascal, a heretic, a traitor, and a murderer of souls". Besides this, in contempt of the law dealing with service as a mercenary, he had engaged himself as a captain in the pay of the Duke of Württemberg and, in order to display his animosity towards the City Council and its protégé, he had driven his horse at a gallop through the interior of the Great Minster.

There is a striking analogy between the condemnations of Zürich under the authority of Zwingli, and those which were to take place in Geneva under Calvin some twenty years later. The same causes operated to bring about the same effects. The drowning of Manz corresponds to the burning of Servetus, and the beheadings of Jacob Grebel and of Bülmann to the executions of François-Daniel Berthelier and Jacques Gruet. Once the legitimacy of the use of force in vindication of the honour of God and the Gospel is admitted, where is one to stop? The two reformers had in common a tenacious will to bring to a successful conclusion the enterprise they had undertaken. It is true that blood flowed everywhere, that the condemnations of Geneva and Zürich weighed but little in the balance, quantitatively speaking, compared with the innumerable burnings which the 16th century witnessed in Germany, Austria, or France.

To what extent did belief in predestination play a part in these sinister decisions? Does the death of an outcast count for much in the eyes of the Lord? Did not St. Augustine once fall into the same error? Again, it must be remembered that in the 16th century human life had not much value. The plague and warfare made death a familiar thing. There is also a certain contagion about cruelty which up to a point constitutes some excuse: "The 20th century", writes Daniel-Rops, "is in a good position to appreciate to what depths of horror the conviction of being the sole possessors of absolute truth and of holding the future in their hands can cause human beings to descend." Let us not forget either that, from 1526 to 1528, Zürich resembled a besieged camp. Alone in Switzerland, the town on the Limmat had decided in favour of an ecclesiastical revolution. Its neighbours surrounded it with threats. Every day its liberty was called in question.

CHAPTER TWENTY

Opposition of the Catholic Cantons: Conversations with Rome

THE ABOLITION OF the mass at Zürich aroused in the rest of Switzerland a wave of indignation. The Bishop of Constance, rendered powerless in the city itself by the firm attitude of the councils, sought revenge on a national basis. The delegates of the Swiss cantons were accustomed to meet periodically sometimes in one town, sometimes in another. At the Diet of Lucerne on March 9, 1524 Claude Hottinger, the iconoclastic bootmaker, was condemned to death. The execution had the value of a warning. The Bishops of Basle and Lausanne supported the efforts of Hugo von Hohenlandenberg. Pope Clement VII for his part required the Swiss to extirpate heresy. Certain districts— Lucerne, Uri, Zug, Schwyz, Unterwalden—declared their refusal to sit any longer at the side of Zürich. In October, 1525, Diebold von Geroldseck, who was obliged to leave the monastery of Einsiedeln, took refuge in the town where the ideas of his former collaborator had triumphed. Once the suspected heretic had been expelled, the monastery was placed under strictly catholic supervision. At Schwyz, towards the end of May of the same year, two partisans of the reformation were solemnly burnt. On August 29, the six most conservative states sent an ultimatum to their compatriots begging them to return to ancient customs or else quit the Confederation.

This pressure induced the important towns of the Swiss plateau, in which Zwingli could count on some solid support, to take counter-action. Vadian at St. Gall, Oecolampadius at Basle, Haller at Berne, could not allow Zürich to be crushed without condemning themselves. Many folk of Glarus remained attached to their former Vicar. Hence Berne, Basle, Schaffhausen, and St. Gall, in agreement with Glarus and Appenzell, openly adopted a conciliatory attitude. At first this took the form of a friendly appeal. The reformed town was implored to retrace its steps, or at the very least to tolerate the mass alongside the new form of worship. But the magistrates of Zürich did not allow themselves to be turned aside. In a letter of September 22, 1525, addressed to Vadian, Zwingli praised their firmness. They had not budged an inch. Only one member of the Council, the old Jacob Grebel—"a sorry jester, your father-in-law," exclaimed Ulrich—sounded a discordant note in the session, but he was interrupted by the murmured protests of the other councillors. As a result of this discussion, the people of Zürich sent a delegation to Berne, which on its side assured them of the support of the powerful republic. A divergence of view on the subject of religious worship, thought the Bernese, is not a sufficient motive for the expulsion of a state from the Confederation.

At a moment of crisis, in 1524, Zwingli had thought of trying to effect an alliance between isolated Zürich and the protestant towns of Germany. At the end of 1525 the same idea was taken up once more, and conversations took place, which however the conversion of Berne in 1528 made useless for the time being.

A piquant interlude deserves to be related here, an interlude which Walther Köhler analyses at great length in one of his magisterial introductions in the *Corpus Reformatorum*. The occasion was a projected letter to the pope drafted by Zwingli towards the end of 1525 on behalf of the Council of Zürich.

In 1521 Pope Leo X, who wished to recapture the towns of Parma and Piacenza, had asked for the help of the Swiss. Zürich, at the urgent entreaties of Cardinal Schinner and the papal nuncio Filonardi, sent a contingent of fifteen hundred

men out of the six thousand demanded, and specified that
they should be used solely for the defence of the papal states.
After the return of the soldiers to their home country. the
authorities of Zürich took note of the fact that the pontifical
client was slow in settling his debt. When Leo X had died,
they addressed their claims to Adrian VI, who announced
that he would pay an instalment of four thousand florins.
So wonderfully well have the archives been kept that the
receipt for this sum of money still exists among the Zürich
state papers, as well as the detailed deductions which justify
the exact amount of the papal debt and fix it at twenty-four
thousand florins. However, the money took rather a long
time to reach the banks of the Limmat, and a strongly-
worded letter was needed, dated April 27, 1523, to bring the
nuncio to produce at last the promised sum. The balance
turned out to be even more difficult to recover. On the death
of the honest Adrian, his successor Clement VII (a Medici)
proved expert in the art of making a creditor wait. Since a
new letter received no reply, Zürich despatched to the holy
city an embassy which reaped an abundant harvest of
fine words. But no money was forthcoming. Two letters
of March 20, 1524, handed to the delegates, sum up the
results of the meeting.

In the first, Bishop Pucci questions the account as presented. He contends that the men of Zürich remained in the
service of Leo X for less than four months, and that therefore
they are entitled to only one-half of the arranged amount
of pay. A recognition of debt for the amount thus reduced
accompanies the letter in which the diplomat pleads exten-
uating circumstances, underlining the *inopia*, the *egestas*
(the poverty and indigence) of His Holiness. The second
document is from the hand of Clement VII himself, who
openly broaches a question intimated at the end of Pucci's
letter. The religious development of Zürich is causing anxiety
to the sovereign pontiff, who accuses the town of yielding
"to the abominable Lutheran heresy". The desired payment
will not be made until order has been restored.

One can imagine the effect of the laying down of this

condition on the minds of people who were already inclined to rebellion. What had religion to do with this question of settling the payment of a bill? But the citizens of Zürich were shrewd folk. Their letter of August 19 shows their keen desire to recover the amount of credit due to them. They humbly presented their credentials to His Holiness, declaring their astonishment at hearing themselves accused of Lutheranism. Pucci, they alleged, must have calumniated them. They insisted that their sole desire was to have the pure Word of God preached in their state.

A long silence was the sole reply to this defence. As we know, the reformation was in the meantime making rapid progress at Zürich. While the pope immured himself in an attitude of reserve which perfectly suited his position as a debtor, the monasteries were being secularized. Reports came pouring in to Rome. Clement VII, once more stung to action, thundered forth in a brief of February 14 which he charged the nuncio himself to deliver into the hands of the citizens of Zürich. He begged them to abandon the errors in which they were entrenching themselves: "Flee, my sons, flee away from such disseminators of heresy, of impiety, and of sedition." An immediate payment by any financial intermediary whatsoever would doubtless have had more weight in restraining Zürich from plunging towards a rupture than the exhortations of a holy father whose hands remained obstinately closed.

Filonardi, who resided at Chur, felt more keenly than the pope in Rome the delicacy of his position. On March 26 he requested from Zürich a safe conduct. The city granted it at once, but the prelate put off his departure, making his excuse on April 11 the fact that he was awaiting a reply from His Holiness to a question which he had caused to be conveyed to him by express messenger. Everything suggests that it was the course of events itself that was the real cause of the delay. On April 12 the Council of Zürich took the decision to do away with the mass. On April 24 Filonardi, refusing to come in person, had delivered to the city, which had now become heretical, the exhortation of the pope. The "*fugite filii, fugite"* of the brief arrived like a hailstorm after the vintage harvest has been gathered in.

The citizens of Zürich did not easily let go their claim. In spite of the schism which had now become manifest, in October, 1525, they sent to Rome a new delegate in the person of the secretary of the Council, Joachim vom Grüt. This choice was significant. In the vitally important sessions which had preceded the introduction of the Lord's Supper, the new ambassador had opposed Zwingli, pleading in vain for the retention of transubstantiation. In the eyes of the papal Curia he symbolized the past, perhaps the future. He was to present to Clement VII several documents in which the city affirmed its will to remain Christian, but always under the sign of the Word of God. It was suggested that the pope should consider the religious question as settled and confine his attention simply to the financial problem.

There was a certain *naïveté* in this effort to separate what the trickery of the Roman administration was only too happy to unite. The Zürich historians accuse vom Grüt of having played a double game and of having betrayed at Rome the cause which it was his duty to defend. But who, in this affair, was not playing on several tables at once? On November 13 the still catholic representative of the heretic city made his pleas before Clement. The latter declared that he was kindly disposed; none the less he castigated the attitude of the citizens of Zürich who had ill-treated ecclesiastical persons, both men and women, and had abolished the Blessed Sacrament of the body and blood of Jesus Christ. His Holiness expressed astonishment that a people hitherto so pious should have so easily been misled by "a few". Vom Grüt attempted— with what feelings in the depth of his heart—to make the pope understand that the events in Zürich only reflected a general movement of ideas. The whole of Germany was madly bent on innovations. Perhaps, he suggested, one should see in these troubles a sign of the wrath of God. Clement VII promised to pay on condition that Zürich without delay returned to the bosom of the Church. Since, in the texts handed to the pontiff, the city affirmed its willingness to be instructed by the Word of God, the pope proposed a discussion within the Swiss framework, whether at Lausanne or Geneva.

In the report which he despatched after this interview, the pious Joachim could not help inserting a comment which reflected his personal reaction: "As for myself, I repeat to you what I have already told you publicly and what I told him privately, namely, with regard to the sacrament, man is easily deceived. I say it and shall not cease to repeat it. . . ."

The pope desired a precise and prompt reply to his offer. Zwingli was summoned before the Council to discuss it. The archives of Zürich possess three more documents of which Ulrich is the author: the autograph rough copy of the speech with which he intervened in the session of the Council and the copy of two drafts, one for the letter to Clement VII and the other for new instructions to be despatched to vom Grüt. All three evince the extreme agitation of the reformer. By the expedient of a discussion at Lausanne or Geneva would not the results attained at Zürich be imperilled? Zwingli imputed Clement's proposal to the intrigues of the secretary who, he surmised, had turned himself into an ambassador. This is possible though not certain. Joachim cannot have been the only one who was seeking means to reverse the reformation. The bishops, especially the Bishop of Constance, through the intermediary of the Vicar-General, Faber, pursued the heresiarch with an impotent hatred. They ardently desired to recover their full authority. Whatever be the truth of it, Ulrich desired that vom Grüt should no longer serve as ambassador. He suggested that Zürich's reply should be delivered to the pope through Captain Roüst who was resident at Rome—a course which seemed to be more secure.

The outlined letter to the supreme pontiff contains, paradoxically enough, yet another attempt at apology. In the teeth of the evidence, Zwingli denies the accusation of heresy: "We have by no means left the catholic church" was, he said, what the Council ought to affirm. We have not been led astray by any false teacher. Our only criterion is the Word of God. The pope gives the impression of deflecting the course of the debate in order to avoid loosening his purse strings. At Piacenza, the Zürich soldiers did not seek any loophole of escape. They did their duty as soldiers and shed their blood. Yet the preaching was then what it has remained. Let Clement too fulfil his commitments, otherwise the injured city will turn back against Parma and Piacenza, which are the sureties of the papal debt. As for the religious dispute, it should take place at Zürich.

The letter in its final form was sent to Rome on January 10, 1526. The Council accepted Zwingli's draft, though softening it. The threat of reprisals against the two Italian towns, in particular, was dropped. As for vom Grüt, he was enjoined not to meddle in religious matters, but to concentrate his attention on the question of payment. The problem of the sacrament has been solved locally; there is no reason to reopen the issue.

The pope received very badly the proposals of the men of Zürich and their perseverance in error. He thundered against *"quidam seductores animarum vestrarum"* (certain seducers of your souls). Normally, he reminded them, a problem of faith is debated at Rome: the offer of a Swiss city as a venue for the conference was in itself an act of great complaisance. As for the money, the city would not receive it until it had made submission.

The debt contracted by Leo X was thus never paid. After Zwingli's death, the Council attempted to make a final approach to the nuncio Filonardi. For the papacy the lamentable bargaining was settled by a spiritual rebuff. Are not souls worth more than florins? Less greed and less cunning might perhaps have retained in the meshes of the Curia a middle class incensed by papal ill will.

CHAPTER TWENTY-ONE

The Baden Disputation

ONE OF CLEMENT VII's proposals was especially borne in mind by the loyally catholic states of the Confederation. They placed the question of religious unity on the agenda of the Diet which was to be held at Baden in the spring of 1526. Faber, the Vicar-General, expected to obtain, by a vote of the delegates, a decision that would be applicable to all the cantons alike. The end of the winter on the shores of the Limmat, as on those of the Lake of Lucerne, was marked by intense diplomatic activity. Would Zürich appoint Zwingli as a delegate, as was desired by the states of the Confederation? The Council, in agreement with the reformer himself, gave a negative reply to the suggestion. Faber, when called to the disputation of 1524, had abstained: it seemed to be only right and proper to pay him back in his own coin. Moreover, would Ulrich be able to stay at Baden in security? This town, a spa, was under catholic domination. The folk of Zürich retained a painful memory of the way in which, in the same place in the year 1524, the affairs of Stammheim and Frauenfeld had been summarily dealt with. Three heads had then fallen to the executioner's sword, in spite of promises made. The bitter experience counselled prudence. Finally, Zürich did not accept the claim of central Switzerland to dictate its line of religious conduct to a state which, although an ally, was none the less independent. The competence of the Diet, it was felt, was limited to political matters.

Berne sent as an advocate of the innovators Berchtold Haller, a cathedral canon, who, bound by ties of friendship to Zwingli, had for six years been struggling in his city to achieve a transformation of doctrine and piety. Basle delegated Oecolampadius, the former monk who had become Vicar of the Church of St. Martin. Both men would have preferred to leave to Zwingli the honours of this battle. His knowledge and his gifts far exceeded theirs. But pessimistic reports reached Ulrich from time to time, with the result that he persisted in a refusal which was approved by the magistrates at Zürich. The abstention was none the less a painful burden for him to bear. He wrote several brochures in explanation of his absence, crossing swords with his adversaries by the use of the pen. Would he not be everywhere looked upon as a coward? However, his very concern for the Gospel forbade him to take imprudent risks. Like a general fettered to his post of command, he felt obliged to pass over his pride and scruples.

The disputation was heralded by the sound of the trumpet not only in Switzerland, but also in Germany. The Duke of Bavaria lent his most brilliant orator, John Eck, who at Leipzig had been the implacable opponent of Luther. He was seconded by a Franciscan from Lucerne, an occasional poet, and a writer with a caustic touch, one Thomas Murner, who was regarded as the decided enemy of the heresiarch: "Zwingli," he had apostrophized one day in the pulpit, "I wish to inform you that you are the seducer of the poor people of Christ." In advance, the mental climate promised to be most unpropitious to a friendly discussion. At Lucerne Zwingli's portrait, and at Fribourg his books, were burnt before the eyes of fanatical, spellbound crowds.

The debates, which opened on Monday, May 21, lasted for four weeks. The situation of Oecolampadius and of Haller was a delicate one. With Louis Oechsli, of Schaffhausen, who supported them, they cut the figure of accused persons rather than of free guests. A daily mass underlined the primacy of the ancient church, while preaching was forbidden to partisans of the reformation. A crowd of high-ranking dignitaries flocked to the spot from all parts. The

Bishop of Constance was represented by his coadjutor, Melchior Fattlin; Lausanne had delegated the provincial of the Augustinians; Basle and Chur had sent canons and doctors in theology; the Abbot of St. Gall had deputed a resolute adversary of Zwingli—namely, Wendelin Oswald. The Abbot of Engelberg, who was personally present for the whole session, presided over some of the debates. A total of eighty-seven ecclesiastics of strictly catholic persuasion stood opposed to thirty-one partisans of Zwingli. During the discussions the representative of catholicism occupied a tall chair, splendidly ornamented, while his adversary found assigned to himself a "wretched and low one".

Shrewdly enough, the first theses of Eck concerned the theory of the sacrament which, from a Biblical standpoint, was the most easily assailable part of Zwinglianism. There followed the redemptive value of the mass, the veneration of images, the invocation of saints, purgatory, original sin, and the power of baptism to efface the effects of the latter. Papal authority and indulgences were deliberately not mentioned.

Ulrich eagerly followed the course of the sittings at which he had refused to be present. The Diet had four secretaries, whose notes were collated each evening under an interdiction against the slightest publication. A young man, Jerome Wälschen, from the canton of Valais, pretending to follow at Baden a cure for his health, used to be present at the discussions, then rush to the baths and hastily draw up a summary of the interchange of arguments, entrusting it in turn to two kindhearted couriers. One of them was another man of Valais, Thomas Platter, whose accounts are still extant, and the other Jerome Zimmermann from Winterthur. At night, one or other of them would travel on foot to Zürich, thirteen miles away, and hand over to Zwingli Wälschen's manuscript. The reformer would then quickly scrawl his impressions and advice for the use of Oecolampadius and Haller. During the whole four weeks of the Diet he hardly slept. The messengers in order to avoid denunciation disguised themselves as poultry merchants, and every evening and morning did their four hours' walk with a basket under their arm.

On the eve of Whit-Sunday, Oecolampadius, in regard to a delicate matter of procedure, once more had recourse to the kind offices of Platter who about midnight rang the doorbell of the Zürich presbytery. All were asleep. At last the porter came to open the door and was followed by an old priest: "What do you want at this time of night? Can't you allow Master Ulrich to sleep for one night? For six weeks now he hasn't been to bed!" "You are incapable of staying still a minute," rang out a moment later the cordial voice of Ulrich, who now appeared in the corridor. "For six weeks I haven't been able to go to bed. As it is the eve of Pentecost,[1] I thought that at last I might get a night's rest. What is it all about?" The point in dispute concerned a matter of procedure, was the reply. "The deuce! only that! Another trick of Eck! Do you know a lad who will go back to Baden for me?" "Yes," replied Platter. "And what about you?" cried Zwingli. "Will you have something to eat? I will awaken the servant so that she may prepare you some soup." "I would rather sleep," declared the author of this vivid account, who wished his interlocutor good night and, before going to bed, sent him another messenger. Ulrich drew up his instructions in all haste. The messenger reached the environs of Baden the following morning at dawn. While he was still some way from the town he caught up with a cart loaded with hay, hoisted himself to the top and stretched himself out on the downy couch. When he woke up, the day had fully dawned on the market square. Realizing in a flash that he had slept and was late, he slid down, frightened, to the bottom of his improvised bed and ran to take the letter to Oecolampadius. It was in such ways that the ardent supporters of a noble cause, great or small, struggled to exert themselves during the sittings of the Diet.

[1] The memorandum of the good Platter has become somewhat distorted with the passage of time. The Diet of Baden did not last for so long. But, as it stands, the anecdote brings before us a vivid picture of the tension in which Zwingli lived.

At their final meeting the delegates of the cantons voted. Eighty-two voices approved Eck and Murner, while only ten deputies declared themselves in favour of Oecolampadius and Haller. The cause of the reformation in Switzerland and at Zürich in particular appeared to be lost. Murner publicly denounced the coward who was hiding in his den. A new decision was taken forbidding the sale of Zwingli's books within the confines of the Confederation, and, furthermore, requiring everywhere the restoration or maintenance of the mass and of the rules relative to fasting. The bishops were confirmed in their right to examine the faith of every priest and to stop the publication of suspect books.

Oecolampadius went back to Basle, anxious in mind and afraid of finding his pulpit of St. Martin withdrawn from him by order of the City Council. But the insolent triumph of the victors provoked almost at once a reaction in favour of the vanquished. Several of those who had, out of deference, voted for Eck, found him too self-assured, and esteemed the more modest comportment of Oecolampadius. Discontent was also aroused by the strange precautions with which the catholics surrounded the publication of the proceedings at these meetings. Concealed from the delegates, the secretaries' notes were despatched to Lucerne, where Murner himself published a text which he had plenty of time to expurgate.[1] In short, each canton clung fiercely to its independence. The Confederation was an alliance concluded between states which were on a footing of complete equality. When on July 29 seven of them presumed to exclude Zürich, which refused to submit to the decisions of Baden, then Berne, Basle, Schaffhausen, Appenzell, and Glarus (where the last meeting of the citizens—the so-called *Landsgemeinde* —had by a majority of twenty votes defeated a council hostile to Zwingli) strongly protested. Was not Faber demanding that all the priests of the Confederation should present themselves at Constance, i.e. outside Helvetic territory, to prove the soundness of their faith? The powerful

[1] Professor von Muralt regards the published proceedings as correct, contrary to the reformers' fears.

republic of Berne, in particular, was not pleased to receive orders from without. On the banks of the Aar, the situation was evolving in favour of Haller and his friends: "The bear", he wrote to Vadian on December 24, "is going forward slowly, but is beginning to manifest its strength."

CHAPTER TWENTY-TWO

Local Opposition Crushed

THROUGH THE REPORT of Thomas Platter we know
something of the state of fatigue in which Zwingli
found himself at the spring of 1526. The correspondence with Vadian, slightly earlier, also shows his enervation.
In a letter of April 26 the reformer confesses his anxiety
to his friend, who, a humanist, and Burgomaster of St. Gall
since the beginning of the year, was in the first instance an
experienced doctor. In the morning, the reformer had
preached, and further, at eight o'clock, had explained some
passages of the Book of Exodus. "When, at nine o'clock,
after my bath, I had had myself cupped, I almost lost consciousness on the way back. After an hour, I recovered a
little, but had difficulty in arresting the breathlessness,
which, as my face showed, was the result of a cardiac weakness. At two o'clock in the afternoon, fatigue gripped me
and I fell asleep, a thing which normally never happens to
me during the daytime. As soon as I woke up, I felt my old
self again. I tell you this, as to my doctor. I have taken
your medicine, according to your prescription. You advised
me, at least once a month, to check the heat of the liver
by taking a rose syrup.[1] On the occasion of a violent fever,
of which there were three onsets in three hours, I had been
very fortunate to have your advice. So I asked my wife to
prepare your medicine at once."

This confidence on the part of a sick man has its value.
Accumulated fatigue overcomes the strength of the most

---

[1] *Saccaro rosato*, probably sweetened spirits in which rose leaves have
been steeped, similar to the ratafia called *rosolio*, still known to pharmacists today, or like the rose honey which is used as a sedative.

resistant. From 1524 to 1527 events followed each other at a harassing speed. Reform of the mode of church worship, organization of the church, disputes with the anabaptists, difficulties on a nation-wide scale, faced him in rapid succession without allowing any desirable interval for repose. In fact, the historian himself has difficulty in undoing the tangled skein of events. He is obliged to deal in separate chapters with events which developed concurrently. Blows rained thick and fast on the tired soul and body of Ulrich. He discussed and decided the most important issues in a frightful hurly-burly. In addition, regular preaching, and study of the Bible with students, were carried on alongside his care for the city and for an increasing family.

To endure such torment, a man of extraordinary constitution was needed. For the scholar, reconstructing the course of events afterwards in the peace of a library, far from the madding crowd, criticism of an attitude, regret for a decision, are easy. But such a one should ask himself whether he would have done better had he been flung into the storm.

From 1523 to 1526 a certain development takes place in the mind of Ulrich. The Renaissance scholar, after the style of Erasmus, enamoured of a lofty idealism, is gradually transformed into an Old Testament prophet. While his former master retains the façade of the man of letters, aloof from the futile quarrels of violent men (though none the less plotting behind the scenes), Ulrich, like another Elijah, descends unmasked into the arena.

At Zürich, a group of disaffected persons had for a long time been seeking some means of getting rid of the reformer. As early as 1520, Zwingli had attacked with all his energy the system of military treaties with foreign powers. Mercenary service horrified him. Blood spilt for the advantage of a foreign prince, he thought, cried out to heaven like the blood of Abel. In 1521, to the great annoyance of those in receipt of pensions for military service, he induced the city to refuse the alluring offers of Francis I. In 1525, the opposition of those who were disaffected on this score was greatly increased by that of the partisans of the ancient faith. The two groups, moreover, to some extent mingled.

A religious revolution is nearly always accompanied by political repercussions. The defence of a form of religious worship is easily allied to sordid questions of vested interests. Without yielding to a materialistic interpretation of history, it must be admitted that the clash between the reformation and catholicism is not of a purely spiritual character.

These engagements of the tough Swiss in foreign military service began with the second half of the 15th century. In the eyes of this impoverished mountain people, the pay of princes stood for both wealth and adventure. The Councils, who were used as intermediaries and whose consent was necessary, received bribes from many sources. At Zürich, in 1497, out of a sum of three thousand one hundred and four crowns paid by the recruiting agents, two thousand went to the city treasury and the rest into the private pockets of the magistrates.

The people muttered protests against this source of revenue. In 1508, long before Zwingli's time, the corporations showed their hostility to the system of pensions of this sort. Nevertheless, the government still liked to see itself as the necessary intermediary of the princes, and forbade individual engagements. It claimed to be actuated more by the fear of mass departures of soldiers such as would leave the country short of troops than by the desire to be the agent in negotiating profitable treaties. In 1519 heavy fines were imposed on recruiting captains. In 1521, the latter accused Ulrich, who made common cause with the humbler folk, of leading them to ruin. This did not prevent some of them—Henry Rahn in particular—from rallying in time to his religious message. In 1522 and 1524 draconian laws forbidding recruitment and departures from the country were introduced. The property of officers in foreign service was confiscated when they were thrown into prison. Instigators risked losing their heads, private soldiers were fined. Penalties increased with a second offence. In 1522 and 1523 the death sentence was twice imposed. The threats which, from 1525, began to overshadow the city nourished among the partisans of mercenary service the hope of a reversion. After Zwingli had been silenced, they conceived that profitable negotiations might well be resumed.

The laws did not prevent, in the years 1525 and 1526, numerous clandestine engagements in the service of Württemberg and Italy. The City Council was busy pursuing the guilty, when, in the middle of September 1526, Zwingli sharply criticized from the pulpit those in receipt of military pensions. He suggested that they were stirring up the other members of the Confederation against the city; at least in part they bore the responsibility for a difficult situation, he claimed. Further, the Council was lacking in firmness.

The authorities swiftly reacted. A commission, appointed without delay, began investigations. Zwingli, when summoned, produced what information he had. Certain indications, flowing from the confidences of third parties, went back ten years. Among the magistrates of the little town, several were receiving or had received pensions in contravention of the laws. Such were Henry Rahn, Hans Escher, and Jacob Grebel. The names of the first two, who were men of war, surprised nobody. The third name astonished everyone. Father of the unfortunate anabaptist who had died of the plague the previous year, an admirer and supporter of Zwingli at the beginning of his reforming activity, Councillor Grebel was a white-haired old man surrounded with every mark of respect. While Rahn and Escher, after a long trial, succeeded in the autumn of 1527 in gaining confirmation of all their rights, Grebel was executed on October 30, 1526. The charge against him was that he had accepted a French pension, which the Councillor cleverly had conveyed to his son, who was at the time a student in Vienna. It was alleged in addition that proofs of high treason had been discovered. On this particular point, present-day historians are divided: it is impossible to obtain conclusive evidence. Several reports of the commission are no longer extant.

Was the insistence of Zwingli decisive in the matter? Certain erudite scholars, Paul Schweizer and Georg Gerig, suppose so. Walther Köhler also attributes to the reformer some responsibility for hastening the course of the trial. Yet Jacob Grebel was not quite the old man of integrity pictured by his compatriots. There is no doubt that he had been in receipt of money. His financial situation, which was not brilliant, in spite of appearances, prompted him to adopt this course. He showed himself very harsh towards the widow of his son, to whom he refused to allot a share of the inheritance.

The fierceness of Ulrich is to be explained by his sense of isolation. In 1526 he tended to see plots and traitors everywhere. Wars have always hardened the human spirit. The ever-multiplying threats against Zürich created on the shores of the Limmat an atmosphere of anxiety favourable to summary judgments. Outside the city, the reformer's friends were troubled in mind: Oecolampadius and Capito questioned Zwingli, who, in a long letter, explained his position. The pressure exerted on the protestant city, after the Diet of Baden, to restore the mass was supported by demands from within. The minority which was hostile to the reform were demanding help. "Our decisions," a catholic delegate is reported to have confessed, "would have been taken less lightly if citizens of Zürich had not pressed us." Hence the institution of a commission of eleven members, furnished with dictatorial powers, was fully justified. "Several have fled, the gates of the city not being closed", notes Ulrich, ". . . one of them in an empty manure cart. It is in a manure heap that those who betray their country for their belly and their dung find their salvation! . . ." Such a quotation illustrates better than long commentaries the exacerbation of minds at this time. Zwingli goes to the length of advocating torture in cases where there are serious presumptions and no proof.

CHAPTER TWENTY-THREE

Scholar and Family Man

T HE EVENTS WHICH, after the year 1522, followed
each other without intermission only rarely disturbed
the rhythm of a life which was dominated by scholarship. In 1523, Zwingli exchanged his charge as priest of the
Great Minster for a canonry, and thus found himself freed
from the many occupations which ceaselessly interrupt the
course of a day spent in the pastoral office. He then left
the presbytery of the Kirchgasse (Church Street), which
was quite close to the Cathedral precincts, for a bigger
house somewhat higher in the same street. In 1525 came
another change of post and another moving of house. Henceforth he was to concern himself with the college for the training of future ministers. Another house was now assigned
to him, in which he was to live until his death.

In the short biography which he wrote in 1532 in memory
of his friend and with grief in his heart, Oswald Myconius
describes a typical day in the life of Zwingli: "Rising early,
he devoted himself until ten o'clock to reading, commenting
on Scripture, study, correspondence, varying these occupations according to time and circumstances. After dinner, he
received information, gave audience to petitioners, chatted
or went for a walk with friends until two o'clock, then set
himself to work again. After the evening meal, he went for
a short walk, then wrote letters, sometimes until midnight.
Besides all this, to the extent which affairs required, he
rendered service to the City Council." Study, notes Myconius
further, was put first, and abandoned only if absolutely
necessary. The annotations in his books furnish the proof

of this assertion: the work begun at Glarus was steadily continued, in spite of the shocks which marked dramatic years.

From March, 1524, Zwingli had set to work on a translation of the Old Testament, comparing the Hebrew text with the Latin and Greek versions. He was able to use the information supplied by Jacob Wiesendanger, known as Ceporinus, who, himself a pupil of the illustrious Reuchlin, had in 1522 left Basle for Zürich. Thanks to his instruction and that of another Hebrew scholar, Andreas Böschenstein, who, before settling on the shores of the Limmat, had been the teacher of Melanchthon, Zwingli came to acquire a fair mastery of the tongue of David. A German Bible, which came from the press of Froschauer in 1524 and 1525, was the fruit of all this labour. But it was especially the theological college, opened on June 19, 1525, which profited from it.

In order to fulfil a plan which he had at heart, Zwingli had to wait until the opposition of his two colleagues, the canons Niessli and Hoffmann, ceased. This pair, who had remained keen supporters of the ancient faith, did their utmost to restrain the new movement. The first died on April 3, 1525, while the second, who had retired to Bremgarten on catholic territory, passed away a few weeks later. The income attached to their posts was at once used to create professorships. First, to Ceporinus was assigned the teaching of Hebrew. The lectures began on June 19 at eight o'clock in the morning in the presence of all the pastors, preachers, canons, and chaplains of the city and neighbourhood. Zwingli opened the session with a prayer; then, each member of the assembly having a Bible open before him, Gaspard Grossmann, called Megander, read the Latin text of the passage chosen for commentary. Ceporinus then read and translated the corresponding Hebrew verses. Ulrich, who followed him, used the Greek Septuagint version, explaining the meaning of the more difficult passages. Finally, Leo Jud came forward to repeat the principal commentaries which had been made in Latin by Megander, Ceporinus, and Zwingli.

By this common study, pastors who at first were often ignorant were transformed into enlightened clergy, capable in their turn of forming the minds of their congregations. The sittings took place every morning with the exception of Friday, which was market day, and of Sunday. Thanks to the notes of Pellican, who in May, 1526, took over the post of the deceased Ceporinus, we know the ground covered in these lectures. At the date mentioned, Genesis and the first fourteen chapters of the Book of Exodus had been gone through. The study of the Pentateuch was completed by the end of the year. 1527 saw the exegesis successively of Joshua, Judges, Ruth, Samuel, and Kings. Isaiah took up the period from September, 1527, to February, 1528; then came Ezekiel and the twelve minor prophets; in 1529 Psalms, Proverbs, Ecclesiastes, Job, in 1530 Ezra, Nehemiah, Esther, and, finally, in 1531 the Books of Chronicles, interrupted at the twentieth chapter by the defeat of Cappel, which decimated the professorial body.

The Old Testament rules these studies. The New Testament does not appear in Pellican's lists. This fact is doubtless to be explained by the course of sermons which Zwingli preached from 1519 to 1524 and which he devoted to the Gospels, the Acts of the Apostles and the Epistles. But the exclusive preaching of the Law and the Prophets for six years is regrettable.[1] Seen in the light of the pressure of a difficult political situation, it probably explains the increasing

[1] In November, 1957, Oscar Farner published the translation of a ms. attributed to Zwingli and containing a homiletic study of Matthew, Mark and John. The text, which appears to go back to a hearer of the reformer, cannot be that of the sermons preached from 1519 to 1524. Farner wonders whether it might not be a question of sermons preached in the Church of the Fraumünster on Fridays, market days, in the years 1527 and 1528. The volume, which has been used, belonged to a descendant of Ulrich, namely the pastor Salomon Reuter (1611-61). A similar text—some parts being identical, others different—was published in the old edition of the works of Zwingli (that of Schuler and Schultess) under the title: *Additamenta ad Zwingli commentarium in evangelium Matthaei a Leone Judae editum*. But, according to this title, it would be a question of commentaries rather than sermons. Is it not possible that the two books—the Reuter manuscript and that used by Schuler and Schulthess—contain traces of the lectures given by Zwingli to the pastors whom he was training? The text translated by Farner has the air of a free explanation. It furnishes precious additions to our knowledge of Zwingli as an interpreter of Scripture.

slide towards a theocracy in which the sword supports the spirit.

In the house where the folio volumes are ranged on the shelves and which now sees a stream of visitors, the atmosphere had ceased to be that of the catholic presbytery where the priest and his assistants lead the studious life of adults. Children's cries were at times to be heard, and the patter of little feet sounded on staircases and in corridors. Zwingli's marriage, which was celebrated in 1522 and kept secret for two years, produced offspring. Four children were born, one after the other, whose names, along with those of the godfathers and godmothers, Ulrich carefully inscribed in a big Bible printed in Venice. The first, a daughter, Regula, came into the world at three in the morning of July 24, 1524. It was on account of her that it became necessary to make the marriage of her parents public. Wilhelm succeeded her on January 29, 1526, at eleven o'clock in the evening. Then came a little Ulrich, "the son of my Ulrich" notes the father, doubtless at his wife's request, the birth taking place on January 6, 1528, "between two and three o'clock in the daytime". Finally, Anna, who was baptized with the Christian name of her mother, was born on May 4, 1530, at ten o'clock in the evening. Opposite this latter name, the same hand has later added "she is deceased".

What emotions surround these four dates and these four lives! But, whereas Luther used to speak on any and every occasion of his dear Katie, Zwingli preserved a disconcerting discretion. The name of his wife hardly appears at all in his correspondence. The reformer's friends addressed their greetings to her, but he himself remained silent. Living continually with her, he had no occasion to write to her. His journey to Berne in 1528 was responsible for a single letter, dated January 11, which contained a brief message of congratulation on the occasion of the birth of little Ulrich: "Grace and peace from God our Father. Dear wife, I thank God that He has granted you a happy delivery. May He give us grace to bring up this child according to His will." There follows a request to send various things, and some advice. "Pray

God for me and for us all. . . . Give my greetings to all your children; in particular to Margaret; console her in my name. Ulrich Zwingli, your husband." The letter is addressed "to the pious Anna Reinhart at Zürich, from her dear husband".

Ulrich was at this time advocating the cause of the reformation to the Bernese. The circumstances were not propitious for long effusions. In its very brevity, this precious document expresses a father's joy. The Margaret about whom he enquires was a daughter of Anna's first marriage, and she had the previous year married Anton Wirz. The poor girl had just lost her firstborn in the cradle; hence her grief was intensified when her own mother, aged about forty-four, brought into the world a very healthy baby.

Anna Reinhart, of whom no portrait is extant, had a dramatic destiny. The daughter of an innkeeper, charming and well built, she married at about the age of twenty-one Hans Meyer von Knonau, a young patrician with a bit of the devil in him. The marriage of this only son, which took place without the father's consent, aroused in the latter a violent and lasting anger. A cousin of the Bishop of Constance, and quite infatuated with his noble rank, Gerold Meyer von Knonau obstinately refused to countenance the decision of his heir. He deprived the young couple of the wherewithal to live, which compelled Hans to engage himself in military service in Italy, where he died on the battlefield in 1517. Remaining alone at home, Anna had great difficulty in bringing up two daughters and a son, whose first name was Gerold, after his grandfather. One day, relates the old family chronicle, the little boy was playing in the street, while the servant-girl was settling the purchase of some fish. The eye of the gloomy old man, who was amusing himself by watching from an upper storey of his house the goings and comings of the passers-by, happened to fall on the tiny tot. On making enquiries, the Lord Gerold discovered that the unknown little child bore his own name. He felt the call of blood. He became interested in Anna's son, took him into his own household to bring him up according to his rank, but refused to receive the mother, who remained confined to the Reinhart family inn, which was called the *Rössli* (little horse).

The old man died in 1518, followed to the grave two years later by his wife. The daughter-in-law took back little Gerold, who had now become the heir of a fortune in which a sizeable hole had been made by the grandparents' liking for display. She found herself in dispute with a tutor of integrity, who was equally incapable of countenancing the unsuitable marriage, and who therefore refused to provide the mercenary's widow with an income. In spite of the fact that her father was an innkeeper, the young wife belonged to a perfectly honourable family which had been accepted into the Zürich middle class in 1432.

Repulsed by those who ought to have supported her, Anna confided her troubles to the priest of her parish, without suspecting that one day she would become his wife. After suffering so much scorn, she certainly found a wonderful consolation in the unwavering affection of Ulrich. Shrouded as it is in silence, their love escapes the biographer's clutches.

Besides the already quoted letter from Ulrich to his wife, one or two allusions have been picked out here and there which shed light on Zwingli as a husband and a father. Thus addressing Faber, the Vicar-General, who reproached him both on account of his marriage and his musical instruments: "The latter are at least useful to me now," he exclaims, "for they enable me to silence the lads." In a message to Vadian of May 28, 1525, his friend admitted that he had concealed from Anna what he knew concerning the secret intrigues of the anabaptists. In 1529, he hid from her the goal of his journey, which was Marburg, and, while on the way there, let her know of his arrival at Strasburg. Was this conduct dictated by the fear of causing anxiety or that of arousing gossip? In the treatise which he dedicated in 1523 to his stepson, the young Gerold, he advised reserve: "For just as silence is the finest ornament of a woman her whole life long, so nothing can recommend a young man more than silence for a certain time." Was this a current adage or does this praise of reserve betray the personal conviction of Zwingli? At the *Rössli*, tongues wagged, and it was generally considered that Ulrich got information from his mother-in-law, who knew all the tittle-tattle of the town. Is it possible that Anna Reinhart was a scandalmonger?

In the short work on the "office of the preacher", the reformer defended himself against those who accused him of having made financial profit out of the religious upheaval of Zürich. He gives the figure of his salary, which was just enough on which to maintain a family, and he refutes the accusation that he had married a rich woman. Anna possessed almost nothing. As for her dress, since her marriage she had ceased to wear silken gowns or jewellery. She dressed like the simplest of women.

If the above is a slender crop of details, the little book which in 1523 Ulrich wrote in Latin and which in 1526 he translated into German expounded his educational principles for the use of Gerold Meyer von Knonau. The elder son of Anna had, like his father, an undisciplined temperament: Hans Meyer, before his marriage, made himself notorious by his escapades, carrying his audacity so far as to force open the door of the Fraumünster, make the nuns there dance and ransack the furnishings of the church. Gerold, the delightful child of 1512, who was a victim of heredity, also had some unpleasant dealings with justice. Zwingli paid assiduous attention to him, and when the boy was seventeen obtained for him the hand of a sedate girl from Basle, Küngolt Dietschi, the daughter of a Councillor, in whose company the petulant young man calmed down. The treatise *How to bring up Young Men of Noble Rank* bears the hallmark of Christian humanism. The first pages recall the unique value of faith. Christian faith, which is inspired by God, none the less is communicated by the lips of men, according to St. Paul's words: faith springs from hearing. The tutor must speak of God with those words that are purest and most worthy of Him, pointing out to the child, in the realm of nature, the traces of a divine agency at work to create harmony. Seeing that all is ordered by God, the child will become accustomed to think of Him as the Master of his life, praying to Him, and asking Him for wisdom and enlightenment, even for wife and children.

Taking Genesis as his basis, Zwingli comments on the drama of the fall and original sin, underlining the necessity of having a pure heart. Jesus alone, who was sinless, and was delivered up for us, can wash away our faults. Faith banishes fear and anguish. Freed by the One who, on his behalf, surrendered Himself to damnation, the Christian does not become lulled into a lazy confidence. Faith urges him to do good. The sacrifices which God desires are the virtues: just dealing, loyalty, and mercy. The growing youth will look to the formation of his inner spiritual life and will learn such languages as Hebrew and Greek, which give us access to Holy Scripture, though at the same time he will not neglect Latin. "Back to the sources!"—such is the central principle governing the instruction. Mathematics and music also have great usefulness.

The young man will discover in Christ the pattern of all the virtues. Zwingli exhorts him to modesty. Let him also avoid flattery, let him practise truthfulness, distrust the excesses of wine, for too much wine makes drunk the "young body which in itself is inclined to violence". His meals will be simple and plain. Eating too much fatigues the stomach and shortens life. Galenus reached the age of one hundred and twenty years simply because he always left the table when still hungry. It is madness to call attention to oneself by the luxury of one's dress. In this regard the pope's mules will always win the day: "Strong as they are, they can carry more gold, silver, and precious stones than any giant." Let us not forget that "the Son of God and of the Virgin Mary wept in a manger, wrapped only in swaddling-clothes".

When love arises in the heart of the youth, let him "remain chivalrous and self-controlled. Let him not yield to the dizzy raptures of love. He will choose a girl friend, whom he will be firmly convinced he will always cleave to and be fond of, in the state of matrimony." Let him remain faithful to her until the marriage takes place, seeing only her in the crowd of women and girls.

After warning his young reader against avarice, Ulrich discusses fencing, which he is not altogether against; but a Christian ought to train himself in the bearing of arms only to the extent required by the general situation and security of the State. The only reason for being skilled in swordsmanship is to defend one's country. Games such as chess are good on condition that they are not abused, and the same applies to sport in general, running, jumping, stone-throwing, and wrestling. However, Zwingli rejects card-playing and dice. Family gatherings, as at marriages and birthdays, have their value. Did not Christ participate in the wedding feast at Cana of Galilee? On the other hand, it is dangerous to take part in popular festivals. It is much better to remain aloof from them, alleging as one's excuse a predilection for study.

The supreme end of life is to offer it to God, which in fact means that our thoughts must not revolve around ourselves, that we must concern ourselves about the common good in a life of self-giving. "In a difficult situation, we must give assistance to authority. To be there the first and the last is an honour."

This summary conveys the spirit in which the husband of Anna Reinhart conceived the education of his children. It is inspired by the Renaissance ideal, but also contains not a little ancient Helvetic wisdom. If Zwingli used it to set right the warped mind of his stepson, he died too soon to be able to educate his own children. This task fell to his disciple and successor, Bullinger, who adopted them after the disaster of Cappel.

Part Six

The Development of the Reformation

CHAPTER TWENTY-FOUR

The Matrimonial Tribunal: Formation of the New Clergy

UP TO THE break of 1525, the supervision of marriages, as far as Zürich was concerned, devolved upon the episcopate of Constance. In conformity with canon law, the episcopal tribunal took cognisance of cases of annulment. The expenses incurred were high. The court allowed these affairs to drag on in order to get as much money as possible out of the applicants.

Cases of separation seem to have been numerous. Unreconciled couples were allowed to go their own way, each partner living a more or less dissolute life. Bastards increased. Zwingli very quickly concerned himself, in this sphere of life also, to establish things on a better footing. In the first place, he wished to prevent the presence of adulterers and fornicators at the Lord's Supper from defiling the solemn rite. The parish, he considered, ought to have the right to exclude the unworthy. A message of April, 1525, envisages this problem. The power of excommunication does not belong to a remote spiritual head, but to the local church. The latter must keep away from the Lord's table all murderers, robbers, drunkards, and those whose sexual laxity is a cause of scandal.

As regards the civic life of the town, the law will maintain purity of manners. A special commission *ad hoc* began to prepare in February, 1525, the plan of an ordinance, and this was published on May 10, of the same year. Six judges —two members of each Council and two pastors—were to meet regularly every Monday and Thursday. Bickering husbands and wives would submit to them their problems, but the six advisers were also to concern themselves with marriages which were about to take place. The age of majority was fixed at nineteen years. Before that term, no guardian could put pressure on his wards to choose one partner rather than another. In cases of impediment, the statutes of Lev. 18 were followed. Orphans without a guardian were allowed to decide for themselves, on condition that the boy had reached the age of sixteen and the girl that of fourteen. It was ruled that a seducer should marry his victim. Proposed marriages had to be announced from the pulpit. Each pastor was henceforth to keep a register in which they were to be inscribed. In cases of adultery, divorce, in accordance with the ruling of Christ (Matt. 19) was authorized. The innocent party would easily obtain permission to contract a new union, while the guilty party was obliged to wait for a long period. Matrimony, divested of its sacramental character (see p. 119), became once more a contract supervised by the State. It was felt that there was no sense in maintaining unions which in the reality of hearts and bodies had already been dissolved. Zwingli wished to avoid the possibility of remarriage being interpreted as an invitation to adultery. The problem which already emerged in 1525 has remained that of the reformed protestant churches and the civil codes which they have inspired.

The new law of Zürich admitted separation in cases of impotency. A sterile marriage could be dissolved. Finally, the judges were invested with authority to declare judgment in grave situations, such as threats of killing or instigation to prostitution.

Walther Köhler has devoted a lengthy study to an examination of the principles underlying the jurisprudence of this tribunal, of which Zwingli, moreover, was not a member. In 1525 an adulterous woman had to wait five years before being permitted to marry again. In a letter to Haller, dated December 4, 1523, Ulrich stated that he had found this term of waiting prescribed in an old manual concerning penance. The judges had doubtless consulted him. On the other hand, in 1531 the term of waiting is reduced in one case to a year, and in another to three months. This last decision called forth a protest from the pastor of Dietikon, the village inhabited by the offender. Often the judges tried to effect a reconciliation between the parties. Calvin's tribunals at Geneva showed far greater severity. In cases of impotency, a trial period was imposed. If the infirmity was not cured, the wife was granted her liberty. Twenty-eight judgments were pronounced between 1525 and 1531. Less indulgence was shown to a husband repulsed by a frigid wife. Out of eighty petitions, quite a small proportion were granted. In three of these households falling to ruin, the husband had so brutally beaten his wife that she could no longer entertain any affection for him.

On May 21, 1526, the burgomasters and the Great Council voted in favour of a plan to widen the powers of the matrimonial tribunal. In consequence, it became incumbent on the latter to supervise the whole moral life of the city. Fornication was thus subjected to strict vigilance. It became possible to compel former priests either to dismiss their concubine or to marry her. Many, who had for years been living with their housekeeper, decided to regularize the situation. The same requirement was imposed on ordinary citizens. "The reports of the sittings", notes Köhler, who has investigated them, "offer us a scandalous chronicle of the life of Zürich, dictated by a concern to raise public morals."

The judges paid no respect to the social rank of the accused. In their books the best-known names in the city pass before us. Their rigidity was not relaxed either in consideration of Councillors or of Diebold von Geroldseck, the former administrator of Einsiedeln, who was asked to dismiss his woman friend, Dorothea Hochholtzerin. Were they not seen together "passing over the bridge"? The eyes of the tribunal, helped by the watchfulness of neighbours, rested on every house, and on taverns in particular. Owners of property were made responsible for the conduct of their tenants. The latter were not allowed to entertain a gay woman. Innkeepers were summoned, questioned, fined. One of them, Heini Genner, who ran the town brothel, had to exclude from it married men. Women go-betweens were forbidden to carry on their dubious trade. However, as was the case at Wittenberg, no measure was taken abolishing prostitution entirely.

As in all authoritarian forms of government, justice made use of the terrible weapon furnished by the system of giving information. Neighbours who heard cries, doubtful talk, or who noted unusual visits, reported to the judges. One citizen found himself summoned to answer for having sat down in an inn beside a servant-girl and having talked to her. One woman had received in her house the bootmaker, another a student. Both were publicly reproved. A man-servant had been found conveying love-letters: this was denounced as a crime which must not be repeated. Melchior Bluntschli was noticed passing too often under the windows of a certain house: he merited a double warning. The judges also concerned themselves with investigating questions of paternity, and studied cases of damages, blows, slanders. From 1529 attendance at church became obligatory, and copious admonitions were meted out to the negligent, to be followed if necessary by fines and imprisonment.

The reign of puritanism at Zürich forms a prelude to that at Geneva. The desire to impose strict morality which actuated both Calvin and Zwingli produced the same effects on the banks of the Rhône and on the shores of Lake Limmat. The two cities became, to use the formula coined by Georges Goyau, church cities. Köhler sums up his appraisal in a sentence which is worth pondering: "The fundamental mistake [of Calvin as of Zwingli] consists in the attempt to attain by legalistic means a certain moral standard, whereas in fact law can only vindicate morality and guard against immorality." Morality, in truth, belongs essentially to the sphere of personal life. Beyond a certain point, coercion destroys it in the very act of claiming to serve it. Or, to be more precise, it proves itself to be painfully inefficient. Puritanism always runs the risk of engendering hypocrisy.

The effort made at Zürich and Geneva finds its justification, however, in the lamentable state of morals which marked the decline of the Middle Ages. The decadence of the Church, the disorders in the life of the clergy, furthered by increasing wealth, had corrupted manners. It was necessary to reascend a slope down which State and Church had for a long time been sliding. As is often the case, the reaction went too far. Encouraging delation as it did, it built a city of artificial moral purity. How was it possible that Ulrich, the self-confessed supporter of liberty in face of the canon law and its inhuman demands, failed to discern this danger?

But it would be unjust to emphasize merely the negative aspect of Zwingli's effort. The jurisdiction over manners exercised by the Zürich tribunal educated the average man who, like the child, appreciated the force of a "thou shalt not" supported by the rod. The level of general morality rose. In 1530 John Eck, at the Diet of Augsburg, thought it good to pour ridicule on the "new law of Zürich which has dropped from the skies". The ethic, which Zwingli's city tried to put into practice, was based fairly and squarely on the Old Testament. Is it legitimate for a Christian country to shape its polity on the model of the first covenant? Does the love of Christ, which alone can produce sanctity in the individual soul, abolish the need to impose respect for the ten commandments? This question goes far beyond the limits of a biography. It is still relevant, however, in all countries where there survives a general—often theoretic—respect for Christianity. Is the command of God limited solely to the domain of the individual life? Or, on the contrary, must we admit that its influence should mark the civil and penal codes? While sectarian Christianity confines its attention to small groups of carefully chosen souls, the Church—be it catholic or reformed—retains the vision of a whole people of believers, a vast community subjected to God. The formula of Köhler which has already been quoted in this chapter leaves the essential questions undetermined, in spite of its apparent precision. For what after all is the meaning of "favouring morality" and "guarding against immorality"? If the divine spark of charity belongs to the transcendental sphere, there is justification for training the people to observe a minimum of orderly and decent conduct. The Christian legislator will naturally be inspired by Moses, as seen in the light shed by the Sermon on the Mount. Let him, however, refrain from being excessively ambitious! Let him not forget the frontier (which it is difficult to trace) that separates individual from social life.

The institution of Zürich became a model for imitation. It was adopted by Berne and Basle in 1529, in 1530 by Schaffhausen and Glarus. The towns of Chur, in 1528, and of St. Gall, in 1547, were inspired by it. Through Berne, Strasburg and Farel, the idea reached French Switzerland. Calvin, a man of the second generation, was treading in a path that had already been cleared, when he set up the Consistory of Geneva.

Alongside moral edification, Zwingli did not lose sight of the aim of converting the people of Zürich by the preaching of the Word of God. The church which had been separated from Rome needed a capable and respected clergy. From 1525, the training of pastors largely preoccupied the reformer, who created for this purpose the Biblical seminar which has been described in the previous chapter. The abolition of the canonries, one after the other, provided the means for the creation of professorial chairs. The college, envisaged as early as September, 1523, in a decision of the Council, gradually took shape.

A great number of Zürich priests remained active. Leo Jud, the impetuous companion of Zwingli at the time of the decisive struggles, made the transition from being priest to being pastor of the Church of St. Peter, which he administered as such from 1522 until his death in 1532. George Stählin, who had been on the staff of the Great Minster with Ulrich, fulfilled various pastoral functions in the canton of Zürich, then in 1528 went to Bienne, in 1531 to Zofingue, and in 1543 returned to the Cathedral where he had once celebrated the mass. It would be easy to multiply examples. From outside, ecclesiastics who were adherents of the new ideas came to take the place of those who went elsewhere as a result of their attachment to the old faith. Myconius, an intimate friend of Zwingli, but a layman, passed without more ado from his professorial post to a pastoral charge offered him by the Council. It was this latter, in close combination with the three pastors of the city, which in effect replaced the bishop and proceeded to make appointments. On the benches of the theological college, students in 1526 began to join forces with aged priests whose Biblical knowledge had to be improved. From 1527 they were housed in a hostel and received grants for clothing and the expenses of their studies. Financially, this operation like the appointment of professors was facilitated by the suppression of chapelries whose holders were deceased, or who were alternatively provided with a country parish.

In this same year, an order provided for the half-yearly meeting of all pastors, canons and chaplains. The first assembly was held in the spring of 1528. It was the origin of the synod which still functions today, and settles questions relative to the general life of the Church. It was ordered that the assembly should also include one or two representatives of each parish, whose duty would be to bring forward wishes and complaints concerning the ministry of their pastors. Not only intellectually, but morally, many of the latter still left much to be desired. Several of them were summoned to appear before the matrimonial tribunal, for they were in the habit of frequenting inns, illtreating their parishioners and in general distinguishing themselves by their bad conduct. The renovation of church life which Ulrich so fervently desired was slow in showing itself.

A little treatise, entitled *The Shepherd* and published in 1524, although directed to a large extent against the debased episcopate of the time, sketches the permanent features of the true shepherd of souls such as Ulrich himself desired to be. As He served as a pattern for the young man in the treatise dedicated to Gerold Meyer von Knonau, so, in *The Shepherd*, Jesus incarnates the virtues with which the pastor must be invested. Did He not exhort His disciples to heed neither father nor mother, but God alone? "O woman, what have you to do with me?" He said to Mary. The preacher and the bishop will listen to the sole word of God, though they may have to chance becoming an object of opprobrium. Self-renunciation means willingness to accept vilification and scorn, for the servant of truth is always exposed to persecution. Emptied of self, the pastor must devote himself to the love of God, in accordance with the narrative of Pentecost. He must try to lead his sheep along the paths which he has himself followed, the paths of the knowledge of God and complete trust in God. External things, such as rich sacerdotal vestments, count for little: "The living example is better than thousands of words." The faithful shepherd attacks the vices of priests and of the great ones of the earth, however eminent their position, as did Elijah of old, who reproved Ahab, and Micaiah, who opposed Jehoshaphat. The prophet warns in time the sinning but he rebukes, should that be necessary, in the spirit of love. Everything should be measured by the standard of Christian charity. "Without charity, man easily slips into pride. Yes, where charity is lacking, there is nothing but pride. . . . Like the shepherd who strikes a few sheep with his hand, makes others go forward with his foot, others again by whistling, draws some to him by offering them salt, carries those that are weak, or leaves them in the cattle-shed until they have recovered, and all that for the good of his master in order that the flock should grow and be healthy, so the pastor, inspired by the love of God, does everything possible to increase and make strong God's lambs." Work of this kind should not be undertaken with a view to material gain.

This short treatise, full of metaphors drawn in part from the Bible and in part from the author's living memory of the Alps with their pasturage slopes and flocks, must be completed by the reading of a work published a year later, *Vom Predigtamt* (concerning the office of pastor). This is a refutation of anabaptism which entrusted the task of preaching to anyone who was apparently inspired. While *The Shepherd* is aimed at the episcopate, the second volume

is an attack on fanatical sectarianism. The pastoral office,
Zwingli considered, should be a commission from the
Church. It depends both on an inward call and on a decision
by outward authority. Only he may occupy the pulpit of a
parish who is called by the parish as a whole to be its head.
The author narrates the following anecdote: One Sunday,
in a church which was administered by a good pastor, a
weaver got up and demanded the use of the pulpit. The
worthy ecclesiastic granted it him for the sake of peace. The
craftsman plunged into an explanation of 1 Tim. 4, and
stumbled over the second verse: "liars whose consciences are
seared". "I don't understand what that means," he muttered. "Stay then," cried the pastor; "I will explain it to
you." But as he started to do so, the congregation cried out:
"Make him come down!" "If I had straightaway told him
to do so," concluded the pastor, "I should have given the
impression of imposing my authority. It was better that the
order should come from you."

The existence of a sacred ministry is many times attested
Biblically. Christ "has appointed some to be apostles, others
evangelists, others prophets and teachers" (Eph. 4). An
apostle is a messenger who proclaims God, His requirement
of holiness, and His love. He is itinerant, and travels around
without taking purse or staff. The prophet, on the other
hand, resides in a definite place. One only speaks at a time
(1 Cor. 14): there must be order in the church. The New
Testament ascribes to the prophet the knowledge of tongues,
which—by a curious exegesis—Ulrich understands to mean
the knowledge of Greek and Hebrew. The anabaptists are
vexed at the idea of an organized ministry, which assigns
to the pastor a house and a salary. But, retorted Timothy,
their adversary, at the bidding of St. Paul, do you not find
in every town married elders appointed, who must be given
to hospitality? How can they welcome the poor if they have
no lodging? With much shrewdness, Zwingli rejects the
system of mendicancy, which, as experience shows, offers
no guarantee against avarice. The parish must provide a
sufficient salary, and the pastor be content with it. "For my

part, I am satisfied with a canon's benefice, for the best thing, in my opinion, is that a pastor should be in receipt of an annual fixed and decent income. . . . He who has grown accustomed to beg, presents himself to everyone as possessing nothing, and he takes all he can get." If he enjoys a regular stipend, no one need take pity on him. He pays for his purchases with his own money. "If you are a true servant of God, you will use your income for the honour of God. If you are not a true servant, which will rapidly become evident, you will aim at base profit, and will beg."

The stable and well trained pastoral ministry does not spell a decline from the liberty of the Spirit. If every one claims to be able to instruct his brother, whether he has been accepted by the Church or not, there will soon be as many sects as individuals. Arbitrariness and improvisation, thought Zwingli, never settle anything. He denounced that spirit with as much energy as he denounced the episcopal abuses of catholicism. The treatise *Vom Predigtamt* justifies on a Biblical basis the pastoral ministry of the reformed churches. He makes a careful distinction between the office of preacher—founded on the twofold call of God and men— and the priesthood of all believers. All are believers, but all do not become pastors. Many protestants of the present day, entangled in the sophisms of sectarian religion, with its proud slogans of the lay priesthood and voluntary clubbing together, would profit from a careful study of the reformer's dissertation. Struggling against the winds and tides of a difficult period of transition, he succeeded in creating an institution which for four centuries has shown itself to be capable of effectively preaching the Gospel to the people of the reformed churches.

CHAPTER TWENTY-FIVE

The Berne Disputation (*1528*)

PROUDLY BUILT ON A rocky peninsula overlooking
for a little way the blue waters of the Aar, Berne
still retains, facing the Alps, the hallmark of a patrician
city. If several of its hotels go back to the 18th century,
its cathedral, the Minster, dates from the 15th century,
and several of its beautiful fountains from the 16th. Its
situation and the architecture of its wealthy streets still
reflect its now dead aspirations to be a sovereign and conquering state. Like Zürich, it possesses a past full of dramatic
crises of various kinds, where sordid intrigue mingles with
heroic strife. Better than the city of the Limmat, which has
been transformed by industrialization, Berne preserves its
ancient picturesque character.

The town, whose coat-of-arms contains a threatening
bear, had in 1526 resisted the pressures of catholic Switzerland, which desired to exclude from the Helvetic confederation those who sympathized with Zwingli. He was able to
count on some faithful friends on the banks of the Aar—
in particular, on Berchtold Haller and Nicolas de Watteville,
who in fact were working in his favour. The arrogance of
Lucerne, which presumed to exercise a censorship in matters
of religious faith, only contributed to the success of their
efforts. On January 4, 1527, Zwingli wrote prophetically:
"The wind has dropped and milder airs [*mitiores zephyri*] are
beginning to blow." On May 6, the elections brought to the
leadership of the state a team of magistrates favourable to
the innovators. "Our greatest joy!" exclaimed Haller in a
letter of May 26.

However, this political success was succeeded by a period of uncertainty and divisions. Supporters and opponents confronted each other daily. Six corporations gave up the masses which they had been accustomed to have said. Some priests were granted permission to get married. Others, who had been exiled, returned. Several preachers thundered denunciations of the mass from the pulpit. On September 4, the Canon of Berne told his friend of the measures taken by a numerous group of priests who were petitioning the Council for authority to go ahead and change the form of divine service. On November 15 the magistrates, following the example of what had been done at Zürich, decided to convene an assembly for public discussion of the issue. The four bishops of Constance, Basle, Lausanne, and Sion were to be invited, as were also several prelates who had taken part in the Baden disputations. The Bernese desired the participation of Zwingli, who was to be accompanied by Pellican, Leo Jud, or Myconius: "Many are calling for you", emphasized Haller in a letter of November 19. "We have got the wolf by the ears, but we haven't yet managed to tame him."

For the reformer who had been solemnly condemned at Baden, the hour of revenge was about to strike. The magistrates, delighted by this unexpected stroke of good fortune, no longer tried to hold him back; quite the contrary. The delegates of friendly cities, such as Schaffhausen, St. Gall, and Constance, gathered at Zürich, where they were given a splendid reception. On January 2, 1528, a hundred horsemen, surrounding Zwingli in his hour of triumph, took the road westwards. The Council had allotted to them a contingent of three hundred armed men, who escorted them as far as the Bernese frontier. The itinerary passed through the region of Bremgarten, which was subject in part to the jurisdiction of catholic cantons. The man who only yesterday had been treated like the plague found himself advanced to become an object of sympathy and admiration as well as of hatred. In the trim countryside villages, the peasants opened astonished eyes, thinking: "Here he comes, the accursed fellow, the heretic!" The journey was completed without incident. When Berne was reached on January 4, Ulrich refused the proffered hospitality of noble houses, and, accompanied by the Burgomaster, Diethelm Roüst, went to the home of his kinsman, Leonard Tremp, who was administrator of the hospital and a member of the Great Council.

The disputation of Berne forms a pendant to that of Baden. The catholic party was hardly represented, so to speak. Eight cantons, including that of Glarus, sulked at the thought of this new contest. Like Zwingli a year and a half previously, the heads of dioceses disdained to be present. Sebastian de Montfalcon alone consented to leave Lausanne for a few hours. If we are to believe his letter of apology, a fall from his horse obliged him to go back, however. He deputed four theologians to represent him, but, not knowing German, they were unable to intervene in the debates. His letter expressing regret betrays his suspicions. He suggested that, taking the Bible as one's basis, one would get only "the husks of Scripture and the inkpots of the theologians". With St. Paul, he proclaimed that "the letter kills, but the Spirit gives life".

The ten theses, drawn up on the basis of a scheme prepared by Ulrich before he left for Berne, were sent round to all the participants. The following is a summary of them:

"The sole head of the Church is Christ. This church is born of the Word of God, which gives it life. It must heed no alien power."

"The Church of Christ cannot legislate except on the basis of the Word of God. Ecclesiastical laws are only binding in so far as they are founded on this Word."

"Christ is our only wisdom and righteousness; He provides the expiation of all sin. To rely on the merits of others to obtain holiness and forgiveness is to deny Christ."

"It is impossible to prove the doctrine of transubstantiation from Holy Scripture."

"The mass, in which Christ is offered to God as a sacrifice for the sins of the living and the dead, implies blasphemy against the very holy sufferings and death of Christ."

"Christ alone died on our behalf. He alone must be invoked as the Mediator and Intercessor between God and believers."

"Scripture is silent about a purgatory after this life."

"The adoration of images contradicts texts from the Old and New Testaments. They must be abolished wherever there is any risk of their being worshipped."

"Marriage is forbidden to no class of men, whereas adultery and immorality are forbidden to all."

"The scandal of immorality is worse on the part of priests than with men in any other condition of life."

The Bernese magistrates had taken the church of the Franciscans. Furnished with pews, equipped with a pulpit, on January 6 it welcomed, in addition to the councillors and their guests, two hundred and fifty priests of the town and country, together with about a hundred chaplains.

It was an old friend of Ulrich, the Burgomaster of St. Gall, Joachim von Watt (known as Vadian), who was asked to preside over the debates. His portraits still show us the picture of a man whose doublet, cut low in accordance with the fashion of the time, reveals too fat a neck beneath the double chin. The face, devoid of beauty, is redeemed by the brown eyes, sparkling with intelligence under their sharply outlined eyebrows, and by the deep wrinkles which imprint on the thick flesh a note of self-control and calm. A man of learning and culture, subtly intelligent and deeply religious, a doctor and a magistrate, Vadian embodies the universal scope of the Renaissance mentality. He was keenly interested in all that concerns man. If he abandoned in midstream the study of law for that of medicine, the reason was that the latter introduced him more deeply to the understanding of nature. After his return from Vienna to his native city, he worked to reconstruct the latter in the new light shed by humanism. His first contact with Lutheran ideas interested him without bringing him to a decision. Although on good terms with Zwingli, he kept his distance during the early years of the Zürich reformation. Would he follow the lead of Glareanus or Faber, with whom also he was in correspondence? He read Luther like a man who did not wish to precipitate matters, and who was scared by the verbal violence of the rebellious monk. At his request, his friends furnished him with books by the new thinker and also with those which were written against him.

Not until October, 1522, did he publicly intervene in the discussions of the day with the publication of a little treatise on the Credo, *Brevis indicatura symbolorum* (a brief study of the creeds), in which he decided in favour of a serious investigation of Holy Scripture as the basis of the faith. He apologized for his intervention as a layman in a theological debate, but circumstances, he said, had brought him into contact with a circle of priests, some of whom were partisans of the new ideas, while others dreaded them as a source of strife. As the discussion was in part concerned with the credal article *descendit ad inferna* (He descended into Hell), he felt unable to refrain from expressing his opinion.

From that moment, the mind of Vadian was made up. He would never go back on the decision: did not both Renaissance and reformation plead in conjunction for a return to original sources? At St. Gall, he energetically pushed ahead in the same direction as Zwingli at Zürich. When the city, deaf to the appeals of the abbey, replaced the mass by the Lord's Supper, the first to receive the symbolic bread (on April 21, 1527, in the Church of St. Lawrence) was Joachim von Watt. For a little more than a year he had been first magistrate of the city, such was his fellow-citizens' confidence in him. No one was better qualified than he to preside over the victorious debates of Berne.

The debates lasted for several days. Alternately, the two priests of the city, Berchtold Haller and Franz Kolb, commented on the articles and asked opponents to express themselves by basing their objections on Holy Scripture. A priest from Appenzell, Theobald Huter, the provincial of the Augustinians, Conrad Träger of Fribourg, and another monk of the same order, Alexius Grat, who was a confessor at Berne, disputed as best they could in favour of tradition. "The struggle was easy for the heretics", notes with melancholy one James of Münster, a priest from Solothurn, who was following the discussions, "for no well-armed adversary opposed them. If the supporters of the ancient beliefs had had some courage and skill, their party would have been maintained at Berne, at least for a year longer. We are receiving the punishment which our contempt for knowledge and our neglect of study have deserved. Our overthrow is absolute. It might have been avoided if our bishops had been more studious and less fond of girls."

During the first skirmishes, Zwingli intervened but little. He did not wish to overshadow his hosts, in particular the modest Haller, whose zeal and seriousness had induced the change of mind in the Bernese. He flung himself all the more keenly into the discussion when it reached the article concerning transubstantiation. A priest of St. Gall, Benedict Burgauer, had made himself the advocate of the Lutheran conception of the sacrament. Ulrich, who for several months had been debating this theme with the Wittenberg reformer, could restrain himself no longer. Suddenly the rising dispute of the theologians echoed beneath the vaults of the Church of the Franciscans. For five days, it was a question of the 6th chapter of St. John's Gospel, of the words which the evangelists ascribe to Jesus when He instituted the eucharist, of the corresponding Pauline texts, of the relation between the Christian communion and the Mosaic Passover. Members of the Council, soldiers, craftsmen, listened unwearyingly. Ulrich led what he jokingly called "the dance of the bears". With admirable skill, he adapted his phrasing to the mentality of his hearers. With regard to the warning addressed to the Corinthians, "Whoever eats the bread or drinks the cup of the Lord in an unworthy manner", he made a distinction between a purely external attachment to the Church of Christ and a sincere faith. The superficial communicant was "like someone wearing an external sign of belonging to the Gentlemen of Berne, but who, in his heart, is not faithful to the people of Berne". Such an unworthy soldier was guilty towards the Republic. The soldier's uniform, a visible sign of an invisible allegiance, committed one. The soldier who had dishonoured it by misusing it or tearing it, had not struck or pierced the Gentlemen of Berne, but he was none the less guilty towards them. The priest Bergauer confessed himself convinced by so much simple logic and withdrew all his objections.

On January 26, at the conclusion of these memorable weeks, Haller once more spoke. He expressed the wish that everyone present should retire with the conviction that a serious and important change had been effected. The dominating motive of the preachers had not been a liking for discussion for its own sake, nor the need to call attention to themselves by the introduction of a few innovations, but the desire to work for the honour of God and the salvation of all believers, and of the Bernese in particular. Out of fidelity towards their sacred office, the pastors had been led to proclaim the Gospel sometimes with gentleness, sometimes with sharpness. The true grace of God which had illuminated them urged them not merely to introduce modifications in church worship, but had also inspired in them a spiritual renewal and change of life. Turning to his colleagues, Haller exhorted them with affectionate emotion to render themselves worthy of the office which had been entrusted to them. In the name of the Council, he then thanked all those who had taken part in the sittings.

The activity of Zwingli was not limited to his interventions in the discussions. With Bucer, Ambrose Blarer, Oecolampadius, Conrad Schmid, and others, he preached in the Cathedral, attracting an immense crowd. On January 19 he gave a commentary on the Apostles' Creed, which made clear that he was orthodox on the essential points of the faith. In addition, he approached the central subject of the mass and justified his own conception of the Lord's Supper. While he was speaking, Bullinger tells us, a priest was officiating in a side chapel. He stopped, facing the eucharistic elements, listened eagerly to the words of the preacher, and, when the sermon was finished, cast off his sacerdotal vestments and threw them on the altar, crying: "If that is the mass, I will not celebrate it again, either today or ever again."

On January 30, in his second sermon, Zwingli encouraged the Bernese to persevere in the way they had just taken. What nourishes faith—and the reformer insisted on this point—is not the visible instruments of devotion, but the inner knowledge of the God of Jesus Christ. Following the example set by Zürich three years earlier, the clergy had already, on January 13, two hundred in favour and forty against, voted to abolish the mass. On January 27, when the sacristans, as was their custom, lighted the wax candles of the sombre Cathedral early in the morning, they observed with astonishment that no priest presented himself to say mass. The bells rang in vain. Alone with the flickering lights, in the vast, desolate sanctuary, the organist, in despair, opened for the last time the organ lid. At his touch there arose under the motionless arches the sorrowful strains of the hymn: "O Judas, how canst thou have betrayed thy Lord?" Then he closed the instrument, which became silent for centuries.

On January 27 the members of the noble Diesbach family gathered in their private chapel for the celebration of an anniversary mass. On the same day, the Council issued an order forbidding the continuance of church worship in its old form. Workmen were summoned to demolish the twenty-five altars of the Cathedral. The images were destroyed and their fragments buried. The only ornaments which escaped this iconoclastic fury were a few pictures from the private chapels, which their owners claimed. A supporter of the ancient faith, Councillor Hans Zehender, entered the denuded church on his ass: "If they wish to make of this place a stable," he said in explanation of his conduct, "my ass must enter it too." The impertinent fellow found himself dismissed from his office.

The people voted and approved the decision of the authorities. Alone, the town of Lenzburg, with Frütigen and Zimmenthal in the Oberland, opposed the measure.

The decision of Berne completely altered the confessional position of Switzerland. It gave Zürich the support of a powerful state. Basle, which until then had been hesitant, rallied finally to the cause of the reformation on February 9, 1529. In the region of the Pays de Vaud, which was subject to Berne, William Farel, who from 1526 had been disseminating protestantism under the mask of his work as a schoolmaster, was now able to promote the cause openly. The districts of Ollon, Aigle, and Bex adopted the religion of their lords and masters in the first fortnight of March, 1528. Then a door opened on what was to become French Switzerland. Neuchâtel was converted in 1530, shortly after the Jura valley of Saint-Imier, which took the decisive step in March of the same year. In the districts of Orbe and Grandson, reformed preaching competed with the mass without producing any authoritative decision. But the matter would soon be decided by the arbitrament of arms. The victorious advance of the Bernese and the collapse of Savoyard domination became the prelude to the disputation of Lausanne, which, on October 19, 1536, surrendered the whole region to the reformers. Geneva took its decision independently on May 21 by a vote of the citizens which provided Calvin with the platform from which the exiled Frenchman was to exercise a European influence.

Hence the decisions of 1528 played a part of capital importance in the religious destinies of Switzerland. Eight years later the confessional map showed roughly the same contours which it has today. Schaffhausen, under the influence of Sebastian Hofmeister, six out of the eight Appenzell districts, a part of the Grisons, half of Glarus, fragments of Aargau and Thurgau, the city of St. Gall, and Toggenburg—all these rallied to the support of the three reformed cities of Zürich, Berne, and Basle. The catholic block included, besides the three original cantons, Zug, Lucerne, the abbacy of St. Gall, parts of Glarus and the Grisons, and Solothurn. In French-speaking Switzerland. Fribourg, the Jura, which was then the property of the dispossessed Bishop of Basle, and the Valais remained attached to the old faith. The Ticino took its stand with the catholic cantons of central Switzerland. Today protestantism counts among its supporters three-fifths of the population, catholicism two-fifths. The churches which were acquired or retained continued to be the property of those who occupied them at the time of Zwingli's death. If the ancient churches of Zürich, Berne, Basle, Neuchâtel, Lausanne, and Geneva now have organs and some of them crosses, the preaching of the Word of God is still the heart and centre of their worship. Their officiants wear the black gown and the bands of Zwinglian or Calvinist ministers.

CHAPTER TWENTY-SIX

Organization of the Church: Development of State Discipline

A FEW MONTHS AFTER the victory of Berne, the politico-religious horizon of Switzerland once more became clouded. The decision taken as a result of the influence of Haller and Zwingli encountered serious resistance in the Alpine villages of the Oberland. The peasants had recourse to arms and were supported by their catholic neighbours of Unterwalden. The partisans of the ancient faith everywhere desired a return to the old ways, and where they were in the majority made every effort to break by force the impetus of the reformation.

The Swiss Confederation communally possessed important territories which had been snatched from the domination of Austria and Milan. In the 16th century the ruling cantons took it in turn to govern the areas which were called "subject countries". It is easy to imagine the prevailing confessional tension. Many wished to follow the lead given by Zürich and Berne. The judges nominated by Lucerne and primitive Switzerland—Uri, Schwyz, and Unterwalden—did everything possible to bridle the new movement. In such circumstances, appeals for help went out to the two protestant cities.

The atmosphere was so much the more electric in that at this very moment the situation in Germany was developing momentarily in favour of catholicism. The quarrel which had brought into confrontation the Emperor Charles V and Pope Clement VII, and which had reached a climax of paroxysm with the sack of Rome in May, 1527, was now subsiding. The enemies of yesterday were being reconciled. Hence the year 1528 witnessed a very definite revulsion, which foreshadowed the second Diet of Spires in the spring of 1529. Ferdinand of Austria issued in his states, in August, 1527, and January, 1528, edicts directed against the Zwinglians, who, placed on the same footing as anabaptists, became liable to the death penalty. In April it was rumoured that the Archduke was preparing an armed expedition against Switzerland.

On all sides fiery protestations were being made. The talk was all of preparations for war. The situation was such that, in most of the states of the Confederation, a minority was hoping that the tide would turn in its favour.

Zwingli was intensely vibrant in face of this terrible ferment. Since 1523, victories, defeats, and new victories had followed each other without intermission. In every city, councils assembled, citizens voted, a majority made or unmade the Church. Centuries would pass before there arose in the human mind a feeling of respect for individual decisions, an awareness that a party can gain power without necessarily destroying its defeated opponents. Toleration is a delicate fruit which ripens slowly and requires for its maturing a climate of mutual trust. The strong, if they are to tolerate the free movements of the weak, must feel assured that the latter would treat them in the same way should the balance of parties be reversed. In the tense atmosphere of the 16th century, this difficult virtue might have been advocated in a few books, but it failed to penetrate and leaven manners. To force which crushed a spiritual development, what answer was there except a countering manifestation of force?

Between 1526 and 1528 there took place in the mind of Zwingli an evolution which we have already briefly noted. The reformer, in his early writings, had clearly distinguished the spiritual from the temporal, but now he was drifting towards a confusion of the two. Is constraint alien to the sphere of faith? St. Augustine, at close grips with the Donatists at the beginning of the 5th century, had reached the conclusion that the Church is entitled to employ coercion. He wrongly based on a Gospel text—"compel them to come in"—his doctrine of the *compelle intrare*. The blind and the lame were forcibly brought into the marriage feast of the kingdom of heaven. The Church, he claimed, had the right to seek the support of the secular arm in order to dissolve heretical communities and restore the dissidents to its own congregations. A distinction must be made between the unjust persecution exercised by the impious and the just persecution with which the Church seeks to coerce them. Nevertheless Augustine, author of the *Confessions*, at the beginning of his career repulsed with horror the idea of using the sword in the service of the faith: "If one came to use such desperate remedies," he said to Fortunatus, "it would be the work of wicked men."

In the mind of Zwingli, caught up in the torment provoked by the reformation, a similar doctrinal change took place. A jurist of Zürich, Alfred Farner, in a remarkable study, *Die Lehre vom Kirche und Staat bei Zwingli* (1930), has traced the stages by which this change[1] was accomplished. On May 4, 1528, Ulrich wrote to his friend, Ambrose Blarer, the reformer of Constance, a letter which is of capital importance. Whereas in his earlier writings Ulrich had carefully distinguished the political community from the church community, the two are now confused. A decision of the City becomes a decision of the Church.

Zwingli is clearly aware of the importance of this change. Earlier, he had shared Luther's opinion: *Regnum Christi non est externum* (the kingdom of Christ is not an external one). He recalled that Erasmus in one of his last letters warned him against what he considered an absurdity: "You will see, Zwingli, what will emerge one day from these paradoxes which you defend to such an extent, and about which I have written to Luther." At that time Ulrich supported the prophet of Wittenberg (Luther) even at the risk of quarrelling with Erasmus, his eminent friend of Basle. Since then his

[1] The reader interested in the reformer's development on this point may also read with profit the thesis of Roger Ley, *Kirchenzucht bei Zwingli* (1948).

eyes have been opened, and on several points he now refuses to follow the Saxon reformer.

The kingdom of God, he now thinks, has external implications also. The temporal authority can compel the Christian to obey certain rules. In the time of Christ, respect for the Sabbath was made compulsory. Did not the Saviour Himself also act with a view to external things when He gave orders concerning fasting or, again, when He commanded the twelve disciples on their missionary tour to take with them neither provisions nor sandals?

Some of these reflections, consciously or unconsciously, are directed as much against anabaptism as against Luther. Zwingli has decided to break with the extravagant ecstatic spirituality to which for a time he deferred. The Spirit, he now thinks, is invested on this earth with a certain form, it becomes embodied and indwells terrestrial realities. In the apostolic church, the apostles, as is shown by the decisions of Acts 15 concerning circumcision and abstention from meats sacrificed to idols, imposed a certain order on church life. The Christian magistrate has therefore the right to issue ordinances binding on his city, though with the consent of the church (*cum ecclesiae consensu*). Does not his role correspond with that of those elders (presbyters) who acted in concert with the apostles in the decisions taken at Jerusalem (Acts 15)?

It would be useless to discuss in detail here the confusion of thought of which Ulrich is guilty. The elder of the primitive church has no direct connexion with the magistrate of the 16th century. But, in the mind of the reformer, the use of constraint in matters of faith is henceforth Biblically justified. Extraordinary as it may seem, Zwingli does not now distinguish between an internal ordinance of the church relevant to believers only, and legislation intended to apply to all the inhabitants of the city, pious or impious, enthusiastic reformers or lingering partisans of catholicism. For him majority is identical with unanimity. The concept of a minority is foreign to him.

The conclusion of this theology can easily be discerned:

the Council of Constance has the right to impose on its town the reformation which the middle class desires. Let it abolish the mass and images. Yet another argument drawn from the Gospels comes to reinforce this invitation to action: did not Christ drive the tradespeople out of the temple by the use of a whip? The important point that violence will thereby be done to the minority is glimpsed for a moment in a subordinate clause. The Council must impose its will "even if many are in consequence injured".

How was it possible that the man of Zürich should rise to the height of liberalism when all around him in Switzerland evangelical Christians were being harried wherever catholicism retained power? The identification of Church and State was universal. The pope and the bishops were temporal princes. For centuries the Church had suppressed heresy with the aid of the secular arm. Zwingli thus relapsed into the medieval perspective from which for a moment he had freed himself.

In conformity with the principle, explained to Blarer, that the spiritual must receive earthly embodiment, the reformation at Zürich began to organize itself. The years 1523-25 were a period of improvisation. The Council of the Two Hundred took reforming decisions, bit by bit, subverting the traditional order of divine worship, creating the theological college and public charity. In the new church, numerous small problems arose which concerned sometimes doctrine, sometimes the person of the pastors, their stipend, and their relationship with their parishes. In January, 1527, a commission of superintendence was set up which included both magistrates and ecclesiastics. It was entrusted with the task of administering the church and of supervising the conduct and the ministry of clerics. The new organism was transformed, after a few months, into a Synod, which assembled for the first time in April, 1528, and which henceforth controlled the spiritual life of Zürich. It required from pastors the promise "to preach truly and faithfully the Gospel and the Word of God according to the Old and the

New Testaments". In practice, this promise meant a promise to obey the orders of the Synod.

Zürich, under threats, was being organized at every level in a defensive position. The last attempts at resistance from within were broken. A restricted council met from time to time. Zwingli, who was called to take part in its sittings, mentions it for the first time in a letter to Vadian dated September 3, 1528. Too many indiscreet persons with their ears to the ground could tell stories in Lucerne or Schwyz of what was happening on the shores of the Limmat. In these secret meetings Ulrich played a preponderant role, on account of which the pen of the contemporary catholic chronicler, Hans Salat, accused him of being "burgomaster, secretary, and council in one".

One of the first measures taken by the new organization was aimed at the Little and Great Councils. It was decided to exclude from those bodies all who refused to partake of the evangelical Lord's Supper. As the Councils were in practice responsible for the church of the city, henceforth only those were to sit on them who lived conformably with the requirements of the Word of God. Zwingli preached on this theme at Christmas, 1528. The Great Council decided shortly afterwards that only those could canvass for the votes of citizens who openly declared that they were communicants at the Lord's Table. The question was put to them publicly. Those who answered it negatively were excluded from the ballot. The confusion of State with Church here reaches its climax of madness. A complementary measure was further decided on in January, 1529. By this, attendance at public worship became obligatory. Without any regard to the will of individuals, all citizens had to go to church on Sundays on pain of being exiled or fined. From 1530, in the city the judges, and in the country the pastor with the collaboration of the lesser magistrates and two members of the parish council, became responsible for seeing that the law was strictly kept. At the same time, attendances by citizens who had remained catholic at masses celebrated in neighbouring cantons became a punishable offence.

Already on November 3, 1528, two men of Zürich who had gone to church at Einsiedeln were penalized by the fine of one silver mark.

On this point, as on others, Zürich and Geneva were alike. The *Ordonnances ecclésiastiques* of Calvin (1541) also provided for compulsory attendance at church. Neglect to do so, after a certain number of warnings, incurred penalties imposed by the magistracy. The extraordinary thing about this discipline, which was exercised on the banks of the Limmat as on those of the Rhône, is that it stands in absolute contradiction to the doctrine of predestination to which both reformers subscribed. On the one hand, all is of grace and God alone inclines the heart to obedience. On the other hand, the police are employed to buttress the faith. As is noted by Alfred Farner, "only the prophetic fire which animated Zwingli could have fused in his mind the liberty of the church, the liberty of faith, and the concept of compulsory religious worship". The legislating Christian often confuses the immediate needs of a cause which he has at heart with the imperatives of his faith. The burnings at the stake which catholicism kindles at the same time throughout Europe are hardly any more logical. Belief in free will, quite as much as predestination, excludes recourse to coercion.

CHAPTER TWENTY-SEVEN

The First War of Cappel (1529)

AMONG THE MANY events of the year 1528, those which shook Toggenburg must have aroused quite a special reaction in Ulrich's heart. The appeals for help which came from Thurgau or Aargau, districts administered in common which were pulled between their catholic and protestant masters, the voting at Glarus which became for both sides an opportunity to count their numbers, could not leave him indifferent. But on September 14 it was his native mountain valley which in its turn was shaken by the clash of beliefs. While the monks were celebrating mass, a group of young men who were partisans of the reformation burst into the monastery of St. John, not many miles from Wildhaus, destroying the organ and images. Had not the abbot just asked Schwyz and Glarus for their help in suppressing the movement which was plunging his subjects headlong into protestantism? Violence was answered by violence.

On September 23, Schwyz, espousing the cause of the prelate, intervened in his favour at the Diet and proposed to punish the guilty. On September 28, Zürich took up the cudgels on behalf of the threatened peasants. Zwingli, in a letter of the same day, contested the rights which the Abbot of St. Gall claimed to exercise over his native district. What was the attitude of his brothers and nephews? We do not know; the hastily written letter merely deals with the juridical aspect of the question.

The confusion was further increased in the first months of 1529. At Wesen, in January, the pictures that had been removed from the church where Zwingli as a child had accompanied his Uncle Barthelemy were burnt before the eyes of the delegates from Schwyz, while the priest, Hans Schindler, demanded help from Zürich. Bremgarten, in Aargau, adopted the new ideas on March 17 after hearing its priest, Bullinger, openly declare himself from the pulpit to be in favour of the innovators. The five cantons of central Switzerland, becoming more and more anxious, turned towards the hereditary enemy, Austria, and on April 22 concluded with her a separate alliance. Only the determination to drown heresy in blood could unite these old republics with the descendant of their former masters. If Zwingli wrote to Vadian on March 12: "The tricks of Ferdinand are more like those of the donkey than of the fox, they show nothing other than an impotent and desperate fear," Zürich for its part was getting ready to meet the worst eventualities. Both camps were furbishing their arms.

In the midst of all this agitation, the Abbot of St. Gall fell seriously ill. Zwingli thought the opportunity a favourable one. His plan was that when the prelate should breathe his last, the monks who had been won over to the reformation should secularize the monastery. The Zürich captain Hans Frey, who lived at Wyl, to which the prelate had retired, would give them every assistance. The secret council of Zürich sent instructions to this effect to his representative on January 28, 1529.

The lands of the abbey, which was a real state, constituted a rich prey. The citizens of the town of St. Gall who were at daggers drawn with their spiritual head had for years been claiming complete independence. Were the views of Zürich, whose territory adjoined that of the dying abbot, absolutely disinterested? Seeing the plans of its ally, Berne frowned. The powerful city coveted to the west the lands of the Duke of Savoy, the county of Vaud, the Chablais, and had no desire to see a war flaring up to the east such as would place it one day between two fires. Terrible combination of a spiritual drama with secret territorial ambitions! The 20th century knows too much of such mixtures of motives for any comment to be needed.

Political problems increasingly occupied the mind of Ulrich. In his veins flowed the blood of a family of municipal magistrates. From his earliest years he had been accustomed to hear the discussion of public affairs. He belonged to a race of people used to voting about all important projects concerning the future of towns and villages. If the abbots of St. Gall, Engelberg, and Einsiedeln were temporal princes, the pastor was essentially a citizen. Beneath the gown of the preacher there survived also the personality of the chaplain of Marignano, familiar with battle and its risks. War, which in 1516 had horrified him, he now felt to be unavoidable. Moreover, it was no longer a question of mercenary service; Zürich was not proposing to fight for any foreign prince, but to defend its spiritual liberty. The destiny of Switzerland was to be staked on a battlefield. An attitude of passive waiting would be fraught with danger. Would it not place the victim of attack in an unfavourable situation?

There is still extant in Zürich a document which it is difficult to date precisely and which contains a plan of campaign drawn up by the reformer. Several scholars think that it goes back to the year 1524 or 1525. Its contents suggest, however, a later date of composition.[1] In it, the confessional division of Switzerland is already that of the year 1528. Zwingli was counting on Berne, Basle, Schaffhausen, Glarus, Appenzell, and the town of St. Gall. The probable enemy has shrunk to the cantons of central Switzerland. Toggenburg itself is regarded as having rallied to the cause of protestantism.

To political counsels—such as, who should be warned, who should be brought into one's game?—are added military suggestions. The reformer wants the people to know about all the affronts which the city has suffered. Patience has proved useless. The only course that remains open is to persevere in truth with the firm intention of sacrificing if necessary "all one's reserves, wealth and property, town

[1] A catholic scholar, Oscar Vasella, in a study published in 1940 in the *Zeitschrift für Schweiz. Gesch.*, proposes the beginning of 1526.

and countryside, body and soul". At the head of the troops should be placed an experienced captain on whose faithfulness the city could implicitly rely. There follows a list of names for all the important posts. Several plans of campaign are outlined. "If the four Forest Cantons [the cantons of original Switzerland and Lucerne] advance from Zug, against us, a camp should be established on the further side of the Albis—eventually on this side—and there five thousand men should be stationed, while one thousand could remain in the city to guard it." But it should not be forgotten that at the same time a body of three thousand men should be flung against the east of Schwyz, in the regions of Uster, Gaster, and March. If the catholic attack came from Baden, part of the Zürich contingent would stop it, while other units, as in the previous plan, would be thrown into the area of Schwyz.

For anyone who knows the region, these names speak eloquently. They evoke valleys and hills. The Albis is that chain of mountains which separates the Lake of Zürich from the Lake of Zug, and which today is pierced by a double tunnel. On its western flank extends the plateau of Cappel overlooking Zug. When hostilities broke out in 1529 and 1531, this was the region occupied by the troops of Zürich.

Another feature of this curious text is its enumeration of various details to which officers must pay attention, such as nocturnal attacks, the condition of the arquebuses, the conduct of the trumpeter, who will keep by the side of the captain and sound the agreed signals. The final sheets are concerned with the spiritual bearing of the leaders. The captain must be pious and disinterested, so that he will not be fighting for his personal glory, but for the good of his men, whose confidence he will thus gain. Ulrich extols the attitude of Alexander the Great, who surrendered his place by the fire to an old soldier sick with cold.

"The chaplain must preach about the necessity for strict obedience towards God and the captain, so that the soldiers do nothing with a bad conscience. For, where there is a bad conscience, courage fails." The chaplain must also remind the soldiers that victory cannot be won without losses, that they should be moderate in eating and drinking, and not tremble when faced by the clatter and clash of arms.

He has put down these notes on paper, he concludes, because of the threats which many are uttering against "the pious city of Zürich". He added, however, that at the same time he prayed God with all his heart that "He would be pleased to protect His city in another way than that which is described in this plan of campaign, and that He would cause the pious people to live at peace within the Confederation."

This prayer—whether it goes back to 1525 or 1528— was not granted. In May, 1529, catholics and protestants, each party independently, were talking about having recourse to arms. The alliance with Austria had not been concluded for nothing. At Lucerne on May 28 the conservative cantons fixed June 4 as their date. The powerful state of Berne alone hesitated, and on May 29 wrote to Zürich to remind her that "patience obtains far better results than force". That same day, a stake was lighted at Schwyz which kindled the flames of war.

The pastor Jacob Kaiser had been appointed to the church of Oberkirch, a village which belonged both to Glarus and to Schwyz. He resided on Zürich territory and went to preach on Sundays in his parish. Arrested on the orders of the Schwyz magistrate, he was taken under a stiff escort to the catholic town and, in spite of the protests of the Zürich Council, there condemned to be burnt. On the shores of the Limmat, anger swept away the last lingering scruples. The troops of Zürich moved off on June 8, while a formal declaration of war was left to the five allied cantons. Since April 8 a number of men had been under arms. Zürich threw part of them into Thurgau, the territory of St. Gall, and the Rhine valley, which were occupied without the striking of a blow, thus cutting off Schwyz from its new ally, Austria. The main contingent crossed the Albis and took up a position at the approaches to the monastery of Cappel, where, firmly entrenched, it faced the little Lake of Zug, a brilliant emerald set in a sombre amphitheatre of mountains. Zwingli, on horseback, with a halberd on his shoulder, accompanied the troops as chaplain. Several letters have been preserved which he wrote to Zürich exhorting the secret council to be firm: "Do something courageous for God," he begged.

The Abbot of Cappel, Wolfgang Johner, had become attached to the reformation and in 1527 had transformed his monastery into a school. Are we to believe the catholic chronicler Salat who sees in him "the chief chaplain and the director of the whole enterprise"? His correspondence shows him above all to have been dissatisfied with the efforts that were immediately made to come to terms with the adversary. The *landammann* of Glarus, Aebli, who presided over the destinies of a canton that was confessionally divided, appreciated the full extent of the catastrophe to which civil war would lead. The whole Confederation would soon be swept with fire and blood. Despite their religious differences, were not the Swiss brothers? Indifferent to the risks he was running, from the very start of hostilities the magistrate went as mediator from one camp to the other.

The chiefs of the two sides hesitated. The armies confronted each other but no order to give battle was issued. The soldiers of the outposts could not believe that, between one day and the next, compatriots had become enemies. If every area of the country has its special dialect, the German Swiss speak essentially the same language. The people of Schwyz, who had been deprived of wheat as a result of the economic blockade which Zürich had ordered several weeks previously, possessed in compensation abundant supplies of milk. Some of them placed a well-filled vat on the frontier. shouting that they had enough milk for all, but lacked bread. The men of Zürich ran forward with their cobs of bread. An unexpected fraternization took place, both sides remaining on their respective territories and eating out of their hands the morsels of bread dipped in the foaming liquid. When one of them reached his fingers too far to the opposite side of the vat, narrates the chronicler, his *vis-à-vis* gave him a friendly tap, crying: "Eat on your own ground." "You

Swiss, you are funny folk," commented the ambassador of Strasburg, James Sturm. "When disunited, you soon associate together again, unable to forget the old bonds of friendship."

The happy spectacle did not delight Zwingli. He could not forget the burning at the stake which had just destroyed one of his companions. Touching embraces, he thought, settle nothing. The adversary was showing affection because he felt weak. Let the Council of Zürich stand firm. Exact conditions should accompany a restoration of peace: the free preaching of the Gospel in all the cantons, the prohibition in the whole of Switzerland of pensions given as a reward by foreigners, indemnification of the family of pastor Kaiser, and of the citizens of Zürich for their mobilization expenses.

The Bernese thought that this was asking too much, and would have been contented with an annulment of the alliance with Ferdinand and a substantial grant to the widow and children of the martyr. "This peace, on which some are insisting, is war and not peace," replied the vexed reformer. His notes to the magistrates show him in energetic action, eager to reach a decisive settlement. Do not yield, he implored them. Has not a prisoner disclosed the fact that Lucerne is without bread and that an important party within the town is urging that concessions be made?

In the end, the diplomacy of Aebli and the conciliatory spirit of Berne triumphed. The text of the treaty concluded with Austria was handed over. The *landammann* of Glarus publicly burnt it.

On his return to Zürich, Zwingli became calmer. The peace was honourable. It placed reformed and catholic on a footing of equality. What the Diet of Spires had just refused to protestants in Germany, the treaty of Cappel granted to their brothers in Switzerland. The reformer's attention moreover was almost at once absorbed by quite a different struggle.

Part Seven

The Eucharistic Controversy

CHAPTER TWENTY-EIGHT

Luther

T HE BIOGRAPHER SHRINKS at the thought of recounting the violent controversy which brought Zwingli into opposition with Luther. The two interlocutors measured up to each other well. Their writings shaped for centuries to come those portions of Christendom which followed them. In a book on the subject of the Zürich reformer, the pages reserved to the man of Wittenberg might well be insufficient to do him justice. It is never easy to be fair. A portrait of Luther is, however, necessary. May it not turn into a caricature!

The clash of the two theologians cannot be explained by a difference in age. They were in fact contemporaries. Luther was born on November 10, 1483, about seven weeks before his future opponent. When Fate confronted them with one another, each possessed a rich fund of ecclesiastical experience. Zwingli went through the mill of training for the secular priesthood, while Luther even in the cloister steeped himself in the study of theology. As early as 1511, his superior Staupitz, Vicar-General of the Augustinians, directed him towards a teaching vocation. On October 18, 1512, the professor Bodenstein von Carlstadt—who was to play an important part later in the discussions on the sacrament—received the monk's oath in the church of the castle. Four days later, Martin, son of the miner Hans Luther of Mansfeld, was awarded the envied title of doctor of theology and soon began to give his now famous lectures on the Psalms and the Letters to the Galatians and Romans. While the priest of Glarus was working with difficulty in the evenings, often after a harassing day, Luther devoted the whole of his time to exegesis. The two writers made contact with Greek at about the same time. The same passion to know and grip the truth made them wrestle with Holy Scripture. Both acquired and annotated the *Psalterium quincuplex* of Lefèvre d'Etaples.

Earlier we drew attention to the hypothesis of Walther Köhler which proposes to explain the divergent evolution of Luther and Zwingli by reference to their scholastic training, the former, a pupil of Gabriel Biel, being imbued with the irrationalism of his teacher, whereas the latter, in the wake of St. Thomas Aquinas, granted much more importance to the light of reason. But does university teaching exercise such power over the student? Does not he quite often react by taking the opposite point of view from that of the lectures he has heard? To quote only one point, was not Luther a decided supporter of predestination whereas Biel defended free will? Did not Zwingli deviate on this same point from Erasmus, whom he passionately admired? The theological student of today still sees numerous theses put before him: some he rejects, others he adopts. If he has at his command a certain breadth of choice, the responsibility for the mysterious discrimination which he makes is in the last resort his own. The choice or the rejection of an intellectual guide depends above all on temperament, on inexplicable sympathies, on the instinctive need to take a new line, sometimes on circumstances.

More than the lectures attended in early days by Luther and Zwingli, difference of upbringing and environment may be the factor which properly explains certain options. Luther several times complained of the excessive severity of his parents. His childhood was passed against a background of harshness which is quite alien to that of Zwingli. Again, the relative isolation of the cloister, the withdrawal into himself, undoubtedly focused the attention of the Saxon monk on the problem of personal salvation. More strongly than Zwingli, he felt the need for some external source of assurance which would deliver him from the inner conflicts in which he was plunged. Zwingli, on the other hand, although tortured by the consciousness of sin, never abdicated his concern for a whole people whose moral and spiritual level he wished to raise. The Holy Communion of Zwingli is not limited to a solemn assurance of pardon, to a redemptive sign which is the bearer of new life. It implies an engagement in the service of Christ and neighbour, the ultimate origin of which—apart from its evangelical basis— is to be found in the ever alert social concern of its promoter.

But the essential factor in the notorious dispute remains the personality of these two proclaimers of the faith. The books that were read in the course of the discussion, as we shall see, made their contribution. Events themselves, and the clash of mind with mind—which does not always shed new light—played their part. None the less, the eucharistic controversy plunges its roots deep into the very hearts of the two believers. In the inner personal reality of meditation and emotion, the Christian with all his subjectivity seeks to find his way as he explores the pages of Holy Scripture. The great certainties are expressed in an individual soul which never exactly resembles another soul. The revelation condescends to indwell vessels of clay, as St. Paul bears witness in an unforgettable warning.

The dramatic conversion of Luther, the sharpness of his spiritual torments, the intense joy which again and again swept away his clinging sadness, classes him among those geniuses whose extraordinary spiritual power is accompanied by a faint mental imbalance. He belongs to the race of mystics in the sense in which the term connotes a special temperament. His exquisite fineness of sensibility is coupled with a formidable violence. "Grace does not eliminate nature" (*Gratia non tollit naturam*)—the theological maxim recurs at once to the mind of anyone who seeks to fathom the mysteries of this extraordinary character. E. G. Schwiebert, one of his most recent biographers, reminds us of the sympathy which he evoked in all who met him. Students, simple people, eminent men, cultured persons—all in turn felt the fascination of his winsome personality. Philip Melanchthon, shortly after settling at Wittenberg, confessed: "If there is one thing on this earth which I love, it is the studies of Martin and his pious writings; but above all else, I love Martin himself."

The memory of the reformer was exceptional, his mind capable of the most audacious new insights. Setting out from scholasticism as his point of departure, by means of Holy Scripture he forged a new theological language. A musician and poet, he was gifted with a rare dramatic sense which was constantly of great use to him in his preaching. His faith was direct and simple, like that of a child. The humanist Urban Rhegius, who heard him pray aloud, was deeply moved by the experience. When necessary, he obeyed in spite of danger, resting on the strength of Jesus Christ. "I would go to Worms even if there were as many devils as there are tiles on the roof-tops." This force, Schwiebert notes, was accompanied by weak health. The mortifications to which he was subjected in the cloister, overwork and strain, the constant nervous tension which drove him on, made him irascible. He suffered cruelly from the divisions which rent the reformation. Hardly had he undergone the supreme test of the Diet of Worms, when he found himself obliged to fight against former allies. The struggle grew sterner. Luther became intolerant.

In the Augustinian monastery he experienced, and in the power of the Gospel overcame, crises of conscience which were characterized by "a formidable violence" and the reality of which is recognized by the catholic historian, Cristiani. Doubts and fears, the "desire to hate and blaspheme against God" of which he accused himself in his confessions to Staupitz, were dispelled; but after the period of joyous relaxation during which he wrote the works which became the basis of protestantism, anxiety emerged again in this too sensitive soul. If Martin no longer doubted God and His love, he tended to see the devil and his fiends almost everywhere at work. His letters are distinguished by a curious mixture of tenderness, hope, and bitterness. When in 1527 were published the principal books which contradicted his views, he said that he was drained of strength and overcome by a mysterious malady. "Zwingli and Oecolampadius have published their works", he wrote to Menius. "I shall not be able to read them until I have recovered. I am absolutely idle, a languishing Lazarus, a sick man in bonds to Jesus Christ."

Zwingli too was in a state of extreme tension. From 1524 to 1528, when the disputation of Berne took place, he had been untiringly militant, fighting at one and the same time against the Bishop of Constance, anabaptism, and the system of military pensions. However, he was able to control himself much better than was his antagonist. The irony which marked his polemics was always restrained. More than Luther, he was anxious about the damage which could have been inflicted on their common cause by a division which delighted the catholics. Doubtless, when caught up in the game, like some Helvetic David, he experienced pleasure at times in loosing arrows at the German Goliath. The chronic hostility of the south against the north then played a part in his opposition. However, we must not exaggerate. When Adolph Hausrath sums up the situation by saying of the two men that they resembled each other as little as the trout of the Swiss torrents resembles the nightingale of Wittenberg, he is simplifying the problem. Luther and Zwingli share the same love of God, of the Bible and of Jesus Christ. The one with revolutionary fervour, the other with prudence, were following essentially the same path.

They were at one in their determination to get rid of abuses and to return to the pure faith of primitive Christianity. Their major disagreement concerned the nature of the eucharist. Apart from this question, there existed also secondary divergences between them, relative to what Luther called the *adiaphora*: indifferent matters. Lutheran churches retained the crucifix and the organ. The chorale was an integral part of the German reformation. Zwingli, on the other hand, emptied the Zürich churches of all pictures and statues, and eliminated the music of the mass without allowing any congregational hymns to replace it. It would be absurd to conclude that therefore his faith was inferior to that of Luther. The difference between the two men was situated, not on the level of the soul meditating the challenge of Christ's commands and promises, but on the level of feeling. The ancient ritual, the mysterious darkness of a cathedral, the flicker of altar lights, were closely bound up with the faith of the German reformer. Zwingli wished his own faith to be naked, divested of all the ornaments of the past. This is the eternal quarrel of the Ancients and the Moderns transposed on to a religious plane.

CHAPTER TWENTY-NINE

Preliminaries of the Quarrel

IN THE ENORMOUS volumes which he has devoted to a
study of the conflict between the reformers under the title
Zwingli und Luther (the first published in 1924, the second
in 1953) Walther Köhler has endeavoured to define in the first
place the position of the two theologians before the direct
clash of Marburg took place. The early writings of Luther do
not contain the theory of consubstantiation. Certain texts,
in particular the *Sermon on the New Covenant* (1520), are
extremely close to Zwinglianism, though never quite identical
with it. Luther emphasizes the importance of faith in
the reception of the sacrament. God takes the initiative in the
covenant relationship; man must accept with gratitude the
promise of salvation. The words of institution, "Take, eat . . .
drink ye all of this" form the principal part of the mass, which
is a memorial service and a sign of forgiveness. "Do this in
memory of me," said the Lord. The Lord's Supper provides
a confirmation of faith, "for, since we, poor men, live in the
domain of the five senses, we must possess at least one
external sign in addition to words". This sign is a sacrament
—that is, "it must be an external sign and yet contain and
signify something spiritual, so that by means of the external
we are led to the spiritual".

Such affirmations are very near to the position which one
day the Zürich reformer was to adopt. Do they in fact express
it? In spite of the identical terms, this is not certain. The
special purpose of the sign seems to be above all to fortify
faith. Luther compares the bread and the wine to the rain-
bow after the flood, and to the circumcision of Abraham.

He also likens them to the seal which the testator affixes to his will. But the two species are "His true body and His true blood".

On his side, the Zwingli of the years 1522 to 1524, while fighting against the conception of the mass as a repeated sacrifice, does not absolutely reject the doctrine of the real presence. Köhler does not rest his argument solely on the sixty-seven theses, the authority of which is debatable, since Zwingli later declared with regard to them that he had taken care to spare the susceptibilities of his hearers. The quotations from the letter of June 15 to Thomas Wyttenbach have greater weight. Zwingli's former master, in a letter which is now lost, had asked his pupil about his understanding of the sacrament. Although in his reply the priest of the Great Minster expressly repudiates transubstantiation, he exclaims: "The eucharist is eaten where there is faith." Communion is particularly necessary to the weak who without it would fail to perceive the body and blood of Christ. The *infirmi* must communicate more frequently than the strong; "the latter will come of themselves to spiritual food". These quotations, despite their relative obscurity, certainly seem to suggest that for Zwingli the principle of a spiritual eating was not to be rejected. The strong also receive in themselves the body and blood of Christ. But this reception does not depend on the frequency of communions. It belongs to the sphere of the Spirit. The firm believer, temporarily absent from the altar, is constantly nourished by the sacrifice of Jesus Christ.

Physical consumption of the elements is thus not indispensable to spiritual feeding; such seems to be the conception of the Zürich reformer in 1523. Köhler notes that the vocabulary which he uses—and which Luther uses also—very probably stems from Erasmus whom both reformers read. Similarly, part of their ideas. The distinction between the strong and the weak was dear to the author of the *Praise of Folly*. The stress on the covenant (*testamentum*), the *memoria*, the term *symbolum* are characteristic of Erasmus. But, from the start, in spite of related modes of expression and a certain haziness of ideas, Zwingli stresses the subjective element in communion, while Luther remains attached to the thought that the vehicle chosen by Christ conveys objective grace.

Is it necessary to dwell on the ceaseless perpetuation of such a divergence? When the protestant of today approaches the holy table and returns from it strengthened in his faith, if he tries to analyse his experience it is very difficult for him to determine precisely whether grace has been dispensed to him *by* the sacrament, or *on the occasion of* the sacrament. He has taken the bread and the wine, and has turned his mind and spirit towards the merciful Saviour. Jesus has nourished him with the divine presence and love, with the radiant certitude of forgiveness. At what point exactly has the spiritual transfusion been effected? Is it reasonable to attempt to fathom these mysteries? Does not the scalpel of reason sever realities which God has united when it makes dangerous incisions? Is not the terrible eucharistic controversy one of those that are dear to the heart of theologians, but which they would do well to avoid?

It was in 1524 that the great conflict about the eucharist and its mysterious uncertainties broke out. Others than Luther and Zwingli must bear the responsibility for the first skirmishes. In Germany, the monk of Wittenberg first of all clashed with the theologian who had formerly welcomed him to the rank of doctor—namely, Bodenstein von Carlstadt, known especially by his second name. At first, the ex-professor had resisted the ideas of his young colleague. But the eloquence of Luther finally tore him away from Thomism. Following an academic discussion of September, 1516, Carlstadt burnt what he had worshipped and devoted himself thereafter to advocating enthusiastically the cause of an evangelicalism closely linked to Augustinianism. He very quickly went further than his master and sharply attacked Eck, who was later to be the able antagonist of Luther at the disputation of Leipzig. In 1519, he accompanied his colleague to the town of the Duke George, and at his side took part in the famous contest which disclosed for the first time the perspective of a schism within the Roman Church. But, by the side of Luther, Carlstadt showed himself to be singularly inferior. Martin was indeed the head of the reformation movement. In the eyes of the whole of Germany, he was its brain and inspiration, and he brilliantly proved that this was so at Worms in 1520.

The part of second fiddle is difficult to play. When Luther, condemned by the anxiety of the Elector of Saxony to withdraw to the Wartburg, inevitably left to his colleague the leadership of the church in Saxony, Carlstadt, though full of good intentions, clearly proved his incapacity. On June 21 he took it into his head to propose an academic discussion in which he offered to sustain the thesis that every priest ought to be a married man. He also asked—which was much more acceptable—that priests living with a concubine should be compelled to marry legally. A few months later he went further and demanded the abolition of organs and images, and with no regard for the reservations felt by the City Council proceeded to put his ideas into execution. Paintings were torn to shreds, statues dashed to pieces. At Christmas 1521, without a word of warning, he celebrated the mass without vestments and introduced administration in both kinds. More and more he came under the thumb of a group of fanatics led by a weaver, Claus Storch, who prided himself on having seen a vision of the angel Gabriel in which the angel said to him: "You will sit on my throne." The prophets of Zwickau, as they were called, not only disparaged all organization, but with them the written Word itself lost its primacy in favour of special revelations of the Holy Ghost. Under their influence, the reformation was being transformed into a new Montanist movement.

Luther hastily left his retreat in the Wartburg. On Sunday March 8, 1522, he once more mounted the pulpit of the parish church of Wittenberg. By a series of sermons, he restored order to unsettled minds. He insisted that everything should be done methodically. Monastic vows, images, liturgy, church rites of marriage and funeral services,—all these things, he claimed, belong to the *adiaphora*, to the category of indifferent matters. Many usages may legitimately be changed, but it is not sufficient to destroy. By the power of his word alone—eight consecutive days of sermons—he restored confidence. Carlstadt, disowned and embittered, left the town. Was it jealousy or vacillation of mind? The man who once had been shy and backward-looking renounced his academic degrees, deliberately dressed as a peasant, and harshly criticized the university he had abandoned. Does not God reveal Himself to the sucking child, rather than to the wise of this world? Furthermore, he began to write with a kind of fury. In the autumn of 1524, five short works signed by him appeared, one after the other, on the subject of the eucharist. He attacked the doctrine of the Real Presence. Christ, he said, was not in the sacrament. The latter cannot therefore guarantee the forgiveness of sins. When He declared "This is my body," Jesus, at the Last Supper, was designating Himself.

The ideas of the one-time philosopher rapidly spread throughout Germany. In the south, in particular, they found a warm welcome. At Zürich Felix Manz made himself their advocate. Zwingli read at least one work of Carlstadt's, and although in agreement with him on many points, on the whole deplored the little volume: "The book pleased me in some places and displeased me in others," he confided to Matthew Alber. His criticism was probably directed more against the tone of the work than against its ideas. Ulrich personally valued the sacrament as a sign intended to reassure troubled consciences.

Luther was annoyed to see Carlstadt, towards whom he had behaved with generosity in 1522, now attacking his doctrine. This first clash led him to formulate it more precisely, and, faced by a theologian who denied the objective reality of sacramental grace, to emphasize the latter. Moreover, the end of 1524 saw the beginning of the troubles which came to a climax, in 1525, with the peasants' revolt. For Luther, this was a source of bitter disillusionment. The Gospel was becoming for the agricultural workers a pretext for repudiating the overlordship of the landowners. If we bear in mind the bond which linked the spiritual leaders of the revolt, the prophets of Zwickau and the anabaptists, to the new rising, we shall understand better the hostility which the German reformer showed towards Zwingli. At Zürich as at Strasburg, the doctrine of the Real Presence was rejected and images abolished. In the eyes of Luther, all these people without exception formed part of the same diabolic clique.

Thus the quarrel between Zürich and Wittenberg opened in an atmosphere of violence. From the very first, Luther considered Zwingli to be in league with the devil. "You would not believe", he confides to a correspondent, "to what extent the dogma of Carlstadt is gaining ground and everywhere attracting support. . . . Now, in Switzerland, look at Zwingli, Leo Jud, and many others who are thinking like him and asserting that there is nothing but bread in the eucharist." *Dogma of Carlstadt!* Zwingli is classed and judged before he has even been read. He is included in the same burst of anger and scorn as the ex-archdeacon of Wittenberg.

In 1525, Zwingli had published by Froschauer the letter on the subject of the eucharist which he had addressed to Matthew Alber. His friend of Basle, Oecolampadius, also entered the lists with an important study: *De genuina verborum domini hoc est corpus meum expositione* (the true explanation of the words of the Lord, this is my body). Both men were distressed by the conflict which threatened to rend protestantism in its very infancy. They studiously avoided any suggestion which might have offended Luther. Oecolampadius' book takes the form of a discussion of a famous medieval work, the *Sentences* of Peter Lombard. But in the main body of the work, where the name of Luther is not mentioned, the distinction between the Roman doctrine of *transubstantiation* (change in the substance of the bread, only the appearance of the host remaining) and *impanation* (the reality of a spiritual presence of Christ mingled with the bread) is reduced to a minimum. Luther affirmed the ubiquity of Christ's body. Christ is everywhere. Hence we receive Him with the bread. Oecolampadius rejected this idea and declared that he supported the theses of his friend of Zürich, Zwingli.

From that time on, the whole of theological Germany took sides for or against the doctrine of the Real Presence. The theory of consubstantiation caused much ink to be spilt. Erasmus himself intervened and supported Luther who "on this point at least has respected the catholic church". By the side of the illustrious protagonists, theologians now forgotten had their say. Luther maintained a pained silence. His partisans defended his ideas: "Zwingli and Oecolampadius", he wrote in October, 1525, "are attacking us; I will leave to others the duty of answering them, or I will scorn them. Satan is raging." He lamented the choice made by Oecolampadius, for whom he had great esteem: "I am distressed to see Oecolampadius, that man who is so noble, falling into this slough, into these wretched thoughts which are worth nothing. It is Satan who is driving him on. May God rescue him."

CHAPTER THIRTY

Zürich against Wittenberg

THE READER WHO wishes to study in detail the eucharistic controversy of the reformation will do well to consult Walther Köhler's work to which reference has already been made: namely, *Zwingli und Luther*. A multitude of pamphlets and letters were exchanged between 1524 and 1526, which for the most part deserve to be forgotten. In this book devoted to Zwingli, our attention must be confined to what concerns him most directly. Through Oecolampadius and the Strasburg theologians, Bucer and Capito, Ulrich became aware of the ill-will of Luther towards him. The respect which he felt for the author of *Christian Liberty* restrained his pen, however. Had not Martin rescued the Church from the *Babylonian captivity*? Had he not been the first to protest against papal omnipotence? Could the reformation of Zürich have been effected had it not been for the courageous refusal of Worms?

In March, 1526, appeared a new edition of the *Syngramma*, a work by Johannes Brenz, furnished with the approbation of fourteen Swabian theologians, published for the first time in October, 1525, and written as a reply to Oecolampadius. The book now left the press, augmented by an insulting foreword which was signed by Luther. He did not condescend to refute the Swiss; that duty had devolved on Brenz. He contented himself with putting the reader on his guard against the "false prophets", the "terrible blasphemy", the "sect". The latter revealed its sad character plainly enough by the fact of its divisions. Those who denied the Real Presence counted not less than five or six heads: Zwingli,

Carlstadt, Oecolampadius, Conrad Ryss, Schwenckfeld, and
an anonymous writer of Cologne. The day would come when
Zwingli, like Carlstadt, would have to confess his error. From
the height of his grandeur, the former Augustinian crushed
his opponent. What was the use of discussing? Has not the
author victoriously elucidated all the relevant problems in
his previous writings? Besides, there is only one dilemma:
faith or the devil. The heresy of these negators is worthy of
that of Arius.

On July 8 Bucer despatched to Zürich a copy of the terrible
reprimand which threw Ulrich into consternation. Oecolampadius was the first to take up his pen. His reply was printed
at Basle by the publisher Thomas Wolff towards the end of
the summer. But Zwingli could no longer feel satisfied by
communication through the interposition of others. Luther's
disavowal stigmatized him in the eyes of Swiss public
opinion. A few months after the Diet of Baden, where the
catholic party had branded him as a heretic, the confirmation
of the verdict by the originator of the reformation was
especially painful to him.

In January, 1526, Ulrich had published a *Brief Instruction concerning the Last Supper of Christ*. He decided to
take up his pen again and this time to address himself directly
to Luther so as to bring their views into immediate confrontation. Moreover, it was rumoured that Luther was planning
to attack him. He felt it would be better to try to forestall
the storm and to reach an understanding before it was too
late. At the end of March there appeared at Zürich the *Amica
Exegesis* (friendly explanation). On April 1 a copy was sent
to Wittenberg. In effect, the colloquy of Marburg was beginning two years before its actual date.

The work begins with a few lines of apology. Zwingli
explains the reasons for his long silence. He would have
preferred to spare the world the spectacle of a disagreement
which is vexing to him and at which the papists jeer. Luther,
however, has not been so reserved. Hence silence is no longer
justified. The Church must avoid subjecting herself to a new
yoke. Christian liberty presupposes frank explanations. Did

not Paul once openly oppose Peter (Gal. 2: 11)? I believe you, says Ulrich in essence, capable of reading me. My work will expound to you in a friendly fashion my point of view and my arguments which are as yet unknown to you. I appeal from the angry and denunciatory Luther to the conciliatory and calmer Luther.

After this *captatio benevolentiae*, Zwingli develops the idea which we have already briefly expounded in our summary of the *De vera et falsa religione*. The "is" of "this is my body" must be taken as meaning *significat*, viz. "this represents my body". If it is affirmed that consolation comes from ritual eating, then we deprive faith of that role. There cannot be two sources of salvation, the death of Christ and the sacramental enjoyment of His body. "Luther, you have on your side the letter [of the Gospel] but not the Spirit." Some closely argued periods deal with the distinction of the two natures in Christ, using it to shed light on several texts and to ridicule the doctrine of the ubiquity of Christ's body. Ulrich throws into the debate some Johannine verses, such as: "I will take you to myself that where I am you may be also" (John 14: 3). "I will take you to myself, that where I am. . . . " he pleads, concerns the human nature of Jesus ". . . for, if the meaning is His divine nature, He was always with them. You claim, Luther, that Christ's body is everywhere? It should follow that wherever the humanity of Christ is, there the elect are also. Since, according to you, Christ is everywhere and fills all things, the elect ought also to be everywhere! . . . " Pitiless logic of a man who does not allow himself to be taken in. What with Luther was essentially a mystical feeling begins to look like a stupid blunder when turned over and over on the grill of Zwingli's caustic mentality. "If Christ is corporeally in the Last Supper, the elect are also. It is surprising that those who eat Christ do not recoil in terror from this Christ-bearer who outdoes the Colossus of Rhodes!" The body of Christ is at the right hand of God. It is useless to seek it elsewhere. "The eucharist is a rite of thanksgiving, an uplifting of the heart, a confession of faith."

The little work ends with a pressing appeal. "Our point of view will triumph", declares Ulrich, "but because of your resistance, the victory will be painfully won. Let us remember that God watches our struggle. It is not only the German people, nor even the whole of Christendom, but all ages to come until the end of time that will be our judges."

Zwingli remains loyal to his past admiration. "I marvelled to see your courage in the affair of indulgences", he exclaimed, "I who had been instructed by my master Thomas Wyttenbach to look upon Christ as the sole price paid for the forgiveness of our sins." He added that he would restrain his pen, that he would not allow it to protest against "the base letters attacking me which you have everywhere sent to your friends". "You have had the courage of a David. You were the Hercules of Christendom. You would have completely cleaned out the Augean stables if you had in addition got rid of the images used in church worship, if you had set aside the conception of a carnal eating of the body of Christ in the eucharist, and if you had perceived, in the light of the Gospel, that the doctrine of purgatory is nothing but a net intended to bring in money."

This summary suggests the tone of the work, which was passionate and ironical and yet conciliatory. Zwingli did not wish to burn his boats, but he was absolutely certain that he was right. The clash of great minds is terrible to see when they are goaded on by an unreserved conviction. In spite of its careful wording, the *Amica Exegesis* sounded like an ultimatum. Luther was implored before men and before God to discuss the theses of his colleague. By a most lamentable coincidence, the adjurations of Ulrich crossed the pamphlet which Martin had just written. "May these words of Christ—'this is my body'—subsist for ever. Against sectarian fanatics."

To the copy of his work which he sent to Wittenberg, Zwingli added a personal letter which, in its candour, went far beyond the message of the book. In this he openly complained of Luther's attitude: "Why have you written to the prince of Hesse intimating that the matter ought to be decided at the point of the sword? This was tantamount to abandoning free discussion for the use of force. No man is omniscient, Luther no more than anyone else. While Zwingli was appealing to the basic unity of the reformation as against the papists, on May 4 Luther was pouring his anger into the bosom of Spalatin: "Zwingli has written me a letter full of pride, calumny, obstinacy, and hatred, and breathing almost total wickedness, all this under the veil of words in appearance the kindest and best." One would like to find in what he wrote a question mark, a reservation, a charitable supposition. In vain. The poor Zürich reformer was knocking his head against a wall. His attempt to engage an objective discussion merely maddened the lion of Wittenberg, who roared furiously against this new Carlstadt. Even had he been able still to do so, he would not have struck out of his book (which appeared at the end of April) a single argument, nor one unjust accusation.

The work of the German reformer was based, however, on a more or less serious study of what was published between 1525 and 1527. He read the writings of Oecolampadius, the *Apology* of Bucer, and the *Commentarius de vera et falsa religione*. His judgment of his adversaries was categorical. Their thesis was that of the devil himself. "The devil never slumbers," he sighed. In fighting against Zwingli and his disciples, it was Satan that Luther was attacking. Their explanation of the Gospel word *est* by *significat* was mere devilish pride. The objectivity and calmness of the debate suffered, it is hardly necessary to say, from this initial judgment. For Luther, his interlocutors would never allow themselves to be enlightened. God rejected them.

Luther's line of argument was over-simple. Only the bare text of the Gospels counted, he maintained. A child of seven knows the meaning of *this is my body*. All the spectacles of all the scholars in the world would not discover any other meaning in the Lord's declaration. The text "remains firm as a rock." I was not aware, he cried out, that when confronted by a verse of the Bible, it was necessary to appeal to reason and accept only what reason authorizes. For the author of *Christian Liberty*, Zwinglianism amounted to a refusal of faith. Ulrich did not wish to, or could not believe, the miracle of the real presence. His interpretation was the fruit of a lack of faith, of rationalism. Martin attacked the argument drawn from the creed, *Christ is at the right hand of God*. It cannot be a question of a "golden chair" to which the Son is chained at the Father's side. The "right hand" designates the almighty power of God which Christ has now received.

But this was twisting the argument. For Zwingli and his friends, the Risen Christ, in virtue of His divine nature, dwelt in the bosom of the Father, closely united to Him and invested with all His attributes. It was to His body of flesh that they refused the privilege of ubiquity. The divine Christ for them was everywhere, while the body of the terrestrial Jesus remained confined to heaven.

The Zwinglians made a great point of the verse: "the flesh avails nothing" (John 6: 63). Luther retorted that if you must have an absolute opposition of spirit and flesh, the incarnation itself will thereby be called in question. If the flesh avails nothing, did Mary really bear the Saviour in her womb? Must the terrestrial life of Christ be considered useless?

From the early church Fathers, the reformer extracted texts counterbalancing those which Oecolampadius had discovered in Augustine or Tertullian. Irenaeus, Cyprian, other passages of Augustine were thrown into the discussion to confirm the doctrine of quasi-physical consumption. The idea of the eucharist as a solemn affirmation of faith was ruthlessly repudiated. Thus understood, the sacrament no longer bound man to God, but degenerated to the rank of "pure service of the belly and gluttony."

The Zwinglians labelled the Lutheran conception as "cannibalistic". Luther reacted sharply to the reproach and in order to vindicate his position wrote the most interesting pages of his little work. In regard to them, Köhler notes that he is trying to purify the concept of consubstantiation. "We, poor sinners, are not mad enough to think that the body of Christ inheres in the bread in any coarse, visible fashion, like bread in a basket or wine in a glass." God has at His disposal more than one way of securing the reality of a presence.

Christ infuses His body into the bread like the Creator of bodies that He is. Hence the consumption is spiritual, not an "external and carnal" eating. It is the same with regard to vision. When the shepherds and Simeon saw the child Jesus, they did not greet the babe of flesh merely, but discerned in Him the Saviour of the world. The Word of God conferred on them the necessary intuition. Spiritual vision or sacramental eating are therefore equivalent to the enjoyment of a spiritual reality, in spite of its carnal vesture. By this line of thought, are we not, however, discreetly returning to the doctrine of transubstantiation? Luther, like Zwingli, clings nevertheless in the last analysis to the sustaining Word of God. "The mouth", the German again writes, "carnally eats the Body of Christ . . . but the heart seizes the Word through the apprehension of faith, and eats it spiritually."

In the eyes of the ordinary man, the painful discussion degrades the solemn rite rather than explains it. Each theologian went on arguing out his thoughts, Luther as much as Zwingli, as much as formerly did Ratramnus, Paschasius Radbertus, or Thomas Aquinas.

Köhler thinks that Luther in his reply to the Zwinglians so much emphasized the spiritual character of sacramental consumption that in consequence he spiritualized the Body of Christ, rather like the monophysites of the 5th century. The flesh of which he makes himself the defender in the end ceases to have any carnal element about it. Zwingli's point of view, on the other hand, is said to have been close to that of Nestorius. In Zwingli's conception, Christ was so closely identified with a real human body that the idea of receiving into oneself His flesh would not imply any degree of spiritual communion. However that may be, hardly had the volume reached Switzerland when a hue and cry was raised against it.

Oecolampadius spoke of it as a "poisonous work". Zwingli when he had read as far as the sixth page wrote to Vadian asserting that the whole thing was nothing but a tissue of "lies, insults, calumnies, hypocrisy, and deceit". However, Luther's work was not without erudition. At the pressing request of Oecolampadius and the Strasburg theologians, Zwingli at once set to work to refute the advocate of consubstantiation. At the same time there arrived from Paris the quite considerable work of the catholic theologian, John Clichtove, *De sacramento eucharistiae*, while from Cologne were flying about all over Germany copies of a writing by the English bishop Fisher, of Rochester, *De veritate corporis et sanguinis Christi in eucharistia adversus Johannem Oecolampadium*. The whole of Christendom was meddling in the quarrel of the two reformers. Moreover, in the eyes of the British prelate, Luther and Zwingli were both heretical, the one every whit as much as the other.

Whilst Oecolampadius was drafting his reply to the champions of transubstantiation—it left the press on June 8 —Zwingli was formulating his own. The new work was dedicated to Luther's patron, the Elector John of Saxony. The letter which constitutes the foreword bears the date, June 20. The title is a manifesto in itself: *That these words of Jesus Christ: "this is my body which is given for you," will always have their ancient and sole meaning, and that Martin Luther with his last book has neither explained nor proved his interpretation and that of the pope.*

To the violence of the Saxon, the Swiss replied with a note of biting and often very subtle irony. He began by wishing his interlocutor "grace and peace from God through Jesus Christ . . . who for our salvation suffered death and departed from this world, as far as His flesh was concerned, then ascended into heaven where He lives until the time when he will return at the last day . . .". "I tell you this", he goes on to explain, "so that you may understand that He dwells in our hearts by faith, and not by corporeal eating through our mouths." But this greeting was intended also to give the book a Christian opening, so as to avoid starting by talking

of the devil, as Luther had done. Zwingli undertook to discuss the matter with restraint, again unlike his opponent:
"In one place you twist the meaning of our words, in another
you falsify Scripture, in yet another you fail to understand
it. . . ." The gentleness of his reply is, as can be seen,
relative only, although Ulrich pledged himself not to use
terms like "fanatic, devil, heretic, murderer, rebel, hypo-
crite" and such-like pleasant descriptions. He affirmed that
he recognized only the authority of Scripture, that he was
not fighting against the devil, but against the flesh which
everywhere he opposed to the spirit. He reminded the ex-
monk, who boasted of having alone brought back the Church
out of darkness into light, of such names as those of Erasmus,
Lorenzo Valla, Reuchlin, and Pellican, whose works had
made possible the present spiritual revival. Glory must above
all be rendered to Him who stood above Paul and Apollos
(1 Cor. 3), to the God who gave the increase. Luther's merit
was none the less indisputable. The humanists had not dared
to attack the papal tyranny. In this direction, Luther had
been a pioneer, worthy of comparison with David against
Goliath.

Thus the heat of the debate did not blind Ulrich. He
realizes what he owes to the militant champion of Worms,
as also to the cultured scholar of Basle. But the greatness of
neither of these men compelled him to agree with them at
every point. "You are only one Ajax, one Diomede, among
many Nestors, Ulysses and Diomedes", he flung at the
proud Saxon. Ulrich also questioned the pessimism of Luther.
You say that the devil is in control of the world. No; God
alone reigns and governs all things by His providence. You
allege that no heretic can be converted. But you have
yourself turned aside from faith in the merit of works to
come to rest in salvation by Christ alone.

As for the doctrinal discussion, Zwingli resumes in German
the essential arguments developed in Latin in the *Amica
Exegesis*. On several points, he formulates his thought more
precisely by reaction to that of Luther. Scripture must
be read with careful thought. It contains some apparent

contradictions. But it is not Scripture which is inconsistent; it is we who lack understanding. One text should be read in the light of another. Thus the words "this is my body" can only be properly understood if they are connected with what follows: "which is broken for you". The bread then becomes the symbol or the memorial of the Body of Christ which was given (once for all upon the cross). In order to prove that "is" corresponds to *significat*, Ulrich quotes several similar texts of scripture, thus Genesis 41: 26 "the seven good cows *are* seven years of plenty"; Matt. 11: 14, "John the Baptist *was* Elijah"; Exod. 12: 27, "it *is* the passing over of the Lord"; John 15: 5, "I *am* the vine, you are the branches."

Zwingli also emphasized the distinction between the two natures. It was in virtue of His divine nature that Christ knew all things (John 17: 25) and by reason of His human nature that He did not know the date of the end of the world (Mark 13: 32). The God in Him performed miracles and spoke the words of eternal life (John 7: 16) while His humanity thirsted, shuddered, was beaten, and died. The conclusion is inescapable: for Ulrich, what nourishes the soul is not the Body of Christ, but the God indwelling Him. This interesting digression should be read if we would estimate the injustice of the reproach of rationalism so often levelled at the Zürich reformer. The latter in fact so deeply revered the divinity of the Saviour that he feared to depreciate it by granting too much importance to the body of the incarnate Lord. *It is the spirit that gives life, the flesh is of no avail.*

The contemporary reader will regret that Zwingli did not develop at greater length the strange mystery of a flesh which is the messenger of the Spirit. It is the incarnate and suffering man who reveals the mystery of the God who is love. Were it not for the body broken and the blood shed, should we know that God loves us as we do know it since, and in the light of, Calvary? Moving exclusively on the limited plane of the eucharist, the debate restricted the extraordinary fertility of the incarnational idea. How can a body become the source of spiritual sustenance? The paradox is accomplished in the world of the spirit where a soul is prostrated, through the sacrament, before the Saviour on the cross. This is why, despite the difference of their theological terminology, catholics and protestants can alike leave the altar or the communion table strengthened in their inner man after reception of the host or the symbolic bread.

Zwingli's treatise ended with a prayer: I beg you humbly, Luther, to abandon your wrath, "for if you are Christ's, we also are His."

In his letters of August 20 and 21, Luther manifests surprise not to have received the work of the Swiss theologian which southern Germany was already discussing. On October 27 his correspondence contains his verdict addressed to the gentle Melanchthon: "I consider Zwingli to be worthy of a holy hatred, for his mind moves in a rash and mad way in contradiction to the Word of God." He very quickly thought of refuting the Zürich pamphlet. On December 29 he was at work. By the end of March, 1528, his work was completed. Yet he did not hope to have any influence on his antagonists who "have turned aside from the light and love darkness to the point of sheer madness".

While, at Wittenberg, Luther was labouring to draft his *Great Confession concerning the Holy Eucharist*, Ulrich was experiencing at Berne the success which we have described. The future of the reformation in Switzerland was assured through the adhesion of this powerful republic. The event did not delight Luther in the least, on the contrary: "Zwingli has been brought back from Berne in triumph, with an escort of a thousand men", he wrote on March 7 to Gabriel Zwilling. "He has carried off a notable victory and is puffed up by it; but soon will come confusion and perdition."

In his new book, Luther fought against four adversaries at one and the same time—Zwingli, Oecolampadius, Schwenckfeld, and Wyclif. It was with the first of these in particular that he was annoyed; he spared his ally of Basle, and condemned the last two only inferentially.

The Saxon monk concerned himself solely with the last book which had appeared at Zürich, ignoring the *Amica*

Exegesis. Like an old refrain, he repeats the affirmation: Zwingli is an instrument of the devil. "I write not against flesh and blood, but against the devil and his host." Oecolampadius vainly criticized this mania for explaining everything by reference to demoniacal influence. Luther would not yield an inch. He declared that he relished a peculiar delight in combating Satan through the persons of his servants. "I confess that as far as I am concerned, I hold Zwingel [*sic*] with all his doctrine to be a non-Christian, for he does not believe nor teach correctly one single article of the Christian faith." He could hardly have gone further than that.

As a proof of his accusation, the reformer of Wittenberg quoted the fact that on several points Zwingli and his friends were in disagreement among themselves. He berated them as though he himself shared in catholic unity. A poor argument, moreover, which every church ought to abandon after twenty centuries of schisms of every kind. Unity stems from love; it does not consist in a slavish identity of doctrine on every point.

Such an atmosphere of peevishness and scorn precluded any serious study of an antagonist's viewpoint. With towering pride and summary dismissal, Luther rejected in totality the demonstrations of Zwingli and Oecolampadius. The pair, he asserted, had not brought forward a single argument legitimating the belief that "is" is the equivalent of "signifies". Paradoxically enough, Luther supported his philippic by invoking the authority of Pope Nicolas [*sic*] who formerly condemned Berengar of Tours.[1]

This new diatribe from the pontiff of Wittenberg contained nothing worthy of the attention of Oecolampadius and Zwingli. With massive emphasis, Luther affirmed once again the miracle of a corporeal presence of Christ in the elements of bread and wine which remained substantially bread and wine, the whole thing being "contrary to all reason". A supernatural union was indeed effected. The communicant who ate real bread ate at the same time the real body of

---

[1] Berengar (*c.* 1000-8) was in fact condemned by Pope Gregory VII on account of his "spiritualism".

Christ. If I take a bag containing a hundred crowns, and say: "There are one hundred crowns," the word is applicable both to the bag and to the money it contains. In this work, Luther for the first time explicitly defined the doctrine which he had so far only implicitly professed, namely the consubstantiality of the bread and the body, of the wine and the blood.

The two Swiss theologians, who had been attacked together, decided after a little hesitation to make a joint reply. Zwingli was given the task of writing a letter to the princes of Saxony and Hesse, while Oecolampadius undertook the duty of a doctrinal study. They both began drafting their documents about the end of June, 1528. The work appeared in September under the title: *Concerning the volume of Doctor Martin Luther, called Confession, two replies from John Oecolampadius and Ulrich Zwingli.* Writing to Blarer on July 21, Ulrich had promised to avoid all violence. Did he succeed in this? His judgment was extremely severe. He asserted that Luther did not know the meaning of impartiality; he was abandoned by God, since he began with the devil and ended with the devil. His book was one big lie. Zwingli himself admitted that he had only skimmed this volume from the pen of his opponent, racing as he did against time. His friend Leo Jud pointed out to him the most important pages, while Henry Bullinger furnished him with the patristic quotations.

It would be out of place here to summarize in detail the arguments of Zwingli or of Oecolampadius, which, moreover, in part overlap. The subject, now broached for the third time, had lost its freshness. In spite of his hurried preparation, the Zürich reformer at times took the discussion quite far forward, calling to his rescue the scholastic distinction between various kinds of identity. A careful discrimination, he said, must be made between *real* identity (*realis*) and *essential, personal* or *rational* identity. As concerning the eucharist, it is only the latter kind of identity which is in question, and it may also be described as *denominative* or *metaphorical*. As France may be said to make war when its king goes off on a campaign, so Christ *is* the cornerstone, the cup *is* the New Covenant. The Bible uses figurative language. These were new variations of an old theme, that of tropes, which had already played its part in this sacramental polemic. Oecolampadius pointed out that when Christ said, "This is my body which is given for you," it was more beautiful than such an expression as: "This is my body which is martyred for you." Was the eucharistic discussion being reduced to a question of literary taste?

Luther had added to his reflections on the eucharist a confession of faith based on the Apostles' Creed. In it he solemnly proclaimed his veneration for the Holy Trinity, and his certainty that Christ is truly God and truly man. Mary was not merely the Mother of Jesus, as the Nestorians affirmed, but the Mother also of the Son of God. Martin condemned monasteries and impious vows, while extolling the priesthood, marriage, and temporal authority. The Holy Spirit, which is the fruit of faith, is externally conferred by the preaching of the Gospel, baptism and the sacrament of the altar. The church of the popes, indulgences, purgatory, the invocation of saints, extreme unction, marriage and penance regarded as sacraments, were all repudiated, while images, bells, sacerdotal vestments, candles were described as belonging to the category of indifferent matters. Both Oecolampadius and Zwingli in turn extracted from this list of affirmations a number with which they declared themselves in perfect agreement. At the moment when, once more, they rejected the Lutheran theory of the eucharist, they considered it important to stress the bonds which on other points united the two branches of the reformation.

As had happened several times already in the course of the controversy, a number of lesser figures entered the lists. Schwenckfeld, Valentine Crautwald, John Rurer, and yet others intervened in 1528 and 1529, either for or against Luther. Some, such as John Other and the Strasburg theologians Bucer and Capito, tried to discover some ground of agreement, striking out in ways which anticipated the position of Calvin.

CHAPTER THIRTY-ONE

The Strasburg Mediators and Philip of Hesse

BOOKS THROWN INTO circulation may provoke a degree of agitation which their authors do not always foresee. In the solitary excitement of composition, replies are silently formulated on the paper. But hardly is the printer's ink dry, when the world seizes on the scathing phrases, grows indignant, roars with laughter, or applauds. Luther's vehement attacks constantly found toadies in Wittenberg. At Zürich and Basle, Oecolampadius and Zwingli received the cheers of their friends.

At Strasburg, which had been won over to the reformation since 1524, the ex-Dominican Martin Bucer was following with anxiety the development of the controversy. Born in 1491, he owed a great deal to Luther, whose ideas he had espoused as early as 1518, but a warm sympathy linked him with Zwingli, whom he accompanied at the debate in Berne. A born organizer, gifted with diplomatic tact, a curious mixture of delicate feeling, pliability, and independence, he was distressed to witness the emergence of a division which endangered the future of the reformation. Together with his friend, Capito, who was his elder by a dozen years, and provost of the Church of St. Thomas, he made an attempt to calm the disastrous strife. In the last analysis, were not Wittenberg and Zürich colliding over a mere matter of words? Did the conception of the eucharist professed by Luther differ so very much from Zwingli's? Bucer and Capito read again those writings of the Saxon theologian which had convulsed catholicism and in which Luther, as yet ignorant of Zwingli, defined his ideas in confrontation with Rome alone.

In April, 1528, Bucer published a review of the Berne disputation, where the question of the eucharist had been debated at some length. He felt it opportune to return to this in an attempt to reconcile the opposing parties. Chapter 6 of St. John he submitted to a new investigation. Christ described Himself as the true bread which feeds us. Wherever He is recognized as Saviour, He sustains the soul. Jesus is speaking metaphorically when He invites men to eat His body. "How many, dear God, eat the eucharistic bread who, all their lives long, have felt nothing of the presence of Christ." Even a child could see that *credere in eum* (to believe in Him) and *edere* (to eat) are synonymous. Did not Jesus say: "He who believes in me has eternal life"? Hence the words of institution refer only to the *manducatio fidei*. The true believer verily eats the flesh of the Lord. This spiritual communion is real, but is not identifiable with the consumption of body and bread corporeally present. Again, although the bread only *signifies* the body of Christ, this symbolism does not imply the denial of a truly effectual spiritual communion. Cleverly apposite references to early Lutheran eucharistic texts enabled the Strasburg theologians to present the quarrel as resting on a colossal misunderstanding.

The peevish reply of a Lutheran fanatic, Bugenhagen, afforded Bucer the opportunity of formulating his views more precisely. Taking up his pen once more in September, 1528, he stressed the deep unity which bound together Luther, Oecolampadius, Melanchthon and Zwingli from the point of view of scriptural authority. All had the Bible. Ah! if only they could avoid falling into disputes which did not edify the Church, such as their "more than famous" controversy about the eucharist. Doubtless it was only proper to seek to discover the exact meaning of the words of the Lord. Doubtless, too, one of the two parties was in error. But if both recognized and preached Christ as our only Saviour, if they confessed, each in his own way, that Christ is present in the Lord's Supper, if they called the bread His body, was there really any grave danger in differing about the way in which the bread is His body? Again Bucer points out that everywhere Christians are being called papists, Lutherans, anabaptists, and such-like names. Those who ought to struggle with all their energy to reduce schism in fact foster it. True Christians, as much as lies in their power, try to live at peace with all men.

In another work, *Comparison or Dialogue between Dr. Luther and his adversaries on the subject of the Supper of the Lord*, published in July, 1528, Bucer, after a detailed study of the Lutheran conception, declared that he considered the Christian of a different persuasion to be his brother, even if the latter, in the fire of his enthusiasm, uttered unjust condemnations. Luther, however, failed to take a single step in the direction of securing agreement. When a moderate, Nicolas Gerbel, sent him the *Dialogus* of Bucer immediately on its publication, the reformer replied by a denunciatory letter in which the eucharistic controversialists were in turn described as "wild beasts, vipers, lions, and panthers", while Zwingli was condemned as "wicked".

Faced by the choleric Luther, the efforts of the Strasburg theologians must have turned out to be quite useless had it not been that they were supported by the developing political situation. The colloquy of Marburg arose, not from any second thoughts of Luther, but from the aggravation of catholic pressure. In 1526 and 1527, the attention of Charles V had been absorbed by the advance of the Turks, whom the victory at Mohacs had made masters of Hungary. The strained relations of the monarch with Clement VII, moreover, led to the sack of Rome in May, 1527. Protestantism used the interval to further its cause. In 1528, when peace had been made between the pope and the emperor, Ferdinand of Austria once again turned his attention to the matter of heresy, and was determined to break its victorious advance. He negotiated with the princes who had remained catholic. In the spring of 1529, the second Diet of Spires revoked the tolerant arrangements that had been made three years earlier by the first, and restored the Edict of Worms. Protestantism, tolerated in those states where it had been victorious, was now forbidden to undertake any proselytizing activity. On the contrary, mass was again to be celebrated both at Wittenberg and Marburg. Where catholics were in a minority they were granted liberty, but where they were in a majority heretics were forbidden to call attention to themselves in any way. This dual claim, which was once more to become a live issue in the 19th century, arose in the 16th. The conservative-minded majority of the Diet drew a subtle distinction between Lutherans, who were for the time being tolerated, and sectarians, who came under an absolute interdict. Ferdinand classed the Zwinglians in the latter category.

On April 19 the reformed party—consisting of six princes and fourteen towns—published the *protestation* which has given protestantism its name. "Concerning those matters which appertain to the glory of God, the salvation and felicity of souls", affirmed the signatories, "everyone will appear before God and will render Him an account of his own individual person, without being able to justify himself by alleging the specious pretext of majority decisions. . . . We *protest* before God, the just Judge who searches the heart, as also before all men and all creatures, that for ourselves, our families and all on whom it is incumbent, we cannot agree to any act or decree which is contrary to God, to the salvation of souls, to a good conscience, and consequently we cannot agree to the aforesaid decree. . . ." In the context of the emperor's threats, the eucharistic controversy seemed more absurd than ever. Melanchthon, who was following the work of the Diet, at last took fright. "I see no remedy for our ills but prayer," he groaned. The pacific arguments of Bucer, which a few weeks previously had irritated him, suddenly won over his sympathy. The sharp revulsion is to be explained by the march of events but also by the energetic intervention of a prince who for long had been convinced of the need for conciliation—namely, the landgrave Philip of Hesse.

The relations between the young sovereign and Zwingli began in 1526. The death of the Elector of Saxony, Frederick the Wise, Luther's protector at Worms, deprived the reformation of its best counsellor. John of Saxony, a worthy but shy man, had by no means the breadth of mind and vision which had distinguished his uncle. In spite of his being only twenty-one, the Prince of Hesse now became the brain of the party. Responsibility did not frighten him. His courageous attitude at the first Diet of Spires attracted to him the attention of all protestants.

An orphan at the age of four, son of the landgrave William II and of Anna of Mecklenburg, Philip began to reign over his principality at the early age of fifteen. At nineteen, he married, for their common misfortune, Christina of Saxony, daughter of Duke George, who satisfied neither his intelligence, nor his heart, nor his temperament. The disharmony of the couple ended in the morganatic marriage which in 1540 Philip contracted with Margaret von der Saal. The scandal —there was never any question of divorce, only of a double union supported by the examples of Abraham, Jacob, David, and Solomon—has left a lasting blemish on the memory of the prince. The affair also impeaches Luther at the bar of history, for he gave his consent. "She is neither beautiful nor affectionate," said Philip of Christina; "she smells and she drinks." The excuse is worth what it is worth. In any event, hardly had his fate been linked to that of the Saxon lady when the prince, who had early been severed from maternal care, threw himself into the disorders brought about by a sensuality and a susceptibility which were alike unsatisfied. His union with Margaret von der Saal seemed to him to afford a means of escaping from an abnormal situation which was painful to his sincere longing for purity. Does the unfortunate man, who has been labelled by succeeding centuries with the ignominious title of bigamist, really deserve the scorn which history has not ceased to heap on him? He was perhaps more sinned against than sinning. His condition of life and his education, his premature marriage, the period, constitute real excuses. His sentimental journey recalls that of several monarchs who were his contemporaries. Compared with the husband of Katherine of Aragon and Anne Boleyn, or with the deplorable rake that was Francis I, the inward struggles of the German prince assume an appearance of moral grandeur. He suffered from his unhappiness and to a certain extent he heeded the advice of his theologians who urged him to amend his life. The 20th century would not have been greatly surprised to see such a one divorced and remarried.

However that may be, Philip as a man was worth far more than the action to which, in religious history, he has owed his fame. He followed his convictions with sincerity and courage, taking risks when necessary. He was distinguished also by the concern for peaceful agreement which caused him in his principality to be nicknamed "the magnanimous". As regards catholicism, after the war which issued in the defeat of 1546 he studiously sought for an area of agreement, read the Fathers of the Church, and tried to define a minimum of doctrine which might gain the acceptance of all. In his testament, he enjoined his sons to avoid—without doing violence to their sincere convictions—whatever might be calculated to promote a renewal of civil war.

On July 24, 1526, Capito drew the reformer's attention to the plan for an alliance between princes and towns that was sponsored by Philip. The provost of Strasburg, moreover, sent to the landgrave a little work which Ulrich, at the time of the Diet of Baden, wrote in self-justification and which he intended for the eye of the Vicar-General, Faber. Quite quickly there sprang up between the two men a sympathy which lasted until Zwingli's death. In April, 1527, the court of Hesse was joking Philip about his admiration for the Zürich theologian. His intimates would describe him laughingly as a Zwinglian. Zwingli, they insinuated, had become his idol.

The Swiss pastor and the German prince had in common a lucid understanding and a sense of political realities. While Luther, lost in the clouds of theology, was repudiating the writings of eucharistic controversialists, without the slightest concern for the danger threatening from catholicism, Ulrich and Philip shuddered at the risky situation in which protestantism found itself. Austria and Bavaria clung to the past. Charles V was in control of the Low Countries. In Brussels, which was totally subjected to his will, the sovereign had in 1523 initiated the era of burnings at the stake. In Germany he was prevented from acting with repressive cruelty solely by the fear lest a war should break out behind him when he was engaged in a struggle with France or the Turks. The friendship of protestant princes was essential to him. The pause from which the reformers were now profiting was none the less a miracle and might cease any day. King Ferdinand, Charles's brother, hated the new ideas. His religious fanaticism, drawing him into sympathy with the cantons of original Switzerland, drove him even to ally himself with the former rebel subjects of the Habsburgs.

In theological matters, Philip, at first a strict Lutheran, was rapidly developing in the direction of Zwinglianism. The theses of Ulrich and Oecolampadius interested him. Capito was delighted at this and communicated the good news to his Swiss friends. Oecolampadius dedicated to the prince his *Commentary on the First Chapter of Ezekiel*. Through the agency of his cousin, the dispossessed Duke of Württemberg, who for a time sought refuge in Basle, in February 1528 the landgrave invited the reformer of Basle to go and reside in Marburg, a plan which was not immediately realized. When at the end of December 1528, there arose at Worms a dispute about the eucharist between a passing Lutheran preacher and the resident pastor, Philip was present and exclaimed in conclusion: "If God so wills, I will bring together at my own expense, and under my own presidency, Oecolampadius and his followers and Luther and his followers, even should the plan cost me six thousand florins."

The second Diet of Spires, as we have seen, brought matters to a crisis. Philip saw salvation in the creation of a vast protestant front, lined up from Berne to Saxony and Brandenburg. But understanding between the theologians was an essential prerequisite. Three days after the protestation of April 19, the courier carried from Marburg a letter earnestly requesting the participation of Zwingli in a debate on the Lord's Supper. The landgrave emphasized the delight with which catholics noted the divisions in the protestant party. Ulrich at once accepted. His reply, dated May 7, expressed enthusiastic gratitude towards the prince who was capable of taking such an initiative.

It was with difficulty that Luther brought himself to agree. Had he not, in contempt of the most elementary common sense, just ruined in the Elector of Saxony's mind the landgrave's plans for establishing a grand protestant alliance? After complicated negotiations, the time and place were settled, thanks to Philip's perseverance. But it was still necessary to overcome the resistance of the Council of Zürich, which hesitated to allow Ulrich to embark on a hazardous journey on unsafe roads. For a time there was some question of transferring the place of meeting to Strasburg. Capito and James Sturm, the eminent magistrate of Strasburg, advocated Marburg; in their opinion the prestige of the landgrave would guarantee the security of the traveller.

Zwingli set off on September 3 about ten o'clock in the evening. It was felt that secrecy would be better assured by this hurried departure, since in Germany it was rumoured that the colloquy was fixed for October. It was only later that Anna learnt the goal of his journey. Ulrich had spoken to her of business which had to be settled in Basle. He was accompanied by Rudolph Collin, a teacher at the Great Minster school. The Council, which still had not given its final consent, was confronted by the accomplished fact. At Basle, Ulrich lodged at the house of Oecolampadius. Early next morning, September 6, escorted by the Zürich councillor Funk, who had joined them, the two reformers left with a group of merchants, as though they were going to Strasburg Fair. The veil was lifted when they arrived in that town, where the magistrates and the clergy gave them a friendly welcome. The Council held an official reception to drink their health. The pastor of the Cathedral, Matthew Zell, insisted on receiving them in his own home, which obliged his wife to become both servant and cook for a fortnight.

After leaving Zürich, Ulrich wrote to the Council begging them to excuse his unauthorized departure. He entreated them not to accuse him of flight. He asked them to warn Anna, from whom he had concealed the true motive of his absence, and to tell her everything "in so far as a woman may be told".

CHAPTER THIRTY-TWO

Arrival at Marburg: the "De Providentia Dei"

FROM TOP TO bottom of the princely castle, valets and page-boys were bustling about. Tongues were wagging. The humblest errand-boy in Germany had heard the name of Martin Luther and desired to see the preacher whose eloquence had shaken the foundations of the papacy. Philip of Hesse was keeping his promise. Nothing seemed to him too magnificent for this theological colloquy which he had initiated. He had planned to lodge the Zwinglians in the palace and the Lutherans in the chief inn of Marburg, but decided at the last minute to quarter both partisans and opponents of consubstantiation under the same roof.

Zwingli and Oecolampadius left Strasburg on September 18 at six o'clock in the morning. Three men of Zürich, the printer Froschauer, the Hebrew scholar Rudolph Collin, to whom we owe an account of the conversations, and Councillor Funk, rode by their side. Basle had delegated a magistrate, Rudolph Frey: Strasburg two theologians, Hédion and Bucer, together with the distinguished layman James Sturm, the best political brain in the city. The journey lasted ten days, including two prolonged halts. From the frontier of Hesse, a detachment of forty horsemen escorted the landgrave's guests. The expedition reached Marburg on September 28 at four o'clock in the afternoon: "The prince", relates Hédion, "welcomed us to his castle with all possible friendliness and greeted each one of us personally."

At Strasburg on September 12 Zwingli and Oecolampadius had preached in the Cathedral, the former at the morning service, the latter at evensong, before crowded and attentive congregations. Behind closed doors, conversations took place bearing on the political situation. Strasburg, which dreaded the intransigence of Charles V, wished to form an alliance with Zürich. The Swiss were given a confidential document in which King Ferdinand, the emperor's brother, revealed his plans of campaign against the free cities of southern Germany. The latter were to be brought to reason, whether reformed or not. Their crime appeared to be of a political as much as of a religious nature. The Austrian sovereign hated the spirit of independence in all its forms. One paragraph related to the future of the Swiss Confederation. In the eyes of Ferdinand, the Swiss were the worst enemies of the princes and the nobility. These frantic republicans, he thought, would be so much the more easily overthrown because they were divided, one party being supporters, the other adversaries of the pope.

Reading between the lines of the texts furnished by Sturm and Bucer, Zwingli and Funk were alarmed to discern the emergence of an immense coalition, which, in opposition to the double cause of the reformation and political liberty, was bringing together those sworn enemies of yesterday, Pope Clement VII and the kings of France and Spain. They hastened to write to Zürich about the matter. The situation seemed to them very grave. The alliance of the three despots threatened the future of the Gospel in Europe. The indications supplied by the authorities of Strasburg were in fact accurate. On June 29, did not Francis I justify the peace with Charles V by stating specifically that it had been concluded "to extirpate the heresies with which Christendom is swarming and to ensure that the Church should be revered and honoured as is meet for the salvation of our souls"? Some months previously, on January 29, signing at Barcelona an identical agreement with the pope, Charles, the master of Spain, undertook to check the plague of the new ideas. Should peaceful means prove insufficient, he specified, he would use force in conjunction with his brother, the king of Hungary and Bohemia. Among those threatened by agreement between the kings and the pope, Zwingli noted that there were, besides the Swiss, the Venetians and Robert de la Marck, the lord of Sedan, Duke of Bouillon. On October 29, the Council of Zürich communicated to that of Berne the information supplied by the reformer.

The letter of September 17, which, in the judgment of the historian Max Lenz, was the most important of all those written by Zwingli, reveals the intensity of his preoccupation during his ride to Marburg. The controversy over the Lord's Supper seemed to him ever more deplorable. At the moment when catholic forces were regrouping, when Spain and France were promising the pope the support of their sword, the separation of Wittenberg and Zürich was weakening the cause of the reformation. It would be necessary at all costs to effect a reconciliation. Zwingli was too clearsighted not to ratify the landgrave's plans. On the other hand, he could not deny his own convictions in order to satisfy Luther.

While gloomy thoughts were jostling each other in his weary head, the protestant cantons on September 24 were affixing their signature to the peace treaty which was the fruit of the Cappel discussions. The agreement, which even at the time of its preparation caused the reformer anxiety, now seemed in the light of the Austrian document to disclose its true nature and scope: was it not indeed a bargain struck by dupes?

The Lutheran contingent did not reach Marburg until Thursday, September 30, after a journey on horseback of fourteen days, the course of which was interrupted by talk and preaching. Philip took advantage of the delay to make the acquaintance of his Swiss guests. On the 28th, Oecolampadius preached in the chapel of the castle on a psalm which had vital relevance to the current crisis: "Why do the nations conspire and the peoples plot in vain? The kings of the earth set themselves, and the rulers take counsel together, against the Lord and His anointed."

The next day it was Zwingli's turn. He discoursed at

length on the theme of Providence. The choice of subject is to be explained both by the political preoccupations of the hour and the subsequent doctrinal discussion. At the request of the landgrave, Ulrich's exposition was published in August, 1530, under the title *De providentia dei* (concerning divine providence).

The reformer began by praising the knowledge and power of God, the source and cause of all life, who controls the development of mankind and of events as He guides the stars in their courses. He created the animals, in particular the eagle and the marmot, which, posted as a sentinel, warns her companions of the approach of danger by emitting a series of hissing sounds. Animals, mountains render homage to God and to His power. "The very hairs of your head are numbered," Christ declared to the fretful disciples.

It is not difficult to discover in this portion of the sermon, where nothing foreshadows the debate on the eucharist, a reflection of the political worries of Ulrich. Face to face with his noble auditor, is it not the mystery of their common future which he is evoking? Above the uncertainties of the moment, above kings and their conspiring, God reigns and is ever in sovereign control of all things. Chance is excluded. Everything depends on the first cause. The orator then explores the world of man, that most extraordinary of creatures, tossed as he is between good and evil. We do not judge dogs which tear and rend each other, he notes, for they are not under the law. The nobility of man resides in the fact that a divine law is ingrained in his heart. In regard to the commandments, we must not be content to emphasize their threats and the condemnation they voice on the wicked. The requirement of love is that which confers greatness on man.

If God has created us such as we are, must we attribute to Him the responsibility for Adam's fall? If He did not foresee it, He is like the unskilful doctor who, badly setting the broken bone, leaves his patient lame. Several philosophers have confessed that without the bitter we should not recognize the sweet. Should we be aware of justice were it not for injustice? God made the fall possible without being directly responsible for it, in this resembling the father of a family who establishes a set of rules in order to prevent his children from indulging in epicurism and becoming lazy. "He who touches the pot of honey will be punished; he who puts his clogs the wrong way up will go barefoot, etc." To make truth and justice apparent to us, the existence of falsehood and injustice was necessary. The possibility of the fall does not overthrow the goodness of God, which, moreover, is revealed in the work of salvation.

Let us go further: if God has foreseen all things, even the moment of a murder, does the responsibility for crime fall upon Him? The brigand who commits the crime is alone guilty. Providence, which incites to kill, foresees at the same time the action of the judge who will punish. Determined to affirm to its logical conclusion the idea of divine omnipotence, Ulrich refuses to accept the solution of Thomas Aquinas, for whom God determines man's fate in the sense that He knows in advance the use which man will make of his liberty. Prevision and determination cannot be dissociated. In God the will is primal; wisdom, justice and foresight are subordinated to Him. The term election, notes Ulrich, is applicable to the elect alone. It cannot be used when speaking of the damned. God rejects them so that they may become examples of His justice.

Since everything flows from God, there can be no question of merit. All derives from the deity, which is supreme goodness. Man is never anything but an instrument. When Scripture speaks of rewarding his virtues, it attributes to the creature what God has conferred upon him. The same basic certitude is applicable to the sacrament. The external signs are nothing in themselves. They do not create faith. The bread is the sign, but it is Christ who saves. The object to which faith is directed is not the symbol itself, but the invisible reality behind it. Faith itself springs from God through the Holy Spirit. The condemnations of the pope have no power to harm the believer. Who will accuse an elect of God?

Thus election precedes faith. The latter makes happy and does not depend on ourselves. He who believes in the preaching of the apostles is saved; he who does not believe is damned. All are not converted at the moment of their first contact with the Gospel. We must not make any judgment except on those who persevere in unbelief up to the moment of death. Basing himself on Rom. 2: 14, Zwingli puts forward the idea that certain pagans believed without knowing the Gospel. God had elected them, such men as Socrates and Seneca, who, although they knew nothing of piety in so far as it is bound up with the Word and sacraments, nevertheless lived pious and holy lives.

Works stem from faith, which is like a hot stove necessarily radiating heat all around itself. Do you debate the question of merit? You are fighting more about a word than about a reality. Faith does not spring from works: it is the converse which is true. While the reprobate turns his whole mind towards the search for wealth and pleasure, the elect are actively occupied in virtuous living. The will of God determines the course of history.

Let us not follow those who groan about the fall of mankind. The fact that Adam fell resulted in the supreme worth of the incarnation. Often ill is the matrix of good. The house that has been burnt down is, after the disaster, so rebuilt that it looks finer than before.

Was the *Providentia dei* preached exactly in the form in which it was later printed? Zwingli redrafted his sermon from memory. Doubtless he amplified it, adding new passages to those which aroused the interest of the landgrave. It has been said that it is his most difficult work. If the reasoning is often closely knit, if the pupil of Aristotle and St. Thomas has not forgotten his masters, the style remains appealing to the mentality of what the 17th century will call the *honnête homme*.

CHAPTER THIRTY-THREE

The Colloquy

PHILIP OF HESSE, who was supported by the chancellor Feige, did not commit the blunder of confronting the two leaders with each other without some tactful preparation. On the evening of September 30, dinner brought together only a part of the learned company. Oecolampadius, in a brief address, tendered greetings to Luther and Melanchthon. Zwingli was absent.

The next morning at six o'clock Oecolampadius and Luther each received a letter inviting them to engage in friendly converse, while Melanchthon and Zwingli were asked to meet each other in a different room. The landgrave deliberately chose to bring into contact a leader and a secondary figure. He knew that Melanchthon was conciliatory and that Luther was better disposed towards the reformer of Basle than towards the reformer of Zürich.

A witness—namely, Brenz—affirms that the first conversation lasted for three hours and the second for six, which seems just a trifle exaggerated. It is true that two theologians face to face, and handling themes of capital importance, can go on talking *ad infinitum*. Luther and Oecolampadius appear to have concentrated on the localization of the body of Christ—a subject which was to recur in the public discussions. Zwingli and Melanchthon passed in review a series of doctrinal points, e.g. the relation between the Word and the Spirit, the conception of original sin, spiritual assimilation in the eucharist, the ubiquity of the body of Christ, and still others. They had to stop to go and eat. The morning had sped by rapidly. Minds had made contact with each

other. Melanchthon awarded Ulrich letters patent of ortho-
doxy. Luther meantime had also made contact with Bucer,
whom he ended by apostrophizing somewhat sharply. "You
are of the devil," he cried out, "and if you have a true faith
and scripture [on your side] you will hand me too over to the
devil, for I am opposed to your opinion."

It was time to pass into the dining-room. The landgrave,
somewhat anxious, drew Melanchthon aside and implored
him to use every effort to bring about an understanding.
He spoke with such urgency and emphasis that, Hédion
tells us, "his eyes seemed to be coming out of his head".
Turning towards the Duke of Württemberg, he exclaimed:
"I would not be prepared to die for this business, but I
would agree to spend six months sick in bed, if necessary,
so that this quarrel might cease." His interlocutor, less
zealous, calmly replied that he would prefer to drain a glass
of beer in peace.

The next morning, October 2, saw the beginning of the
formal debate. A carefully chosen audience gathered at six
o'clock—they were decidedly accustomed to early rising—
in a room among the private apartments of the landgrave.
Besides the four speakers of the previous day, the Strasburg
participants, a few theologians from Hesse and Saxony, the
two princes of Hesse and Württemberg, the chancellor Feige
and the Swiss who had escorted Oecolampadius and Zwingli,
made up an audience estimated by Zwingli at twenty-four
members, and by the Lutheran Brenz at sixty. There was
no official report. Several of the witnesses, however—Collin,
Hédion, Brenz, and Melanchthon—later drew up an account
of the conversations.[1]

The chancellor had seated around one table the four
principal debaters: Luther, Melanchthon, Zwingli, and
Oecolampadius. Luther opened fire. He confessed that two
years previously he would have refused to take part in such
a discussion, in the conviction that the writings already

[1] The principal one, by Collin of Zürich, has been translated by Canon
Cristiani in his *Luther tel qu'il fut* (Fayard). W. Köhler has used them all
to give as complete an account as possible of the colloquy in *Das Marburger
Religionsgesprach* (1929).

exchanged were sufficient. But in consequence of the Diet of Spires and the prince's invitation, he had agreed. Not that he was willing to change his opinion on any point whatsoever, but that he considered it would be useful "to give an account of his opinions and to demonstrate the errors of other people." He then enumerated a certain number of points—the Trinity, the doctrine of the two natures, original sin, baptism, justification, the preacher's office, purgatory —on which his interlocutors and he differed.

The historian is obliged to note that Luther had accepted the landgrave's invitation with great reluctance. His letters of July and August show that he was very unhappy about his decision, going even so far as to urge Brenz to give up the idea of the journey to Marburg. Did he wish to torpedo the debate from the very start? Oecolampadius and Zwingli reminded him that the theme of the conference was the eucharist. It was necessary to stick to the point.

Luther, however, had no intention of evading the subject of the eucharist. Before the discussion began, he had lifted up the tablecloth and had chalked on the wood of the table: *Hoc est corpus meum* (this is my body), clearly marking his intention of not yielding an inch of ground to the partisans of the symbolist theory. Hence he began to speak again and passed directly to the offensive. The *ratio naturae* (natural reason) asserts that a body cannot be in two places at once. Hence can Christ be at one and the same time in heaven and in the sacramental bread? That was the point made by the symbolists. But natural reason has no relevance to such matters. "God can do far more than our thoughts suggest." Hence the German reformer rejected all arguments drawn from geometry and mathematics. The Christian should adore the words of God with amazement and wonder (*verba dei cum stupore esse adoranda*).

Oecolampadius affirmed his loyalty to and belief in Scripture. He fully recognized its authority, but considered that the message of the Bible needed interpretation. The arguments brought forward in the course of the previous controversy reappeared. The word "is" must not be taken literally as Luther wished. It is no more than a figure of speech as we see from such examples as John 15, *I am the true vine*, or 1 Cor. 10, *that rock was Christ*.

Luther admitted that Scripture contained metaphors. But, he added, it was not enough for an allegorical interpretation to be possible. Its necessity also had to be proved, which Oecolampadius at once tried to do by attacking the exegesis of John 6. The debaters then became involved in a long discussion concerning the mentality of the people of Capernaum. For Luther, the Jews believed that it was necessary to eat Christ "as one eats from a plate bread or meat or a piece of roast pork". It was that error alone that the Lord wished to combat. His warning did not exclude a more spiritually exalted eating of the body of Christ. When Oecolampadius flung into the debate certain patristic texts, the Saxon set them aside with the remark that they must confine their attention to Christ alone. He also stressed that they should not fasten their minds solely on the extraordinary nature of the command, but should consider its author. "You must not think only of what is said; you must pay attention to who said it." If God commands we must obey: "All must adhere to His word without being curious about other matters. . . . If Scripture commanded me to eat dung, I would do so. . . . A servant does not murmur against the wishes of his master. . . ."

The humanist in Oecolampadius revolted against this call for blind submission. He protested. Intervening for the first time in the discussion, Zwingli compared the attitude of Luther to that of a forgotten heretic, Helvidius, who, supporting his argument on the mention (John 7: 3) of the brothers of Jesus, denied that Christ was the only son of Mary. Luther had sufficiently accused him of heresy for Ulrich to feel pleasure in paying him back in his own coin.

He did not, however, forget the aim of the conference, and hastened to establish it as a fact that the discussion had produced relative agreement. Luther had expressly repudiated the error of the Jews of Capernaum and admitted, like his opponents, the idea of a spiritual assimilation. But he

added to it that of corporeal assimilation of the eucharistic
elements. The agreement was only partial. Ulrich also
returned to the question of the *humilis intellectus*. He was,
he said, basically in agreement, but besought them not to
indulge in puerilities such as the example of dung. God is
light. All that He commands is for our salvation and our
good. "The oracles of the demons are obscure, but not the
words of Christ." Hence we must not introduce an element
of essential reality, of flesh, into the words, *This is my body*.

Zwingli had spoken for long and with vivacity. As though
fearing that he might have gone too far, he ended by begging
them not to misunderstand his words, or take them amiss.
He expressed his delight at seeing Luther and Melanchthon.
Luther in his turn declared that he wished for peace to prevail, but at once he set the ball of the debate rolling again
and, to begin with, repudiated the unflattering comparison
with Helvidius. His interlocutors had by no means proved
the metaphorical character of the *hoc est corpus meum*. The
setting aside of the idea of a carnal coarse eating did not
eliminate the possibility of a real spiritual eating. "We eat
in faith that body which is given for us." The mouth receives
the body of Christ. While the soul believes in the words, the
mouth eats the body. "You assert that God commands
nothing that is incomprehensible: I cannot admit that."
How many extraordinary things are told us, such as the
virginity of Mary and the forgiveness of sins.

Zwingli could not bow to the accusations of his opponent.
One by one, he went back over his own arguments: the
necessity for exegesis, comparison of texts, possibility of a
symbolic interpretation. It is easy, he said, to accuse him
who refuses to accept everything blindly of lacking faith
(this wicked reproach is as old as theological quarrels). The
Lord's Supper is not the same as the Annunciation. When the
angel addresses Mary, his message is clear: *the Holy Spirit
will come upon you*; the virgin understands that a miracle is
in question, and is submissive. Renewing the question of a
spiritual presence and going as far as possible in the direction
of his contradictor, Ulrich pointed out that if Christ is present

there, He is not there "for the comfort of the body, but for that of the soul".

In a cutting reply, Luther magnificently brushed aside arguments concerned with exegesis, and returned to his annihilating thesis of the incomprehensible element in religion. Mary was aware of being confronted by a mystery, since she said: "How can this be?" Abraham hoped against all hope. "Your arguments are weak," he concluded. "Abandon them and give glory to God." On the other side of the table, Zwingli got red in the face: "We too," he cried, "we ask you to do the same thing; we ask you to give glory to God and to abandon your begging of the question." "You are twisting the argument. I shall not allow myself to be turned aside." "I remain firm at this place, John 6, verse 63. I shall oblige you to return to it. You will have to sing a different tune with me." "You are speaking maliciously," replied Luther, suffocated with rage.

Ulrich insisted on a clear reply. The tactics of Luther, invoking faith, emphasizing the element of mystery, instead of adducing exegetical arguments, infuriated him. How should the famous verse of John 6 be understood? he demanded. "The text," replied Luther, "has nothing to do with the matter under discussion." "No, no," shouted Ulrich in triumph, "this text will break your spine." "Do not boast too much," interrupted Luther. "Here, necks are not broken. You are in Hesse now, not in Switzerland."

The discussion was turning into a wrangle. The allusion to the too speedy execution of justice in Zürich—Luther was in fact alluding to the condemnation of the anabaptists —was insulting. Zwingli, however, was the first to control himself and apologize. "To break one's neck" was a rather crude Swiss mode of expression. The landgrave made a sign that he understood and accepted the apology, but nevertheless he felt it wise to interrupt the colloquy at this point.

At two o'clock in the afternoon the discussion was resumed. Zwingli at first tried to make Luther contradict himself by quoting a former sermon of his adversary. Against Melanchthon too he produced the witness of the *Commentary on the*

Gospel of John which the humanist had published in 1523. But, without realizing it, the Zürich reformer was interpreting his opponents in the light of his own conceptions. He was brought up sharply against a haughty refusal to admit the claim: "All this concerns neither my sermon nor Melanchthon," exclaimed Luther. "Even if I were of your faith, you would not have contradicted these words: *This is my body*." And, penetrating to the heart of the conflict, he affirmed that the body of Christ nourished the body of the believer for all eternity. The Word of God is fulfilled, he added, whatever be the quality of the priest who administers the sacrament. Zwingli protested at once against this idea, which seemed to him singularly near to catholicism. "It is not at all absurd," replied Luther. "The foundation of our salvation lies in the Word of God, independently of our dignity or indignity."

The dispute was merging into the old Donatist controversy. It very nearly became bogged down in it. Oecolampadius saved the situation by referring to St. John, chapter 3. The Saviour teaches Nicodemus that salvation depends on a second birth. Hence it is not essential to receive the body of Christ. Luther rebutted the argument, which was very quickly succeeded by another. The Basle theologian pointed out that Christ said (John 16: 28): "I leave the world and go to the Father." Consequently, He could not be in the sacrament. The duel went on between the two men while the minutes rapidly flowed away. Disappointing as is a dialogue in which the incapacity of the parties to understand each other becomes manifest every minute, this one was not lacking in greatness. Both sides must have loved Jesus Christ with an equal love to attach so much importance to the nature of our communion with Him. More zealous than any of his guests, the landgrave followed with passionate interest the progress of this astounding spiritual match. He listened without flagging to Oecolampadius' evocation of the passible and mortal nature of the body which clothed the Saviour when He was on earth. It is not a question, replied Luther, of that terrestrial body, but of the body which is the bearer of the promise.

261

Zwingli, who had for a long time been silent, intervened once more to suggest that an inadequate Christology should be elucidated by reference to Phil. 2: 7: "He took the form of a servant": "He therefore had a limited humanity." As was to be expected, Luther rejected this argument. Zwingli had also referred to Heb. 2: 17: "Christ like His brethren in every respect." "So He took a wife, had black eyes!" snarled the Saxon ironically. The wretched man, sometimes serious, sometimes joking, had an answer to everything. Ulrich, clearly annoyed, went back to Phil. 2: 7, quoting the Greek text. "Oh do speak in Latin or German, not in Greek," interrupted Luther. Zwingli apologized: for twelve years he had been accustomed to read the letters of Paul in the original and no longer used the Vulgate. Then he came to his argument. If Christ was made like His brethren, He was limited (*finitus*) as we are. "I agree," Luther answered this time, but immediately he added that God can cause the body not to be in a particular place and at the same time to be in that place, for God controls space. The two Swiss, in their turn, marvelled to see that the divine omnipotence could cause a body to be in several places at once, but this possibility did not solve the problem of the eucharist. In the Gospel, Zwingli pointed out, Christ is always in one place, whether it be the manger, the temple, the desert, on the cross, in the tomb or at the right hand of the Father. He challenged Luther to prove that He was in several places at once. Luther replied that the burden of proof was not incumbent on him. "It would be disgraceful," exclaimed Ulrich, "to hold to such an article and to teach it while not being able, or not wishing, to adduce any scriptural argument in support of it." Luther did not allow himself to be abashed. Lifting the tablecloth he pointed with his finger to the chalked writing: "My dear sirs," he cried, "as the text of our Lord Jesus Christ is there, *hoc est corpus meum*, I cannot set it at naught, but must confess and believe that the body of Christ is there." "But, doctor," protested Ulrich, "you therefore accept a localization of your body of Christ in the eucharist. You say: 'the body of Christ must be there', and 'there' in truth is an adverb of place."

With this dramatic altercation, the sitting was broken off. Night was falling. It was necessary to have a meal. Sleep, which we might imagine to have been somewhat agitated, soon separated the debaters.

Early the next morning, before the first repast, the contest was renewed. The hope of agreement lessened. Most of the important arguments had figured in the previous day's theological tournament. Once again they wrestled over Phil. 2: 7, argued about the ubiquity of the body of Christ. Zwingli read a quotation from Fulgentius, to which Luther replied by quoting another text of the same author. Threatened at times in the positions he had taken up, the Saxon returned to rest in literalism pure and simple, invoking the power of God. "One thing suffices me," he went on repeating, "*this is my body.*" "A man prepared to argue," Ulrich once interrupted, "might assert that John was the son of Mary since Christ said: 'Behold your son.'" But every objection was dashed to pieces against a wall. Zwingli eventually shut himself up in a weary silence.

Oecolampadius tried unsuccessfully to revive the discussion. Two quotations from Augustine were rejected by Luther as contributing nothing positive, while he himself offered a third, which was favourable to his thesis and in his opinion alone valid. Augustine, he noted, must be judged by Scripture, not the reverse.

Sunday afternoon was filled with vain skirmishes. Themes already broached emerged again: on the one hand, Augustine, his authority and that of the Fathers in general: on the other, the localization of the body of Christ. Finally, Oecolampadius and Zwingli confessed that their resources in argument were exhausted. Luther declared that he maintained his opinion unchanged. The protagonists were tired out. Several times in the course of the debates, Luther had protested his weariness and called for the help of Melanchthon, who however remained strangely silent.

The struggle ended with an exchange of compliments. Luther expressed his gratitude to Oecolampadius for the friendly way in which he had defended his point of view. He also thanked Zwingli, although the latter had shown more acrimony, and he apologized for having at moments expressed himself with violence: "But, after all, I am flesh and blood." Ulrich voiced similar sentiments. He desired nothing so much as the friendship of Dr. Martin. Tears came into his eyes, noted several witnesses of the scene.

A false note disturbed for one moment this harmonious end. Oecolampadius having begged them to bear in mind the afflicted Church, Luther brusquely retorted: "Pray God that He will open your eyes," which drew down on him the reply of the conciliatory man of Basle: "You too should pray for that. You have equal need of it."

The men of Strasburg and the landgrave, alike racked by their keen desire for a public affirmation of unity, were by no means satisfied. Philip of Hesse stressed that he wished to secure an understanding. Through the mediation of Osiander, the Lutherans then produced a formula which they thought would be conciliatory. It affirmed that the eucharist was not a pure memorial: "We confess that in virtue of the words *this is my body, this is my blood* the body and blood of Christ are veritably present and distributed in the holy eucharist." Was it a question of a corporeal or a spiritual presence, of a natural or supernatural reality? The Swiss revolted and refused their signature, an attitude which later on brought upon them keen reproaches from their adversaries.

On the evening of October 3, the princely host once again brought representatives of both parties together round his table. The following morning was filled with a flurry of secret meetings, in which Bucer and Hédion tried to obtain intercommunion in spite of divergences. At the time of the conflict about the date of Easter which arose between Asia Minor and Rome at the end of the 2nd century, had not a harmonious arrangement been reached, in spite of incapacity to agree? Luther pointed out that the current disagreement was "far more considerable" and refused.

Bucer, who for his own part was ready to believe that the

reality of Christ was bestowed in the eucharist, disputed that he had accepted a corporeal presence. He explained the refusal of Zwingli and Oecolampadius as being due to the fear of confusion: the people would have materialized the conception of spiritual presence. The hope of an alliance between Lutherans and Zwinglians was fast fading. At the urgent entreaty of Philip—"the prince required it", notes Bucer—Luther jotted down on paper a summary of the points on which the protestants had established their unity. This constitutes the famous articles of Marburg, which turn on the doctrines of the Trinity, the incarnation, the unity of the two natures in Christ, original sin, redemption by faith in the sacrifice of Christ, on the nature of faith, the futility of the doctrine of works and merit with all its consequences, the uselessness of monastic vows, on the doctrine of the Holy Spirit and of Holy Baptism, of good works, the confession of sin, and on the repudiation of human traditions and accretions. With regard to the eucharist, the declaration enumerates first of all the points on which agreement was reached: communion in both kinds, repudiation of the mass regarded as a work deserving of grace, recognition of the rite instituted by Christ as a sacrament. Spiritual participation in the body and the blood is especially necessary to every true Christian.

A fifth section sums up the difference between the parties: "Although we have been unable to agree on the issue as to whether the true vine and blood of Christ are corporeally present in the bread and wine of the eucharist, nevertheless each party will prove towards the other its spirit of Christian love, in so far as his conscience will permit. Both will fervently pray to God Almighty that He may grant us and confirm us in true understanding of the matter." The chief participants: Luther, Jonas, Melanchthon, Osiander and Brenz on the Lutheran side, Oecolampadius, Zwingli, Bucer and Hédion on the opposite side, affixed their signatures.

The declaration of Marburg ill concealed the failure of the colloquy; none the less, it underlined the unity of the protestant world on an impressive number of doctrinal issues. The basic unity of the reformation was clearly apparent despite the emergence of differences. The subsequent development was to justify the insistence of the landgrave Philip. If there still exists a type of narrow-minded Lutheran who refuses intercommunion with the Reformed Christian, in many regions the doctrinal difference has become blurred. At the heart of the 16th century Marburg is manifestly a first step in the direction of the ecumenical movement.

It would be wrong, however, to exalt in an exaggerated way the scope and depth of the harmony achieved. Very soon the two parties showed a tendency to present Marburg as a victory from their own point of view. The correspondence of Zwingli is in this respect as disappointing as that of Luther.

Before leaving the landgrave, Ulrich had with him further important political conversations. With their keen sense of political realities, the two men, in spite of the diversity of their origins, were well fitted to understand each other. Between the prince and the commoner there arose a friendship which expressed itself in the letters exchanged during the two following years. On October 5, Luther preached, and chose as his theme the first verses of Matthew chapter 9, the healing and forgiveness of the paralytic. This was probably the last time that Philip of Hesse heard him. He soon left on horseback. A rumour was spreading throughout the district that a new epidemic of the plague had broken out. In the afternoon, the Lutherans and the Zwinglians left the castle, each party setting out in their different directions. By October 13 the reformed party had reached Strasburg, where the Swiss separated from their companions. After passing through Basle, where he parted from Oecolampadius, Ulrich got back to Zürich on October 19 at five o'clock in the afternoon.

The next day, although wearied by the journey, he took up his pen and sent to Vadian a confidential description of his preliminary interview with Melanchthon—whom he found excessively polite and consequently somewhat evasive —and also of the official debate. Luther, he noted, attached a great deal of importance to trifles. Thus, "he said that the body of Christ was given by these words *this is my body*, even supposing that they were spoken by a rogue", and many other such "stupidities and absurdities". On the other hand, he admitted that the body of Christ was limited and that "the sign of the body of Christ might be called eucharistic [action of thanksgiving]". "The truth," added Ulrich, "won him over in the end." The truth was evidently Zwingli's own point of view. Terrible human nature of ardent believers, each sure that he is right! The colloquy, however, rendered at least this service, he affirmed in conclusion—namely, that as a result of the signing of the doctrinal articles "the papists will no longer be able to cherish the hope that Luther still belongs to them". John Eck, who at Leipzig and Baden had been the champion of catholicism, had publicly rejoiced to see a rent in the reformation and had entertained the conviction that Luther was returning to the bosom of the Roman Church. Marburg made manifest the chimerical nature of such a belief.

Part Eight

Last Struggles

CHAPTER THIRTY-FOUR

Projects of Alliance: Venice and France

SO SOON AS HE had returned to Zürich, Ulrich found himself absorbed by the usual run of affairs. The students of the Great Minster school were awaiting his lectures, the secret Council his advice. The thousand and one little problems of the church in Zürich always ended by penetrating the presbytery in the Kirchgasse. Anna and the children were greatly delighted by his return. On October 24 crowds thronged the Great Minster to listen to him reading and commenting on the Marburg articles.

In the midst of his normal work, Zwingli could not forget the exciting theological discussions of the recent colloquy, nor the political conversations which had preceded and followed them. The correspondence of the last two years evinces the anxieties of the reformer. If several of his letters are lost, those of his correspondents, which are much more numerous, preserve the memory of the subjects discussed and enable us to fill in several gaps.

Between Cassel and Zürich, lasting links had been forged. The prince and the pastor of peasant stock understood and appreciated each other: "The time seemed to us too short", notes the latter on November 2, "not only because of the discussion, but for many other reasons as well." He proposed to his host of yesterday that synods should be inaugurated in Hesse, a counsel which Philip was to follow, and he also talked to him of a closer alliance with the Swiss—a plan which the hostility of the Bernese, on the contrary, was to ruin. The landgrave on his side treated the Swiss reformer with friendly confidence and called him "dear Master Ulrich".

From February 7, 1530, the use of a key enabled the two correspondents to discuss with relative security the problems of European politics.[1] Zwingli, who was blindly followed by the people of Zürich, had been trying since November to parry the imminent assault of the catholic party. The German cities, reformed Switzerland, the prince of Hesse, and his cousin, the Duke of Württemberg, formed a chain of states capable of cutting in two the Austro-Spanish empire. The question arose as to whether Venice, which was on bad terms with Charles V, might not be able to block the still open road to Italy. Zürich flung itself into the adventure of embarking on negotiations with the doge, the head of the Venetian state. The ambassador appointed was none other than Collin, Zwingli's companion at Marburg. This honest Hebraist set off on the road to the south of Europe and reached the Adriatic about Christmas-time, equipped with instructions from the secret Council. On December 28 the Senate of Venice gave him audience, but his proposals were received with glacial silence. Part of his travelling expenses was defrayed, to the extent of twenty-five crowns; an absurdly small contribution. The fact was that the Venetians five days previously had become reconciled with the emperor. The information given by the too-confiding Swiss was immediately communicated to the enemies of protestantism.

This cruel setback induced Ulrich to adopt a more prudent attitude. At first he listened with reserve to the advice of those who urged him to come to an understanding with France. The question was whether Francis I, now liberated, would really detach himself from Austria. On January 18, 1530, two mercenaries, the captains Hans Kaltschmid and Hans Junker, assured him of the kind intentions of the very Christian monarch. The two soldiers, who were worried about the future of the Confederation, took the initiative of engaging in conversation with the ambassador Boisrigault. Would not Zürich be prepared to join the

---

[1] The document giving the real significance of the names used still exists in the archives of Cassel.

French alliance? Boisrigault proposed an interview in Aargau, at Bremgarten or Mellingen, a short distance from Zürich territory.

Did Ulrich suspect that Junker had been commissioned to pay royal pensions in Switzerland? Although he did not immediately reply to the invitation, the prospect of a political combination with France penetrated his mind and awakened old hopes. Was not Farel only recently counting on the influence of Margaret of Angoulême to bring her brother to an acceptance of the Gospel? The situation, however, had not yet reached that stage. The Zürich reformer appreciated the importance of an alliance with France which would buttress the frail barrier of tiny states made up of the Swiss, the German cities, Hesse and Württemberg with the support of the powerful French kingdom. In the end he outlined on paper a scheme of alliance which he submitted to the secret Council, and, shortly before February 15, he entered into relations with the new envoy of Francis I, Lambert Maigret, whose protestant tendencies caused anxiety to Ferdinand of Austria: "The French ambassador", he wrote to his brother, Charles V, "shares the opinions of the Swiss in that he eats meat on Fridays." Then the reformer, after twice refusing to do so, communicated to Maigret through the mediation of Collin a summary of his ideas, hoping that the plan would get as far as Paris and be submitted to the monarch.

On the religious plane, Francis had nothing in common with the people of Zürich. Persistent illusions, however, fostered in him an inclination towards the reformation, which his actions periodically contradicted. Politically, on the other hand, he shared with the reformers—whether German princes or Swiss towns—the desire to hold in check the formidable Charles V. His conception of a European balance of power foreshadowed the ideas of Henry IV and Richelieu.

The text delivered to Maigret has been lost, as has also the copy despatched to the citizens of Strasburg and a summary sent to the landgrave of Hesse. But a second and more complete version of the plan has survived,[1] and this too was intended for the French ambassador.

Zwingli points out that the Swiss cities and the most Christian king have in common their opposition to "the violence and tyranny of the Roman empire". Left to themselves, the Swiss would have difficulty in bearing the burden of a war against their powerful neighbour. France and the Swiss towns must combine "in defence of the Christian religion". In case of attack, the allies would come to each other's help. The king would send to Switzerland arms, provisions and cavalry; the Swiss would place at his disposal an army which he would pay. Furthermore, Francis would pay annual pensions to each town. The final clauses stand in absolute contradiction to the efforts which Ulrich had formerly made to obtain the abolition of mercenary service and pensions. Now his desire to establish the security of reformed Switzerland wrested from him concessions which shocked his friend, Commander of the Grisons. The latter, informed of the plan by a recruiting officer named Travers, wrote from Chur on July 25 a letter blazing with anger. Travers was everywhere boasting of having gained the consent of Zwingli. "For three years now", declared Commander, "our fellow citizens, thanks to the Gospel, have repudiated the alliance which was sealed in blood and have thrown the French envoy Grandisius out of the town." French gold was turning the heads of highly placed persons. May God grant "that these Jebusites be at last expelled from our church".

On January 23, 1531, Zwingli was pleading with his Bernese friends, Haller and Megander, in favour of James May, who was enrolling mercenaries for the advantage of the Duke of Württemberg. He advised leniency and used the opportunity to give his opinion concerning military pensions. If they are granted with a view to the maintenance of peace,

[1] Köhler, whose keenness has driven him to investigate all the minor problems of Zwinglian history, supposes it to have been written in July, 1531. The old edition of Zwingli's works (Schulthess, 1842), however, prints it after the letters of February, 1530; Lenz and Mörikofer also took this point of view.

they may be retained. This, he thought, was especially true in the case of those paid by the French king. Although it is the case that money has often corrupted our republics, he suggested, there must be tact and shrewdness in all matters. It is private pensions which ought to be abolished, not those directly paid to the State. "Moreover, we shall not solicit them, but we will accept those which are offered. Solomon received handsome gifts from the Queen of Sheba."

In spite of the information given him by several correspondents, Ulrich persisted in nursing the chimerical vision of a Francis I rallying to the cause of the reformation. This was a curious piece of obstinacy on the part of a man who in other respects was so clear-sighted. On March 30 Oecolampadius warned him: "I place little hope in the French. They will be persuaded by any and every reason rather than by the light of the Gospel. Ah! if only they might become sensible!" On January 14, 1531, Bucer spoke to him with indignation about the pitiable situation of the "brethren" in France. None the less, Ulrich continued to negotiate with Maigret, and at the end of March, 1531, sent Rudolph Collin once more to discuss with him the political situation.

Ulrich prided himself somewhat too easily on having at his command convincing arguments. In regard to Luther, this feature of his character for a long time concealed from him the depth of their disagreement. He persuaded himself that, confronted by the appropriate Biblical texts, the reformer of Wittenberg would do him justice. Hence the greatness of his disillusionment at Marburg.

In his blind confidence, it was for the frivolous Francis I that in the spring of 1531 he wrote his last work: *Short Exposition of the Christian Faith*. The little book was handed to Collin, who took it to Paris in July, 1531. Doubtless the sovereign to whom it was addressed spent no more time on it than he had done on the *Commentary on True and False Religion*. The manuscript still lies today on a shelf of the *Bibliothèque Nationale* in Paris. A copy which had remained in Zürich enabled Bullinger to edit in 1536 the last work of the deceased reformer.

CHAPTER THIRTY-FIVE

In the shadow of the Diet of Augsburg

IF ZWINGLI CLUNG so obstinately to the shadowy hope of a conversion of France to protestantism, his attitude was in part due to the difficulties which he was encountering in Germany. In the wake of Marburg, nothing might have seemed more natural than common action by all the protestant states. In spite of theological differences, the landgrave had secured from the participants a declaration on fifteen points enabling protestants to present a united front publicly. But the conflict over the eucharist arose from its ashes at the meeting held at Schmalkalden by the delegates of principalities and towns at the end of November, 1529. It was the wish of the majority of Lutherans that military alliances should be subordinated to theological agreement. The representatives of Ulm, Strasburg, Lindau, Constance, Memmingen and Kempten constituted a strategical balance which Philip of Hesse, distressed by this dispute, reckoned at no less than fifty thousand men. Can we join in with heretics? asked in all seriousness the counsellors of Duke John of Saxony. An alliance with pagans gives rise to no sort of ambiguity. But the hand outstretched to mistaken Christians seems to signify approbation.

The discussions at Schmalkalden proved awkward from the start. In vain did the landgrave invoke the precedent of Spires, where all protestants had acted in concert without taking into consideration controversial doctrinal questions. Lutherans insisted on grouping themselves around a banner on which they had inscribed their persuasion in all its details. Already Charles V was declaring his intention of devoting his attention to the religious affairs of Germany, from which he had for years been distracted by the wars in which he was engaged. The protestants, divided by the intransigence of Luther and Melanchthon, constituted two distinct federations: the group of the princes completed by the addition of Nuremberg, and that of the towns. The former drafted for the notice of the emperor, who indicated his desire to listen to every party, the so-called Confession of Augsburg; while the four cities—Strasburg, Constance, Memmingen and Lindau—united on the basis of a text prepared by Bucer and known as the *Confessio Tetrapolitana*.

The bitterness of Zwingli, who was kept informed by his friends of the course of the negotiations, is easily understandable. Marburg had apparently been useless. He, the Swiss, the republican, was classed as the heretic of heretics. Luther presented himself at Augsburg before the scion of the Habsburgs as a relative conservative: "We ask for reforms, but do not wish the eucharist to be modified; we are a moderate party", is what, in substance, he could say to Charles V. Melanchthon, who more even than his master entertained the hope of an understanding with the catholics, could not but emphasize the gulf which separated him from the reckless Swiss. The Elector of Saxony, for his part, was not displeased to divorce his cause from that of the towns whose spirit of independence was offensive to Spanish authoritarianism. The landgrave of Hesse, who desired conciliation in the teeth of all obstacles, signed the Confession of Augsburg, though with a reservation concerning the eucharistic article.

On January 21, 1530, the emperor despatched invitations to the Diet, which was to meet in the first instance at Augsburg on April 8. The Elector of Saxony, convinced that the emperor had developed since the period of Worms, lulled himself with the illusion that the assembly would witness the reconciliation of divided Christians. Philip of Hesse, whose attitude was to be justified by future events, remained sceptical. Was it important that Zwingli should go personally to this historic rendezvous? The Swiss cantons, who had gradually been liberated from Austrian dominance by a series of wars, were by no means anxious to revive the memory of their original connexion with the Germanic Holy Roman Empire. Strasburg, however, through the mediation of Oecolampadius, on May 22, advised the sending of a delegate who could speak French and who would be capable of expounding to Charles the Zwinglian point of view, though without presenting himself in the guise of a vassal.

The preparations for the Diet were lengthy. The emperor, without consideration for the princes who were already on the way or had arrived, announced a delay of several weeks. In the interval there was plenty of time for correspondence to function between Strasburg, Basle, Ulm, Constance, Cassel, and Zürich. At one moment rumour had it that Ulrich, escorted by Oecolampadius, would go personally to Augsburg. On May 31, however, Sturm, writing from this town and describing to Zwingli the prejudices which it fostered against him, advised rather the preparation of an apology for the attention of the emperor, on the model of what was formerly done by "Christians and martyrs in their approach to pagan princes."

Neither the reformer of Basle nor the reformer of Zürich felt prepared, for the sake of peace, to modify their eucharistic symbolism. At the precise moment when the stakes were being laid at Augsburg, they welcomed, in succession, Luther's sworn enemy, Carlstadt. Oecolampadius remarked that the poor theologian who had been obliged to flee from Germany was indeed very different from the terrible account of him which Luther and Melanchthon had given. He is a man "much more cultured than many. . . . I fear that we are unworthy of such a guest."

In a missive of June 19, Sturm described to Ulrich the march of events: the impressive entry into Augsburg, four days previously, of Charles V, accompanied by his brother Ferdinand, by Cardinal Campeggio, papal legate, by the cardinals of Salzburg and Trent, the dukes of Bavaria, the count Frederick, brother of the Elector Palatine, and a large number of Spanish bishops and officers. An escort of a thousand foot-soldiers, who had to be paid by the city of Augsburg, displayed in the sunshine the power of the monarch who was then at the height of his glory. This Diet, like every self-respecting assembly, was agitated from the start by a drama of protocol. King Ferdinand would have wished to walk in his brother's procession, with the papal legate on his left. The princes opposed this. By virtue of a constitution dating from the time of Charles IV, they asserted that the privilege of surrounding the emperor was *their* right. In the end, Charles V decided to walk alone, followed by the group of electors.

Poor petty victory of tradition! Hardly had the emperor dismounted from his horse, when he asked the princes to take part with him on the morrow in the procession of the Blessed Sacrament. The protestants apologized for their inability to agree to this. Early the next morning the emperor, bare-headed, and accompanied by the catholic princes, went in procession to the Cathedral, where the Archbishop of Mainz, in magnificent vestments, celebrated mass.

What would Zwingli and the Swiss have done amid these splendours, at once imperial and catholic? The reformed princes, as is shown by Sturm's account, constantly found themselves in a delicate position, despite all their desire for harmony. Charles V had taken the precaution of forbidding any protestant preaching, and intimated his desire to the electors through his brother Ferdinand, who discharged the office with painful violence. John of Saxony was struck dumb with stupor, while the two princes of Brandenburg and Hesse audaciously retorted that the emperor was not the master of their consciences: "Before denying my God and His Gospel," exclaimed the margrave, "I would prefer to kneel before Your Majesty and offer my head to the executioner."

After such a beginning, one could hardly expect to see any important result emerge from the debates. Only the situation created by the new advances of the Turks prevented a complete breakdown. Vienna was once more threatened. At first Charles tried the method of persuasion. For a month and a half the two parties parleyed in vain. At a solemn meeting on August 3 the emperor expressed his irritation in the tone of a Spanish despot. He declared that he would not suffer schism to arise in Germany. The princes and the towns must submit to his will. Philip of Hesse, carried away with indignation and fearing the worst, furtively left the town.

While these palavers, doomed to failure, were going on, Ulrich was drafting the defence which Sturm had demanded. During the last days of June he worked without intermission. On July 3 he was putting the final touches to a work containing under the title *Fidei ratio* (systematic exposition of the faith) the essentials of his doctrine. In its plan, as also its occasion, the little book resembled the one which a year later he handed to Collin so that the latter might offer it to Francis I as an act of homage. The same truths were handled in both. However, the tone of the volume written in 1531 is akin to the typical tone of the humanists. The text of 1530 is shorter and more incisive, the digressions are less numerous, and the style more concentrated.

If Zwingli had obeyed Sturm's suggestion, he did not share the hopes which some still placed in Charles V. His correspondence with the landgrave of Hesse and with Bucer shows that for some months he had been extremely sceptical about the good will of the monarch. "All his actions are deceptive", he wrote on July 22 to Philip of Hesse, whom in consequence he urged to remain vigilant. "The French ambassador", he added in the same letter, "reads the Gospel . . . and the king himself is very well disposed." The unfavourable course of events in Germany threw Zwingli back more and more on the hopes he entertained in regard to France. While he showed penetrating insight into the character of Charles V, he gratuitously believed that Francis I would come to embrace the cause of the reformation.

On August 8 Bucer warned him of the turn taken by events at Augsburg. The invitation to return to the bosom of the Roman Church provoked a stiffening in the attitude of protestants. Vadian too commented on the most recent news. In that world without newspapers, letters fulfilled the function of discussing the events of the day. Ulrich, however, found it difficult to understand the attitude of the landgrave, and begged him for a word of explanation. Philip answered him on September 4, apologizing for his long silence. If he left Augsburg, he said, it was especially because of Melanchthon, who was ready to yield at every point. Dreading the outbreak of civil war, Luther's collaborator went further and further in the direction of concessions. The Elector of Saxony, who was ill, was also inclined to flinch. The rectification of this came from the Nuremberg delegates, who were supported by the Saxon chancellor, Bruck. Luther, who had for a long time trusted his friend, decided at last to disavow him. Faced by the propositions of the catholic negotiators, he made short work of them: "This is bacon in a mouse-trap to catch us. To accept such conditions would be to slay Jesus Christ and deny His Word." The protestants could not be content with secondary satisfactions, such as the marriage of priests and the extension of the cup to the laity. Luther wrote in feverish agitation to Melanchthon, Link, and Jonas. Shortly afterwards the negotiations were broken off.

On September 22 the emperor granted the protestants an interval of six months in which to return to catholic unity. In the meantime, princes and towns were to desist from any attempt at proselytizing and to help the catholics in their struggle against the anabaptists and "all those who reject the Blessed Sacrament". To offset this, Charles V promised to use his influence with the pope to secure the convocation of a General Council.

The Lutherans, dismayed by the result of the Diet, from that time on began to lend an attentive ear to the advice of the landgrave. Saxony had played the chief part at Augsburg, and its desire to reach agreement had been broken by the sheer intransigence of the catholic party. The protestant world unanimously revolted against the prospect of total submission, of a return, pure and simple, to the catholic fold. On German soil itself, the gulf between Lutherans and Zwinglians was being bridged. The Duke of Luneburg suggested a meeting between Bucer and Luther, and this took place at Coburg on September 26. A year after Marburg, the Hessian conception of an alliance between protestants of all kinds was returning to favour. Had it not been for the tragedy of the situation, the landgrave Philip would have had the right to smile at this reversal of things.

From Coburg, Bucer slowly travelled back to Alsace, hawking from town to town his call for harmony. After a first stop at Nuremberg, he stopped at Ulm, then at Memmingen, Lindau, and Constance, which he reached on October 10. On the 12th he crossed the boundary of Zürich, where Zwingli, in conciliatory mood, told him that he was prepared to accept a formula such as *verum corpus vere dari* (a true body truly given). The Coburg talks did not authorize the simple affirmation of an agreement between all those who believed in Christ and accepted the authority of Holy Scripture. The question of the eucharist had been raised with such emphasis that the princes and towns considered it necessary to publish a formula which would do justice to the convictions of both parties.

As soon as he had returned to Strasburg, Bucer set to work and drew up for the attention of the Duke of Luneburg an optimistic report, in which he tried to demonstrate the affinity between the Lutheran and Zwinglian points of view. After the doctrine of the Saxon reformer had been spiritualized, there would be no further difficulty, he felt, in the use of his vocabulary by his opponents.

About the middle of November, Ulrich became acquainted with his friend's memorandum. It gave him a shock. The assent which he had given to Bucer at the time of their interview in October, presented without the necessary precautions, had the effect of ranking him among the Lutherans. After the way in which he had been dragged in the mud, any ambiguity rankled. In agreement with him, the pastors of Zürich on November 20 instructed Burgomaster Roüst, who was meeting the Strasburg delegates at Basle, not to

commit Zürich—and that in spite of the advice of Oecolampadius urging conciliation. The opportunism which
Ulrich sometimes had shown yields in this instance to a
feeling which may be variously interpreted. Excessive
susceptibility, inability to forgive, insinuate some. Ardent
need of truth, horror of falsehood and of anything resembling
it, answer others.

The league of Schmalkalden, which grouped together all
the protestants of Germany, was organized at the end of
December, 1530, without the participation of Zürich. But
in January, 1531, Zwingli seemed ready to abandon his
intransigent attitude. The Strasburg theologians assured
him that in the confession of faith eucharistic differences
would be minimized. Ulrich could appreciate the importance
of what was at stake politically. Berne, normally in favour
of strict neutrality, but now worried about the manœuvres
of catholic Savoy around Geneva, seemed disposed to sign.
But Luther in his negotiations with Bucer insisted that
Zürich and Wittenberg should speak the same language.
The Saxon was bitterly insistent that an objective presence
of Christ in the eucharist should be professed. He would
have liked to have felt sure that for Oecolampadius and
Zwingli even the wicked receive the body of the Lord,
whether or not they derive any spiritual profit from it. On
February 12, 1531, Ulrich refused to grant such satisfaction
to his antagonist. The Swiss never signed the articles of
Schmalkalden, preferring isolation to compromise. "They
have a mass almost more papist than the papists themselves," exclaimed the Zürich reformer. "We know that the
body of Christ is in the eucharist, but it is not there naturally
or corporeally, it is there sacramentally, that is to say, by
the contemplation of faith. . . . We must not say: what does
it matter if the people say this or that . . . for we occupy
the position of prophets."

For seven years, partisans and opponents of the doctrine of
an objective Real Presence had clashed. The long discussions
had been useless. Luther remained Luther, and Zwingli,
Zwingli.

CHAPTER THIRTY-SIX

The Royal Writings

TWO WORKS, MENTIONED in the course of the preceding chapters, appeared in 1530 and 1531: the *Fidei ratio* and the *Expositio fidei*. They have in common their dedication to foreign princes, Charles V and Francis I, and they are also alike in their conciseness. In the popular edition of the works of Zwingli at present in use, the first numbers about forty pages of the size used in novels, the second about fifty. Passing from one book to the other, the reader will note many repetitions, while many passages correspond to those of the *De vera et falsa religione*. None the less, they are original works, written in a single flash of inspiration by a writer whose matured thought easily finds its appropriate form.

The plan of the two volumes is that of the Credo: God, Christ, the Holy Spirit, the Church, forgiveness, eternal life. In the pages dedicated to the emperor, the frequent repetition of the "I believe" aims at persuading the monarch of the seriousness of the author. Zwingli wishes to be a Christian as devoutly as does the catholic and Luther. The important place given to consideration of the two natures of the Saviour is manifestly the result of the eucharistic discussions. Ulrich has thought out for himself the Chalcedonian problem—how Jesus Christ can be both true man and true God. The reflections on original sin echo the discussion of the theme with Luther and Melanchthon. Sin is an hereditary malady which each one assumes through his own particular faults. Little children, who have not yet sinned in the personal sense of the word, do not die condemned.

Their position is like that of the descendants of a prisoner sold as a slave for his misdeeds: they share in his state without being directly responsible for it.

The great themes of the previous writings reappear: faith is given through election, not through participation in the sacrament. The latter is no more than a sign of a holy spiritual reality. In a series of paragraphs, Zwingli dispenses to Charles V the teachings which were developed and amplified in the eucharistic controversy. Two or three pages which introduce newer ideas extol the value of preaching. It is preaching which conveys the liberating message of God. The office of the prophet is therefore essential; through it election is visibly accomplished. The presence of faithful pastors in the Church is a sign of grace. The temporal power must welcome and support them. Do they not render it a service in return by providing it with good subjects?

Although opposed to the doctrine of purgatory, Ulrich affirms the reality of hell. The seriousness of his undertaking is attested by his life and erudition, as also by the morally uplifting influence of the Gospel. The effect of sermons is to make falsehood, incredulity, pride, immorality, quarrelling recede. The emperor can observe the progress of a people enlightened by the Word of God. Such fruits are incomparably superior to the frivolity of the popes and of individuals assured that salvation is to be gained by paid masses.

The chapters written for the attention of Francis I differ from those dedicated to Charles V more by their style than their substance. Convinced that the king of France will listen to him with the attention of a humanist and a Christian, Zwingli addresses him as one who is capable of understanding. He tries to dissociate his cause from that of the anabaptists. There is nothing in common, he asserts, between the authentic reformation and this spurious branch of it. The anabaptists outwit old women and extort from them the money they need for their maintenance. They are like tares in the wheat, a plague, the enemies of military service, of oaths, of taxes, of the slightest participation in the responsibilities of state authority, advocates moreover of the community of goods and even of women.

Ulrich repudiates among other calumnies the accusation of despising the saints which was often addressed to the reformers. There is no truth in this allegation. But the place of a saint is not on an altar. The venerated person would be the first to protest against such excesses. The Christian must be content respectfully to imitate the good examples set by pious people.

The paragraphs devoted to the sacraments, apart from the inevitable texts about Christ seated at the right hand of God, contain a fine description of the feelings of communicants. "When you approach the table of the Lord to enjoy spiritually the body of Christ and you give thanks to the Lord for the ransom of your soul, for the end of despair, and the assurance of eternal felicity, and when you share with your brethren the bread and the wine which are the image of the body of Christ, you are experiencing a symbolic communion. You do inwardly what you manifest outwardly, for your soul is strengthened by this faith, to which you bear witness by the sign (which is the sacrament)."

The eucharist sustains faith, Ulrich notes further. Faith is constantly being tested by the Tempter. He seeks to destroy it by means of our body. If the senses are occupied in a way which prevents them from giving heed to the suggestions of Satan, then his attacks will have little success. The sacraments deliver the senses from the dominion of the devil. The four most important are freed from the desires of the flesh: hearing, when instead of the sound of musical instruments, it hears the promise ring out: "God so loved the world that He gave His only-begotten Son"; the eyes when they behold the bread and the cup, which represent the goodness of Christ; touch, when the hands take the bread which is no longer bread, but a symbol signifying Christ; and finally taste and smell which measure the goodness of the Lord (Ps. 34: 8) and the blessedness of the man who trusts in Him.

Ulrich without ceasing to be himself seems here, despite

his denials, to be advancing in the way marked out by Bucer. In such a description does not the reader palpably feel both the greatness and the vanity of the effort to define the exact nature of spiritual participation in the sacrament? In the last pages of the treatise a few famous lines carry us to heaven to see enthroned Abel, Noah, Abraham, Isaac, the holy Virgin Mother of God, John the Baptist, Peter and Paul, along with the most virtuous heroes of Graeco-Roman antiquity: Hercules, Theseus, Socrates, Aristides, Antigone, Numa, Camilla, the Catos, the Scipios, the list being completed by the ancestors of Francis—namely, Louis, Philip, and Pepin. Luther, who read this enumeration in 1544, fulminated a posthumous excommunication. Zwingli, he declared, had turned pagan; there was cause for doubt whether he was truly saved.

CHAPTER THIRTY-SEVEN

Switzerland under the Shadow of Anxiety and Suspicion

VENTS IN GERMANY, interviews and correspondence with the authorities of Strasburg and Cassel, led Zwingli to feel increasingly that the peace of Cappel was a bargain concluded with dupes. During the year 1530 the political situation in Switzerland developed under the shadow of growing tension. The troops of Zürich, which had occupied the lands of the Abbot of St. Gall, refused to give them up. The diplomacy of Vadian and the firmness of Berne were needed to secure the arrangement whereby on August 23 the town of St. Gall took possession of the conventual buildings. Zürich strangely mingled a desire for self-aggrandisement with a concern to extend the sway of the reformation. Crusades are rarely disinterested. The crusader fights as much for himself as for God.

In the protestant coalition, Zürich was the motor, Berne the brake. On the banks of the Limmat the pastors urged bellicose adventures. Doctrinal absolutism, flung into the world of politics, resisted all compromise. Already, when the mediation of Glarus had reconciled the divided states of the Confederation, Ulrich had resented the restoration of peace. He spoke as if the treaty had settled nothing. On the banks of the Aar, although men like Haller were in line with Zwingli, the magistrates had too keen a sense of political realities to wish for a new conflict. Whereas in Zürich the Council was no longer anything but an instrument in the hands of the reformer, at Berne the laity retained control. The preachers were listened to with respect, but were not obeyed

The very admiration which surrounds them hardens the judgment of great men. Usually Zwingli's correspondents were too closely allied to his views to be in a position to reason with him. "You are the sole eye and the vigilant guard, not only for the whole country, but of all Christendom", Haller wrote to him.

Like a sentinel, Zwingli could assess the dangers which threatened the cause of the reformers. Rather than wait for the completion of imperial preparations, would it not be better to take the initiative, he asked himself. At the beginning of 1531, rumour had it that the alliance between Austria and the five catholic cantons had been re-established. In January, 1531, the latter were sharply protesting against the way in which Zürich was behaving on the territory of St. Gall and the districts administered in common, where the representatives of the heretic town were conducting themselves as though they alone were the owners. If the Forest Cantons could speak with such assurance, was it not because of a new alliance with King Ferdinand? A treaty torn up and burnt can be rewritten and signed afresh by the parties. Did not the first magistrate of Schwyz, *landammann* Rychmuth, say this openly in a public meeting?

Most protestant historians judge with severity the way in which Ulrich acted during this crucial year. Köhler remarks that in instigating a new outbreak of hostilities he was only apparently strengthening the position of his party. The network of alliances on which he prided himself had the solidity of a house of cards. How many armies had he at his disposal? "All was planning, hope and faith."

At the beginning of March an incident brought to a climax the general ferment and irritation. An Italian freebooter, Giangiacomo dei Medici, lord of Musso on the Lake of Como, at the head of his men, invaded the Grison area of the Valteline, seized two delegates returning from France and gave orders to execute them. The Grisons appealed to the Diet. Zwingli transformed this purely local incident into a vast and sinister intrigue against the reformation. Charles V had, he thought, schemed to bring about the expedition. The troops sent to the help of the Grisons would be lacking at the centre of Switzerland when the attack of the catholic cantons against the protestants took place. The only support for this theory is the refusal of the Forest Cantons to send troops to the states of the Confederation that were attacked.

Zürich, extremely disturbed, began preparations for war. In vain the French embassy offered its services to effect a reconciliation of the divided Swiss: "I hope it will come to nothing", wrote Myconius to Thomas Platter on May 2. "No peace with the godless is possible even if the latter desired it. Three days ago we appointed a new captain. . . ." Nevertheless, Maigret, in his brief missives, was copious in his use of appeasing words. At the same time he intervened at Lucerne in an effort to calm the ferment there too. Francis I desired mercenaries. A civil war could only impoverish the sources on which he might draw. Sympathetic as he was personally to the reformation, the ambassador was under no illusions about the dispositions of the king. Moreover, on Zwingli's behalf he sincerely dreaded the adventure of a war. On May 14, in a letter longer than usual, he begged him to consider the dangers of his position. On the previous day the delegates of the protestant towns had met at Aarau. Zürich had repeated its complaints. If war broke out, pleaded the ambassador, it would mean the ruin of the Confederation. The victor would be no better off than the vanquished. Did not the adventure of the lord of Musso give reason to pause and reflect? False friends, after inciting him to embark on his risky undertaking, left him and joined his enemies.

Five days later, Maigret, accompanied by his colleague, Louis de Boisrigault, went to Zürich and reiterated his warnings. Taking occasion to make use of the exhortations of the Gospel, he adjured the magistrates to forgive injuries.

Zürich refused to listen to such counsels. If the influential voice of Berne prevented the issue of a formal declaration

of war, the protestant cantons none the less decided on an
economic blockade, which irritated in the highest degree the
catholic cantons. Zwingli insisted not only on obtaining
apologies—the catholics, he considered, dragged his name
in the mud, ceaselessly vituperating his heresy—but on
gaining an assurance that at Lucerne and Schwyz the
preaching of the Gospel would be authorized. He was for-
getting that in Zürich itself the mass had been forbidden
for the last three years. Let us point out, however, in excul-
pation of Zwingli, that on catholic territory the sword and
stake were used to secure the maintenance of pure doctrine.
At Lucerne on May 12 a citizen of protestant Winterthur
was condemned to death. The judges accused him of railing
against the "five districts" (the catholic cantons of central
Switzerland) and of having married again after divorcing
his first wife.

The economic sanctions decided on made Ulrich indignant.
He felt this to be a half-measure. Its effect would be to
deprive the weak of bread. Children and old women would
be compelled to go without nourishment. Nor would the
political conflict be settled in this way. On Whit-Sunday,
May 28, the measure which the authorities had decided to
adopt was announced from the pulpits. The reformer who
was preaching on that day did not scruple to criticize, as
pastor, the decision which he had vainly opposed in the
secret Council. It was necessary either to strike or not to
strike, he urged. The sanctions enforced would not fail to
provoke a reply with armed strength.

Zwingli's situation in that extraordinary spring of 1531
was not unlike the situation of Savonarola, who, a few
months before his fall, was demanding from the rulers of
France, England, Spain, Austria, and Hungary the calling
of a general Council for the purpose of deposing the pope,
Alexander Borgia. It is often the case that religious leaders
think their power and influence greater than it is.

Although in Zürich itself the authoritarianism of the
reformer was beginning to become wearisome, in the spiritual
sphere his doctrine continued to gain ground. Rapperswil,

at the other end of the lake, decided in favour of the reformation. At Appenzell the Diet adopted measures which favoured the innovators. At Augsburg and Ulm and other German cities, Zwinglianism carried off brilliant victories. Was not the political struggle, which the reformer led with such ardour, harming his essential cause? As though tormented by a bad conscience, in his correspondence he pleaded for the measures adopted. "The five Districts will not accept the preaching of the Word", he explained to Oecolampadius. And in similar terms he wrote to his Ulm friends: "The sole obstacle to peace is the refusal of the Five Districts to authorize the preaching of the Gospel."

At Berne discontent was growing. It was being said there that the Five Districts were less to be feared than the imperialism of Zürich. On July 11, a new round of negotiations between protestant and catholic delegates took place at Bremgarten, but they failed to produce any concrete result. Zwingli journeyed to this city, met the Bernese delegates there in secret and submitted to them a plan which would have revolutionized the Helvetic constitution had it been accepted. Was it not abnormal, he suggested, that in the country's affairs the small cantons should enjoy voting rights equal to those of the two republics of Zürich and Berne? The two states, he asserted, were the "pillars" of the Confederation. They ought to possess in the districts administered on a communal basis an influence proportionate to their real importance. Collaboration with the Five Districts was no longer possible, for they had abandoned all discipline and all justice. The protestants should hasten to pass to a military attack now that these cantons were weakened by a blockade of food-supplies.

This was the dangerous advice of a fanatic. Five years of incessant struggle had wrought a change indeed in the one-time admirer of Erasmus. Nothing now remained from the pacifism of his early years. The militant Confederate had gained the upper hand. Zwingli was now reasoning as a statesman resolved to take into consideration brute facts and necessities rather than rights. He felt that the Swiss constitution had become out of date: it was necessary to renew it. All the changes proposed were to the advantage of Zürich and Berne, who would pull the Confederation along "like two oxen in front of the waggon, pulling under the same yoke".

The Bernese, confronted by this amazing programme, maintained their coolness of judgment. In their opinion the advice of Ulrich would have led straight to a war, which was the last thing they wanted. Did they express their astonishment to the Zürich delegates? This is not known. A fortnight later, on the banks of the Limmat, the general agitation was such that Zwingli begged the Great Council to accept his resignation. Moved by emotion, he recalled his eleven years of faithful service as a preacher. How many times had he not put the citizens of Zürich on their guard against the Five Districts dominated by the pensioned mercenaries? He was no longer listened to. In the Council itself he numbered several enemies. The city was rushing to its ruin. He no longer wished to shoulder the burden of such a responsibility. The magistrates retained him in power, but this dramatic sitting of July 26 betrayed deep uneasiness. Plebiscites arise from anxiety to consolidate a power which is being challenged.

When the crisis had been dissipated, Ulrich continued to insist that the city should prepare itself for the worst eventualities. The reign of austerity went further. From 1530 wedding parties celebrating at inns found their jollities curtailed; dancing was forbidden. On August 16 Zwingli boasted to his friend Conrad Sam of Ulm about the good will of the Council of Zürich which was ready to give help to anyone desiring it. A comet appeared in the skies. Several people saw it three days in succession, "I, once only; it was, I think, the 15th of August. Today, which is the 16th, I don't know what we shall see." Myconius, in his biography, tells us that Ulrich discerned in the mysterious flying star a warning from heaven foretelling sinister events "for himself and one other". This other unnamed person, supposes the writer, was probably Oecolampadius. Gloomy presentiments thus haunted the mind of the pastor of the Great Minster. Twice, in the fortnight preceding the departure for Cappel, Myconius heard him give voice to his restless anxiety from the pulpit: "I know very well what's going on. They want to get rid of me. I've got to get out of the way. . . ."

CHAPTER THIRTY-EIGHT

On the Battlefield (1531)

POLICY AT ZÜRICH fell short through insufficient military preparation. Democracies often shout about their intentions without possessing the military strength they require for their purpose. During the years which followed the triumph of the reformation, Zwingli and his partisans had ceaselessly struggled against the military pensioners. The city had fewer officers than before. Some military personnel had left it. After the first war of Cappel, moreover, an edict was issued diminishing the authority of professional soldiers to the advantage of members of the Councils. In a recent study[1] a historian, Georg Gerig, maintains that the defeat of Cappel was due to these dangerous purges. Zwingli, it is asserted, anxious not to leave too much power in the hands of political adversaries, superseded a whole series of capable men. May there not be some exaggeration in this thesis? Köhler, however, instances the dismissal of Hans Berger, one of the most competent of captains. "You should pay attention to the fear of God, to faithfulness and truth, rather than to the art of war", wrote Ulrich with reference to the character of the Christian officer in his *Plan for an armed expedition*. In a technical sphere, to prefer correct opinions to competence is to run great risks.

Those minds that were more aware of the trend of things were becoming disturbed. Not until September 9, 1531, did the Council of Zürich appoint a council of war consisting of devoted supporters of Zwingli, and under orders, in the

---

[1] *Reisläufer und Pensionenherren in Zürich (1519-32).*

event of an attack by the Five Districts, to mobilize the army at once and march to meet the enemy. A leader was chosen in the person of captain Hans Lavater, formerly an officer in the papal service, who had early become attached to the reformation and for several years had fulfilled the office of administrator of Kyburg. But the Council, which had reserved to itself the right to take final decisions in preliminary measures, did nothing. Good citizens were convinced that the catholic cantons would not dare to declare war. Lavater, infuriated by their inertia, after a few days returned to his castle at Kyburg.

Ulrich, while keeping an eye open, was none the less busy with his various duties during these tense and anxious months. On August 17, at the request of the humanist Grynaeus, a theologian of merit settled in Basle who had been commissioned by the king of England to take the advice of the universities with regard to his possible remarriage, Zwingli gave his opinion of this delicate problem in a letter which is unfortunately lost. The text of it, however, was summarized by the English writer Burnet in his *History of the Reformation in England*. While Grynaeus and Bucer, considering an annulment of Henry VIII's marriage with Katherine of Aragon impossible, suggested the strange solution of bigamy, their Zürich correspondent advised that the marriage, which was vitiated by the close kinship of the partners, could well be dissolved. The divorce, he said, should be invested with all due legal forms, and the queen should retain her title and prerogatives. Oecolampadius also adopted Zwingli's point of view: "Let us take care", he wrote on August 20, "not to give heed to Mahomet rather than Christ."

Of the last two extant letters of Zwingli, the first, which is dated September 3, shows him still absorbed in his grand political designs. In it he invites the Duke of Milan, Francis II of Sforza, to ally himself with the people of Zürich. The second is addressed to Vadian, his old friend as ever. It is a simple letter, seeking help and advice, which was despatched on September 17. Ulrich was concerned about the lot of a cousin of his, two years his senior. Liable to fits of dizziness, the poor man could no longer get about alone. He had a modest private income. Could not a servant of the lower classes be found to take care of him? On the eve of the drama which was to carry him off, the reformer showed his tender concern for his neighbour. Christian charity still dwelt in his heart, though mingled with passion for the cause he served.

Zürich had promised Berne not to let loose the hounds of war. The blockade was only partially effective. Through the passes of the Alps provisions arrived from Italy. None the less, in the Five Districts exacerbation increased. While the protestants were drowsy with good feeding, the empty stomachs of the catholics drove them to seek extreme solutions. Lucerne, Zug, Uri, Schwyz and Unterwalden were secretly mobilizing. The rumour of this reached Berne and Zürich in the days preceding the declaration of war. Couriers galloping from one town to another scattered panic in their train. Along the frontier of Zug, the three hundred soldiers of Zürich who were quartered there could observe troop movements and were demanding reinforcements. Two thousand men at the very least were needed to hold the position. On October 9 and 10, contingents from Schwyz and Uri were grouping in the region of Baar. The wind carried the sound of drums and fifes as far as the threatened territory.

Cappel, standing at a height of over seventeen hundred feet, and Baar, situated four hundred feet lower (it was the first important locality in the plain which extends from the Lake of Zug), were roughly one hour's march from each other. The frontier runs about a quarter of a mile to the south of the ancient abbey of Cappel, the towering arches of which are today still prominent in the centre of the little village. The meadows, cut by deep ravines and studded with forests, constituted a terrain where manœuvring was difficult. The men of Zürich by their very situation enjoyed a decided advantage, on condition, of course, that they could profit by it.

The Five Districts had assembled for the attack about eight thousand men. On the shores of the Limmat, the magistrates, faced by the disturbing reports which reached them from Cappel, believed that the news was exaggerated. The troops were not alerted until October 9. A first detachment left Zürich the following day about noon and hastened to the threatened region, where it arrived in the evening, wearied. At its head the Council had placed an officer who had distinguished himself in foreign service, the chevalier George Göldli of Tiefenau, member of a conservative-minded family. His brother in fact was fighting in the catholic camp. The company from Zürich took up a position on a dominating plateau less than half a mile away from the abbey. As the commission of enquiry appointed after the defeat noted, this position entailed a double disadvantage. In the rear, marshes and a ditch full of water made retreat difficult. Eastwards, the forest of Kalchofen enabled the enemy to turn the flank of the Zürich soldiers. Their security required the occupation of the wood, which Göldli refused to do, in spite of reiterated demands.

Early in the morning of October 11 an enemy dispatchrider brought the declaration of war from the Five Districts, a long document in which they summed up their grievances. It was handed to the chief of the Zürich army. An advance guard of five hundred men followed at a distance. It was perceived by the sentinels when it reached the northern edge of the wood of Schönenbühl, a little way south of the monastic buildings. Anxious at heart, the defenders of the abbey began to shoot about midday.

The wish of Berne had been respected. The responsibility for the outbreak of hostilities could not be laid at the door of Zürich. The victim of aggression, Zwingli's city could plead its innocence, but the situation of its troops was no less delicate for all that. After the arrival of the detachment commanded by Göldli, an important reinforcement under the command of captain Lavater had hastily set out early in the morning of the 11th. The attackers nevertheless had at their command an overwhelming superiority. Compared with their eight thousand well-armed and well-prepared men, the garrison of Cappel could count no more than fifteen hundred soldiers.

Hence the battle was engaged inauspiciously for the soldiers of Zürich. If they repulsed the frontal attack which the catholic troops flung against the abbey, the latter, after retreating, lost no time in thinking of turning the enemy position. They had to advise them one of their chaplains, Rudolph Weingartner, a former monk of Cappel, who had settled at Zug after the secularization of the cloister and who knew the locality perfectly. On the catholic side as on the protestant, hearts of warlike strategists beat beneath ecclesiastical dress. The main part of the troops, across fields and through woods, wheeled around Cappel, leaving a company to occupy the cloister in order to safeguard the security of the manœuvre. About three o'clock in the afternoon, the men of Zug and their allies established themselves in the shelter of this very wood of Kalchofen where Göldli had refused to engage his men. The odd attitude of the Zürich captain may perhaps be explained by the fear of dispersing too much a comparatively small troop of soldiers. Moreover, a frontal attack might be resumed at any moment.

While the catholic army was thus securing the mounting of a second assault, part of the protestant reinforcements —a company of about seven hundred men—under the command of Lavater, climbed to the peak of the Albis. A short distance away, as the crow flies, the glance of the chiefs could at once discern the perilous situation of those whom they had come to help. A council of war was held, in which Ulrich participated. Must they wait until contingents gradually mobilized in Zürich arrived on the scene? Could they allow the advance guard to be crushed, without other support? "If we are to assemble slowly here," advised the reformer, "our good people, I fear, will arrive too late. We ought not to wait while lower down our men suffer. Gladly, in the name of God, I will die with them or promote their deliverance." The desire for solidarity got the better of prudence. The troop hurried down to the foot of the mountain and joined

the threatened detachment. On the way they did not forget
to ease the tension by touches of humour. With a hearty
laugh, the baker Burkard turned to Zwingli: "Master Ulrich,
what do you think of this business? Are the carrots salted?
Who will eat them?" "I and many an honest man who is here
in the hands of God to whom we belong, dead or alive,"
answered Ulrich. "I will do my utmost to help," rejoined
the other in confirmation, "and to stake trustfully my body
and soul."

The united Zürich soldiers now numbered upwards of
two thousand men (i.e. they were one against four) and
they had at their disposal fifteen pieces of ordnance. It was
about four in the afternoon. On the horizon, the autumnal
sun was sinking. The chiefs of the catholic party, unaware of
their numerical superiority, hesitated to attack. A few short
hours and darkness would fall on the combatants. One of
them advised concealing three hundred marksmen of Uri
in a still unoccupied beechwood which extended a curtain
between the adversaries, and from that protected site to
start harassing the enemy. The main attack was then
launched by a second detachment, which, from a position
more to the south, concentrated its fire power on the plateau
where the Zürich soldiers had been stationed since the morning. The latter, caught in a sort of pincer movement, recoiled.
Their best men were struggling against the marksmen of
Uri. The new wave of attack caught them unawares. They
fought on energetically, but, once the height they were
occupying was lost, they had to retreat. An order of Lavater
which Göldli, deliberately or unintentionally, misunderstood,
disorganized their defence. Meantime, the catholics kept
up their attacks unremittingly. Seeing the embarrassment
of the Zürich soldiers, they profited by it to the utmost.
Soon the retreat turned into a rout. The marshes situated
behind the protestant contingents slowed up their flight.
Defeat became panic and confusion. Five hundred men
perished or fell mortally wounded under the blows of the
assailants, who lost only a hundred of theirs. The banner of
Zürich only just escaped falling into the hands of the

pursuers, thanks to the prodigies of valour achieved by two peasants, Uly Denzler and Adam Naef, each of whom was later rewarded by a farm and the freedom of the city.

The group surrounding the flag was cruelly decimated. Zwingli, armed with helmet and sword, made every effort to check the headlong flight. "Good people," he said, "have faith, do not fear. Trust in God, who cares for His own. God reigns." The numerical superiority of the enemy made any attempt at resistance useless. Blows came thick and fast. Did Ulrich personally take part in the fighting or was he content to exhort his fellows? Opinions differ. Köhler thinks that he used his sword, while Staehelin asserts that his action was confined to words. Helmeted and armed, his appearance at all events did not distinguish him from the other men of Zürich. Twice struck in the thigh by enemy lances and bleeding copiously, finally he received a violent blow on the head which knocked him to the ground gravely wounded. He still breathed. His friend Bullinger depicts him with his eyes turned heavenwards, his lips murmuring a last prayer, while the catholic chronicler Salat presents him on the contrary with his face turned towards the ground. The faithful Myconius, who does not altogether escape the deviations usual in hagiography, makes him cry out before collapsing: "They can kill the body, but not the soul."

When the battle was over, the soldiers who were rifling the corpses on the battlefield offered the dying man the assistance of a confessor. Ulrich still had enough strength left to refuse. In the light of torches which lit up the entangled bodies, a captain from Unterwalden, Vockinger, suddenly recognized the heresiarch and gave him the finishing stroke. From that moment, insults rained thick on the beaten enemy. The painful scene was continued the following day. A procession was organized. The men of the Five Districts all wished to behold with their own eyes the man who had shattered the religious unity of Switzerland, and to heap upon him coarse insults. One word of mercy, however, shed a luminous ray on the sordid shroud. A septuagenarian priest of Zug, Hans Schönbrunner, formerly a

canon of the Fraumünster and in that capacity for years
a colleague of Zwingli, gazed with compassion at the face
of him from whom he had long been separated as a result
of the religious upheaval of the country: "Whatever your
religious faith, I know that you were always a loyal Confederate. May God pardon your sins." The pity of the old
canon was not shared by the crowd, which, setting itself
up as a tribunal, handed the body over to the executioner
to be quartered. This punishment, reserved for traitors,
was later considered insufficient. The bloodstained fragments, mingled with dung, were solemnly burnt.

Thus died the pastor who had endeavoured to rescue
from abuses the Church of the 16th century. Ferdinand
of Austria, to whom the happy news was communicated
at Spires, was all eagerness to convey it to Charles V: "I
hope much from this," he remarked, "for it is the first event
which has been favourable to the faith and the catholic
church." A few months later, Erasmus laconically triumphed
at the happy event, to which was now added the premature
death of Oecolampadius: "It is a good thing", he wrote,
"that these two leaders have succumbed. If Mars had been
propitious to them, it would have been the ruin of us." As
for Luther, he was no more generous. He saw in this lamentable end a sign of the divine judgment: "The Zwinglians",
he wrote to a correspondent, "have made peace with the
other Swiss cantons, but on the most shameful conditions,
to say nothing of the ignominy and disaster which have come
upon them through the so unfortunate death of the head of
their beliefs. Such is the end of the glory which they sought
through their blasphemies against the Lord's Supper." And
to another correspondent: "We see the accomplishment of
God's judgment, first in the person of Münzer, and now in
the person of Zwingli. I was a true prophet when I said that
God would not suffer the impious blasphemies with which
their minds were filled. They mocked our God, they called
us eaters of flesh and drinkers of blood. They have brought
this on themselves." He seized this opportunity to impress
on the mind of Prince Albert of Prussia a salutary terror:

"Do not tolerate the Zwinglian heresy, do not argue with them, do not allow such people in your states. I have pity on their misfortunes, but they are not martyrs."

The Bible narrates that Job, when crushed by misfortune, found no consolation from his friends. Even Blarer, Bucer, and Vadian saw in the disaster of Cappel a warning sign from God. Outside Zürich, Oecolampadius was almost alone in defending the memory of the companion of his struggles. He wrote to the pastors of Ulm telling them that the Swiss custom was that the most prominent ecclesiastics should accompany the flag on the battlefield: "Our brother was not mobilized as the captain of a troop, but as the good shepherd who wishes to die with his flock." In the defeated city, Leo Jud, Myconius, and Bullinger pleaded energetically for the defeated prophet. Myconius published the short biography to which reference has sometimes been made in this book. In the ashes of Zwingli, he tells us, four days after the battle, the heart of the reformer was found intact. This miracle appeared to him as a sign from heaven.

Epilogue and Conclusion

THE MOTHERS AND the widows of Zürich wept for their dead. Among them, none was more grievously afflicted than Anna Zwingli. The poor woman learnt of the loss not only of her husband, but of her eldest son, Gerold Meyer von Knonau, the fine child of the mercenary; of her son-in-law, Anton Wirz, of her brother, Bernard Reinhart, and of a brother-in-law whose name cannot be traced. Supported by the respectful sympathy of her fellow-citizens, she lived for another seven years. From a material point of view there remained to her nothing but to look after her children. Bullinger gave her a home along with two of them, and these two, after the death of their mother, he brought up as his own. The third was entrusted to the care of Leonard Tremp of Berne, Ulrich's kinsman.

Genealogists have amassed a great deal of information about the posterity of the married priest. His younger daughter, Anna, died at an early age, only a few weeks after her father. Wilhelm reached student age, but the plague carried him off in his sixteenth year while he was studying at the university of Strasburg. Regula, who had married the Zürich pastor, Rudolph Gwalther, also succumbed to the plague when she was forty-one years of age, while Ulrich, pastor at the Great Minster and teacher of Hebrew, died of an attack at the age of forty-three. Regula and Ulrich, both married, left numerous descendants, some account of whom is given by W. H. Ruoff in a study published in the year 1937. In many families of Switzerland, Germany, and the United States there still flows a few drops of the blood of the Zwingli couple. The male line of the reformer died out in the 17th century, but it is estimated that several thousands can claim him as their forefather according to the flesh. It is a curious fact, but, according to the documents collected by pastor O. Sartorius, the living posterity of Luther is much less numerous (only five hundred persons in 1926).

Spiritually, Zwingli's influence is perpetuated by his writings, as also by the tradition of the communities which he reformed. Protestant Switzerland, in its German section, is connected with him, as also is a part of Germany. The Zwinglian churches are characterized by extreme sobriety. The form of worship allocates to preaching a preponderant part. Although the organ and the singing of hymns have reappeared, the liturgical aspect has been gradually reduced. The figure of the Zürich pastor remains popular. He is loved for the pluck with which he flung himself into the dramatic crises which marked his career. Less passionate than Luther and less cold than Calvin, his robust faith speaks to the heart of the layman, to whom his simplicity seems preferable to the ratiocinations of theologians. The prophet in him stimulates the pastor.

Zwingli restored the Bible to a central position, making it the fontal source of piety. Like Luther, he fought against the anxiety to achieve salvation by works. Asceticism, ornamentation of churches, repetition of prayers, yield to a religion which is dominated by the concern for the weak, a religion which is eager to translate itself into practical concrete terms, which develops works of public or private charity. To be sure, Zwinglianism runs the risk of intellectualism and of moralism, but it deeply embodies a faith in individual and social realities as reflecting the divine command: "You shall love your neighbour as yourself." Through Ragaz and Kutter, and also through his education, Karl Barth, who quotes Zwingli relatively little, owes much to him. At the present time the Barthian movement, which is opposed to any permanent insertion of the divine into the stream of immanence, is putting the brake on the liturgical renewal—of Anglican inspiration—which is more and more modifying the form of Calvinist worship.

Calvin owed much more to the author of the *De vera et falsa religione* than appears at first sight. Through the mediation of Farel and the Strasburg group, part of Zwingli's conceptions—how much it is difficult to say—penetrated the *Institutes of the Christian Religion*. The reformer of Geneva nevertheless judged with severity the reformer of Zürich. A pastor of Orbe, in the district of Vaud, one Zébédée, had dedicated to the memory of Ulrich a quatrain beginning with this cry: *"Majorem sperare nefas"* (It would be wrong to expect a greater). The eulogy displeased Calvin as head of a theological school of thought. On February 27, 1540, he expressed his displeasure in a letter addressed to Farel, a colleague of Zébédée: "It would be inhuman to slander the departed and impious to speak of such a man otherwise than with respect. But there must be restraint in praise and I cannot subscribe to that of Zébédée. I see at the present time many who are greater [than Zwingli] and I hope for others. I desire even that all should surpass him" (*"aliquos sperem, omnes cupio"*). Already the apostles were caught by Jesus discussing who should be the greatest. Two years later, in a letter to Viret, the author of the *Institutes* defined his criticism more precisely, admitting that he had not read the whole of Zwingli's work; the last writings toned down the errors of the earliest; the man of Zürich expressed himself profanely about the doctrine of the sacraments. "None of us can have a full understanding of this mystery."

The defeat of Cappel abruptly checked the expansion of the reformation in Switzerland. The war did not last long. The contingents of Berne, Solothurn and Basle, together with the soldiers of Zürich, soon amassed on the slopes of the Albis nearly thirty thousand men to whom the Five Districts could oppose no more than ten thousand. But the Bernese were not anxious to fight. Their chief, Sebastian von Diesbach, remained opposed to the reformation. In Zürich itself a movement of reaction was in progress. The flower of the citizens had fallen on the battlefield. The enemies of Zwingli accused him, along with his friends, of having involved the country in a wild adventure. Leo Jud had to go into hiding for some days.

On October 23 a detachment of the protestant army which had advanced as far as the Zugerberg was surprised by a night attack and lost a hundred men. Basle insisted on negotiations. The Zürich peasants, weary of camping far from hearth and home, were likewise clamouring for peace. Berne turned a deaf ear when Zürich asked for reinforcements.

Finally, the Council of Zürich initiated negotiations, and on November 16 signed an agreement with the Five Districts, which guaranteed its political independence, but sacrificed the minorities in the areas administered in common and in St. Gall. A week later, the Bernese subscribed to the treaty, which guaranteed the right of each Swiss state to decide for itself its religious future. Several communes of Aargau and Thurgau, in which the majority had already decided in favour of the reformation, retained the new form of worship; in the others the mass was restored. Henceforth changes in religion became impossible, as is proved by the exile of the protestants of Locarno in 1555. The Abbot of St. Gall recovered his cloister and the lands dependent on it. Glarus and Toggenburg adopted a liberal solution.

In Zürich itself, the Council, condemning the political attitude of Zwingli, undertook never again to engage in war without the consent of the country districts, and dissociated itself sharply from those who had never accepted the first peace of Cappel. The secret Council was solemnly dissolved and the pastors were entreated never again to meddle in political matters. They were enjoined to stop accusing, from the pulpit, persons who were displeasing to them and to "devote all their zeal to teaching in a Christian, friendly and virtuous way the word of God and scriptural truth as enshrined in the two testaments". This limitation of pastoral power contained by implication the decision not to return to catholicism.

Protestantism survived the terrible crisis. Zwingli's successor at the Great Minster—namely, Bullinger—helped to relax the atmosphere by his level-headedness. Thirty-five years after Cappel he concluded with Theodore Beza the doctrinal agreement known as the *Confession Helvétique postérieure* (March, 1566) which was signed by the pastors of Zürich, Schaffhausen, Chur, Mulhouse, Bienne, and Geneva, the pastors of Neuchâtel, Glarus, Basle and Appenzell associating themselves later. Thus Zwinglianism, becoming officially united with Calvinism, wiped out the failure of Marburg. The value of the document was recognized by the reformed churches of France at the synod of La Rochelle in 1571. In 1566 it was countersigned by the Church of Scotland at the synod of Glasgow, in 1567 at Debreczen by the Hungarians, and in 1570 it was adopted, with a few modifications, by the protestants of Poland under the name of *Confessio Polonica*.

The political activity of Zwingli during the last three years of his life reminds the church of today of the frontier separating the temporal from the spiritual sphere. Where exactly does the frontier lie? In democratic countries the servant of God remains a citizen among others. He may, he must at times mix with the life and affairs of his city, but his office does not confer on him an incontestable political wisdom. Beneath the sacerdotal garb, the priest remains a man, subject to passions and to error. "My kingship," said Christ, "is not of this world."

Sometimes neutrality borders on cowardice; the Christian must live with the life of his time, and bear his part of responsibility for the decisions which are taken. There is a way of leaving all to the decision of the Holy Spirit which amounts to comfortable slumber. Zwingli's activity, as on the catholic side that of Ignatius Loyola, is not without its grandeur.

The power of the Christian, his vision of the future, his duty of intervening in affairs, stop, however, at a point which it is difficult to determine. Beyond, God alone can act efficaciously. "Tomorrow will be anxious for itself." Abdication, silence, withdrawal, impose themselves at certain moments. The *hic et nunc* of obedience are discoverable in prayer.

Calvin, sheltered behind the ramparts of Geneva, advised the French protestants not to have recourse to violence. Shortly after the massacre of Wassy, the Admiral de Coligny was awakened in the middle of the night by the sobs of his wife: "Sir," she said, "I have on my heart and conscience so much blood shed by our men; this blood and your wife cry to God in heaven and in this bed against you, to warn you that you will be the murderer of those whom you do not prevent from being murdered." Zwingli's reasoning was that of the courageous Charlotte de Laval. He did not admit that it was legitimate to remain at peace in Zürich while at Schwyz and Lucerne reformed Christians were being burnt. If he went beyond the bounds of his vocation, who will feel himself to be sufficiently pure in heart and single-minded in his zeal to cast at him the first stone?

Eucharistic Piety

A THEOLOGICAL EXPOSITION is inevitably incapable of grasping the richness and complexity of an act of faith. In order to elucidate the Zwinglian conception of the Lord's Supper, it may be useful to translate a document currently in use. The following prayer, intended to be recited by the faithful before communion, is taken from the hymn-book of the reformed churches of German Switzerland (edition of 1952):

"Faithful God and Father! In the name of our Lord Jesus Christ who shed His blood for us, I ask Thee in all sincerity to make me to know the richness of the holy meal, in which Thou dost grant me forgiveness of sins, life and blessedness. Fill me with Thy Spirit. Help me to forget and to pardon with all my heart the humiliations and the hostility which I have suffered, to be conciliatory towards the men among whom I live, since I myself have need of reconciliation. If bread and life are offered me from Thy table, allow me to find consolation and peace in the communion of the body and blood of Jesus Christ. Nourish our souls hungry for the bread of life, and make us to share now in the great banquet which Thy Son will take with us in Thy kingdom. Amen."

After communion a second prayer completes the first:

"Faithful God and Saviour! Thou hast once again assured me at Thy table that Thou hast died for me too, and that Thou hast covered all the unrighteousness of my life by Thy obedience which went as far as the death on the cross. O Lord, I thank Thee with all my heart for this pledge of Thy mercy.

"I implore Thee now: keep me faithful in communion with Thyself and Thy church, so that I may courageously confess Thy name and remain firm amid all the temptations of the Evil One. Help me to love my brethren, in praise and thanksgiving for the goodness which Thou hast shown towards me. May it be that, consoled and joyful, I live in the faith that Thou wilt not cease to gather together and protect Thy church, to feed it and to instruct it, until the day when, according to Thy great promise, Thou wilt celebrate the Feast with us in the kingdom of Thy Father.   Amen."

APPENDIX II

On Visiting Zwingli's Country Today

ZWINGLI CONDEMNED pilgrimages. He was convinced that the Spirit was never enshrined in wood or stone. Nevertheless, a visit to the localities where the reformer lived can provide a stimulating and refreshing experience. *Wildhaus*, in Toggenburg (about three thousand three hundred feet up), a winter sports centre and summer holiday resort, twenty-two miles from Buchs in the Rhine valley (good road and mail bus service) shows the traveller the house in which Zwingli was born.

Wesen, situated on the shores of the lake of the same name and at a distance of ninety-six miles from Zürich, is a small, picturesque old town. *Glarus*, about sixteen miles further south, offers no specially interesting feature unless it be Zwingli's chalice among the treasures of the church (which was rebuilt in the second half of the 19th century). The sanctuary is used for the worship of both confessions, protestant and catholic. *Einsiedeln*, linked by railway to Wädenswill on the Lake of Zürich, deserves a visit, however. Its altitude (about two thousand six hundred and sixty feet) makes it a centre of excursions. The Benedictine abbey, rebuilt between the years 1674 and 1735 and affording a good example of the baroque style, contains no vestige of the sanctuary in which Zwingli preached. Inside the cloister, the traveller may visit the sumptuous library.

The old part of *Zürich*, with the Norman church of the Great Minister (*Gross-Münster*) built between the 11th and the 13th centuries, together with the churches of the *Frau Münster* and St. Peter, the houses of the guilds and the town hall, as also the curious *Wasserkirche*, constitute a picturesque block at the heart of the modern city. The town library (*Zentralbibliothek*) contains the Zwingli museum, in which several documents are exhibited. The National Museum includes among its treasures the reformer's helmet and sword. From Baar, on the Zug line, a rail-car takes one in a few minutes to Cappel. The ancient abbey, recently restored, is worth visiting, as is also the battlefield which is quite near.

Connected with Zürich by excellent rail communications, *Basle* and *Berne* (an hour and an hour and a half by rail or road), with their medieval sanctuaries and their old streets, evoke for the visitor the time when Zwingli listened to the lectures of Bünzli and Lupulus.

Bibliography

THE PREPARATION OF this book has benefited from a number of studies successfully concluded by scholars over the past eighty years. Of these we must mention, among those now dead, the names of Martin Usteri, Emil Egli, Rudolph Staehelin, Herrmann Escher, Georg Finsler, Walther Köhler; and among those still living, the names of Leonard von Muralt, Rudolph Pfister, Oscar Farner,[1] and Fritz Blanke. The advice of the two latter has been of invaluable help to us and we desire to express here our warm gratitude to them.

The reader who wishes to fill in the gaps of a work which is inevitably incomplete will do well to use in the first place the twelve volumes already published in the *Corpus Reformatorum* (*Huldreich Zwinglis sämtliche Werke*). edited by Emil Egli, Georg Finsler, Walther Köhler, Oscar Farner, Fritz Blanke, Leonard von Muralt, Edwin Künzli, Rudolph Pfister (1904 onwards). Its highly valuable notes make it preferable to the less unwieldy popular edition still in course of publication (Zürich, 1941 onwards) under the title *Zwingli Hauptschriften*, translated and edited by Fritz Blanke, Oscar Farner, Rudolph Pfister.

Among biographies, that of Staehelin (2 volumes, Basle 1895-97), while valid as regards essentials, contains not a few errors of detail. For the years 1484 to 1526 it is better to consult the three volumes by Oscar Farner[2] (*Huldrych Zwingli*, 1943, 1946, 1954). We owe to the same author two precious volumes of letters translated into modern German and covering the years 1511 to 1526. In addition, at the end of 1957 Oscar Farner edited under the title *Aus Zwinglis Predigten zu den Evangelien Matthäus, Markus, und Johannes* a precious volume which completes the extracts from Isaiah and Jeremiah published at the beginning of the year (see note to p. 168, above).

Walther Köhler, fiercely industrious, has published a

[1] Oscar Farner died in 1958.—Ed.
[2] The fourth volume, which he was unable to complete, appeared in 1960, thanks to the care of Rudolph Pfister.

series of monographs. Some of these we have referred to in
the course of our study, in particular *Zwingli und Luther*
(*Quellen und Forschungen zur Reformationsgeschichte*, vi and
vii; 1924 and 1953). The collection in the journal *Zwingliana*
may be profitably consulted (*Mitteilungen zur Geschichte
Zwinglis und der Reformation*, 1904 onwards). This journal
is indispensable for serious students.

Other studies by the scholars mentioned above include:

Fritz Blanke, *Brüder in Christo*, 1955.

Emil Egli, *Die Schlacht vom Kappel*, 1873; *Aktensammlung
der Zürcher Reformation*, 1879.

Herrmann Escher, *Die Glaubensparteien in der Eidgenossen-
schaft*, 1822.

G. Finsler, W. Köhler, A. Ruegg (translators and editors),
Ulrich Zwingli. Eine Auswahl aus seinen Schriften, 1918.

Leonard von Muralt, *Die Badener Disputation*, 1926;
Zwingli als Begründen der reformierten Kirche (in "Mélanges
Charles Gilliard"), 1947.

Johann Martin Usteri, *Initia Zwingli*, in "Studien und
Kritiken", 1885, 1886.

Also quoted or referred to in the course of this book:

Alfred Farner, *Die Lehre vom Kirche und Staat bei Zwingli*,
1930.

Georg Gerig, *Reislaufer und Pensionherren in Zurich
1519-1532*.

Walther Köhler, *Das Marburger Religionsgesprach*, 1929.

Roger Ley, *Kirchenzucht bei Zwingli*, 1948.

Oswald Myconius, *Life* of Zwingli, 1532, publ. Basle 1536.

Arthur Rich, *Die Anfänge der Theologie Huldreichs
Zwinglis*, 1949.

André Siegfried, *La Suisse, démocratie témoin*, 1956.

A note on books for English readers:

Selections from Zwingli's writings have been translated
into English by S. M. Jackson (Philadelphia, 1901) and by
G. W. Bromiley, *Zwingli and Bullinger* (Library of Christian
Classics, xxiv, London/Philadelphia, 1953), pp. 47-279, with
Intro. pp. 13-40.

Life by S. M. Jackson (New York/London, 1901); shorter
studies by S. Simpson (London, 1903) and Oscar Farner
(Zürich, 1917; Eng. tr. *Zwingli the Reformer*, London/New
York, 1952).

Index

315

Zwingli, Ulrich—cont.

31-4, 47; chaplain to Swiss mercenaries in Italy, 35; studies Bible and the Fathers, 36-8; influenced by Erasmus, 38, 39; chaplain of Einsiedeln Abbey, 41-4; appearance and character, 45, 46; friendship with Cardinal Schinner, 46, 47; appointed to the Great Minster, Zürich, 47; preaches course of sermons on St. Matthew, 48, 50, 51; discovers Luther, through his books, 50, 51; near death in the great plague, 52, 53; continues his Biblical preaching, 57-62, while maintaining friendly relations with church authorities, 64-6; clashes with authorities on fasting, 68-70; marries Anna Reinhart, 71, and is involved in further clash on the marriage of the clergy, 72, 73; publishes the *Architeles*, 73; accused of heresy, 74; requests a public debate, 75, and draws up sixty-seven theses which form the charter of the Zürich reformation, 75-7; supported by city Councils of Zürich, opposed by church authorities, 77-9.

Sponsors further reforms, 83-91, in conjunction with city magistrates, 85; publishes his sermon on *Divine and Human Justice*, 84, 87-9, and *Essay on the Canon of the Mass*, 85; backed by the Council, he inaugurates the change from Mass to Lord's Supper, 92, 93; the *De vera et falsa religione*, 99-128; breaks away from Erasmus, 131-8; induces the Council to suppress anabaptists, 139-47; opposed by catholic cantons, 148, 149, and by the pope, 149-54; refuses to attend Baden Disputation, 155, 156, but is kept in touch through secret messengers, 157, 158; shows signs of strain, 161, 162; attacks system of mercenary service, 162-5; promotes Bible study among the clergy, 167, 168; home and family life, 169-72; writes for his stepson *How to bring up Young Men of Noble Rank*, 172-4; concerned with reform of morality at Zürich, 177-82, and training of pastors, 182-186; *The Shepherd*, 183-6; attends Berne Disputation, 187-94; political opposition inclines him towards compulsion in matters of faith, 198-203; organizes military campaign against opposing cantons, 206-8, and accompanies troops as chaplain in first war of Cappel, 209

Opposes Luther in eucharistic controversy, 213-39; *Brief instruction concerning the Last Supper of Christ*, 227; the *Amica Exegesis*, 227-9; manifesto on the words *This Is My Body*, 233-6; replies jointly with Oecolampadius to Luther's *Confession*, 238, 239; friendship with Philip of Hesse, 245, 246, leads to Philip's invitation to debate with Luther at Marburg, 246-51; heads deputation of theologians to Marburg, 249; preaches on *De Providentia Dei*, 252-4; at Marburg colloquy, fails to reach agreement with Luther on nature of eucharist, 255-64, but signs articles of Marburg which indicate the unity of the parties on other doctrinal issues, 265-7.

Seeks fresh alliances, 271, particularly with France, 273-5; is classed as a heretic by German protestants, 277, and stands aloof from League of Schmalkalden, 283; writes the *Fidei ratio* for Charles V and *Expositio Fidei* for Francis I, 275, 284-7; fosters political struggle against catholic cantons, 288-94; consulted about the remarriage of Henry VIII of England, 296; on declaration of war with catholic cantons, accompanies Zürich troops as chaplain and is killed in battle at Cappel, 297-303; estimate of his work and influence, 305-9.

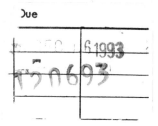